True Poetry

True Poetry

Traditional and Popular Verse in Ontario

PAULINE GREENHILL

McGill-Queen's University Press
Montreal and Kingston, London, Buffalo

© McGill-Queen's University Press 1989
ISBN 0-7735-0697-7

Legal deposit fourth quarter 1989
Bibliothèque nationale du Québec

Printed in Canada on acid-free paper

This book has been published with the help of a grant
from the Canadian Federation for the Humanities, using
funds provided by the Social Sciences and Humanities
Research Council of Canada.

Canadian Cataloguing in Publication Data

Greenhill, Pauline, 1955–
    True poetry
    Includes index.
    Bibliography: p. 221
    ISBN 0-7735-0697-7
    1. Folk poetry, Canadian (English)–Ontario–History
    and criticism. 2. Canadian poetry (English)–Ontario–
    History and criticism. 3. Canadian poetry (English)–
    20th century–History and criticism.I. Title.
    PS8225.O6G74 1989   C8ll'.5'09   C89-090157-0
    PR9193.8.G74 1989

Contents

Maps and Figures

Preface

This preface is directed at folklorists, anthropologists, and other academics who will be interested in the context of my research on traditional and popular verse in Ontario. Those who are mainly concerned with the poetry itself – what it is, what it means, and how it is used – should proceed to the first chapter without stopping off here.

This study of Ontario folk poetry is based primarily on field research. Most of my work was done between 1983 and 1985, though I had earlier located, contacted, and interviewed a few poets and performers. I chose to survey the use of verse in southern Ontario from a research base in Toronto rather than to use the more conventional ethnographic method, living in and studying a single community. When matched against other research techniques current in folklore and folklife studies, the field survey could appear dated or anomalous. But folklorists have not done much collecting at all in Ontario, and folk poetry has been explored in only a limited fashion in other culture areas, so I wanted to obtain the broadest possible perspective on the area and the material.

In addition, I wanted to forestall the objections that some of my professors at the University of Texas and even some of my Canadian folklorist colleagues had raised to my initial research reports – that I had located an unusually poetic community and/or a unique group of poets rather than a pervasive and highly significant Ontarian cultural phenomenon. The results, in which I was able to show an enormous variety of verse from across Ontario, more than justified my methods. However, an intense, single-community ethnographic investigation would be an immensely valuable contribution to the literature of folklore and anthropology.

My goals in field research were threefold: to clarify the genre's range by gathering as many texts as possible for comparative purposes; to interview participants – poets, performers/presenters, collectors, and audiences; and to observe poetry being performed or presented. My understanding of the cultural context derives from my own experience as a long-time resident of urban Ontario and observer of the rural scene, from such ethnographic, autobiographical, and social historical documents and publications as were available; and from directed or open-ended interviews on rural and urban community life with Ontarians.

Verse-gathering took several forms. I searched through archives and libraries for historical examples, contacted other fieldworkers, and sifted through current newspapers. The legislative library of the Ontario government at Queen's Park, which subscribes to over one hundred weeklies, provided me with a good sample of local newspapers, from which I obtained a large collection of popular and locally composed poetry, mainly dating from late 1982 to early 1984.

Following leads established by the newspaper research, I interviewed poets and newspaper editors, recording our discussions on audiotape and making fieldnotes on circumstances and context. While visiting each community, I inquired at the local newspaper office and library for poets, poetry collections, and collectors. The poets themselves provided information about their audiences, which I often followed up with informal interviews. When researching verse about Terry Fox, I contacted local Canadian Cancer Society offices and interviewed *Toronto Star* reporter Leslie Scrivener, who had covered Fox's run and was his biographer. On this topic I also conducted telephone interviews and sent out a questionnaire.

I was pleasantly surprised by the positive response to my research in Ontario communities. Only one of the poets contacted, who said that he no longer had any interest in poetry, declined to discuss his work. However, several newspaper editors refused, expressing a complete lack of interest in the project and in local poetry.

Locating and observing the cultural scenes and performance events where verse was delivered presented some difficulties. It soon became obvious that poetry was presented orally in public only on rare occasions; usually its public delivery was in written form. Because I didn't concentrate my fieldwork on a single community, I lacked a social base that would provide easy access to these occasions. I relied instead on local contacts to keep me aware of future events, and through them I was fortunate enough to be a participant observer at a community shower, a local concert, and a meeting of a Women's Institute group at which verse was read.

Conducting this survey proved in some ways to be more difficult than conventional ethnographic research. In standard anthropological fieldwork just about any social act – visiting a friend, shopping at a grocery store, or going out for an evening's entertainment – may be relevant to the study. Participant observation of such occasions yields information about everyday activity, communicative forms, situations for performance, and so on. Simply living in the community advances the researcher's understanding of the material. In contrast, my survey required constant evaluation and re-evaluation while in progress and redirection into potentially fruitful areas.

Because of the incredible amount of verse I located during the two years of my intensive research, it was impossible to discuss every example. Though personal interest naturally influenced my choice of poems and poets to be considered, they were selected as much as possible on more objective bases. Where there were alternatives, I discuss here the best-documented or most complete examples. For instance, though I located great quantities of verse written for wedding showers, the poem presented here was the highlight of a celebration at which I was a participant observer. Other examples were unique in my collection but illustrated significant points in a telling fashion, such as the duel in verse between the newspaper editor and the United Church minister, or the poem and letters to the editor concerning the same topic. When I felt that a series of illustrations would best serve my purposes, I included every available one in my collection.

The majority of people I contacted had either no idea or an inaccurate one of what to expect of a folklorist's research. Ontario's anglophone city residents perceive the entire province as a centre of urbanization, mass communication, and modernity – in fact, as the very antithesis of anything conducive to folklore. Anglo Canadians, the group to which most informants belong, have never been particularly eager to recognize their own folk culture, generally equating folk with ethnicity and with non-English-speaking groups. Further, Ontario has been almost completely neglected by folklorists and ethnographers, both Canadian and international. With few exceptions (for example, Farber 1983, Greenhill 1981, and Inglis 1983), ethnography in the province has concentrated on native peoples, historical and currently inactive traditions like lumberwoods singing (see, for example, Fowke and Cazden 1970), or non-Anglo ethnic cultures (Giuliano 1976).

Another explanation has been advanced for the current lack of awareness of folk traditions, including folk poetry, in Anglo Canada. John P. Matthews's comparative analysis of nineteenth-century poetry in Canada and Australia contends that both countries had two parallel streams of literature, the academic, "based on sophisticated English models of the central tradition" and associated with the universities, and the popular, "folk literature and ... literary adaptations of it, based upon less sophisticated models of the central tradition." Matthews maintains that "Academic poetry received the greatest attention in Canada, virtually driving Popular poetry beneath the literary surface" (1962, 113). This has remained true to the present day, when popular poetry is almost completely unrecognized – especially as part of a current tradition with contemporary significance – by academics, writers, and journalists.

Most nineteenth-century published collections of verse give the impression that there was no indigenous Anglo-Canadian tradition of popular poetry and song. Matthews indicates that "popular" and "family" songbooks contained mainly English and American material (132). Early twentieth-century attempts to infuse a Canadian spirit into popular song employ few traditional texts, although W. Roy Mackenzie's collection of folksongs and ballads from Nova Scotia was published in the 1920s, and others (for example, Creighton 1932) quickly followed. E.K. Brown's reference to "the meagre treasure of our [indigenous] popular song" (1943, 58) shows that the pervasive academic ignorance of published examples of the Anglo folk tradition lasted well into the twentieth century. Compilers usually included French Canadian folksongs in popular verse collections (see, for instance, Macmillan's *A Canadian Song Book*, 1929), but they seem to have been unaware of comparable material in English and often resorted to composing original verses on classical and popular airs to fill the perceived gap in the repertoire. An odd example of this was John Murray Gibbon's "Old Ontario" (1939), written to Papageno's birdcatcher song from Mozart's "The Magic Flute":

I come from old Ontario
Where grapes and pears and peaches grow,
And apples and tobacco too,
And fragrant flow'rs of fairest hue.
Cool rivers flow on ev'ry hand
By forest, rock and meadowland
With wonderworld of mines below
Enriching Old Ontario.

Niagara our waterfall
Unchains a giant power from thrall,
And wheels in busy cities whirr
To keep the working folk astir;
A thousand miles from east to west,
And ev'ry mile with beauty blest

There is no fairer land I know
Than lovely Old Ontario. (Gibbon 1939, 10–11)

Ontario's folk traditions went unresearched until very late because the perspective of most central Canadians precluded the possibility of mainstream Anglo Canada having a folk tradition; only backward Maritimers, French Québécois, and non-Anglo ethnic groups did. Edith Fowke's discovery that there were folksongs in Ontario must have been a revelation to many. It came very late, however; she began collecting in the province in the fall of 1956.

Yet my own research, including the present work, has revealed a wealth of folklore in urban, suburban, and rural areas alike. There are traditional customs and beliefs such as water witching; internationally and historically documented festive practices like charivaris[1] and mock weddings; folk artists; craftspeople; and, of course, poets. In some genres folk artists or performers attempt to reproduce their notions of traditional behaviour; in others, folk poetry in particular, the creators innovate and see themselves in dialogue with tradition rather than merely maintaining it. Contrary to common assumptions, Ontario is a place where folklore in all its manifestations is flourishing. This is by no means surprising but is, rather, inherent in folklore's nature and its dialectical relationship to culture and society. Traditional and popular culture generally provide an alternative to or critique of mainstream ideology. Perhaps that is why folk poetry receives so little attention from the representatives of elite culture or is met with ridicule on the rare occasions when it is noticed. This book contends that traditional and popular verse are unquestionably vital to Ontario's communities and that what we can learn from folk poetry about the province's culture and society cannot be discovered elsewhere.

NOTE ON PRIMARY SOURCES

Excerpts from audiotaped events or interviews are designated T with the last two digits of the year in which the tape was made and a sequence number. T84–33, then, is tape number 33 made in 1984. Questionnaires are designated Q, letters L, and fieldnotes N, with the date on which they were done. All published works are reproduced here as they appeared on publication. Ellipses are the authors', and do not signify omissions. I have avoided the use of *sic* except where usage in the original might be ambiguous.

Acknowledgments

It is a pleasure to acknowledge some debts to my teachers, colleagues, and informants. Roger Renwick supervised the dissertation on which this book is based. I learned more from him than I can express, and I enjoyed almost every minute of it. Encouragement and moral support from Dick Bauman, Magnus Einarsson, Kenny Goldstein, and Stan McMullin have meant a lot to me. Steve Jones assisted in chipping the academic obfuscation away from a very early – and very drafty – draft of this work, and Susan Kent Davidson copy-edited the final version. For their time, patience, and correction when I didn't get things right, I thank Betty Bohlender, Anne Boyes, Betty Burton, Valdine Ciwko, Tina Cohen, Costas Cokkinos, Roy Cowieson, Bill Crewson, Kathleen Dyer, Gerry Eagan, Grant Filson, Jeanne Greenhill, Dorothy Herridge, John Herron, Bonnie Hind, Lyda Johnson, Vern Kennedy, Ross Knechtel, Andrea Koziol, David Laycock, Margaret Laycock, Shirley Laycock, Jim Merriam, Ed Miller, Helen Parkin, Shadrock Porter, Bob Raymes, Astrida Reader, Ken Reynolds, Evelyn Sample, Mose Scarlett, Bob Shrier, John Slykhuis, Katherine Smith, Joe St. Denis, Mac Swackhammer, W.S. Tomlinson, Bill Wilkinson, Margaret Wilkinson, Millie Wilkinson, Laurena Wright, and Cora Yuill. I appreciate their permission to quote them and their verses. And I thank my friend John Junson for everything.

I am also very grateful for financial support from several institutions. The research on which this book is based was funded in part by graduate fellowships from the Social Sciences and Humanities Research Council of Canada and the University of Texas at Austin. The Canadian Studies Program at the University of Waterloo provided assistance with several incidental expenses.

A portion of this work was previously published in *Western Folklore* 46 (1987): 77–96. I appreciate assistance from Composers Authors and

Publishers Association of Canada (CAPAC) and Performing Rights Organization of Canada (PROCAN). The following have granted permission to quote previously published material: *Acton Free Press, Alliston Herald, Arthur Enterprise News,* Fitzhenry and Whiteside, *Grand Valley Star and Vidette, Haliburton Echo,* Mika Publishing, *Manitoulin Expositor, Rainy River Record, Smiths Falls Record News,* and *Stittsville News.* I have made every attempt to contact those who may hold copyright to the material published here. I would very much appreciate being notified of any omissions so that they may be rectified in future editions.

True Poetry

CHAPTER ONE

Appropriation, Appropriateness, and Ontario Folk Poetry

Look through any weekly community newspaper in Ontario and you're likely to discover a piece of verse such as this:

HALIBURTON
O' Haliburton
With your setting so rare
Not many villages
With you can compare.

Your places of business
Are varied and many
Your scholars are the best
Not surpassed by any.

The numbers who flock
To the Skyline Drive
Assures every tourist
Haliburton is alive.

The surrounding lakes
And beautiful hills
Are the finest scenery
And provide many thrills.

Your forests in colour
Are a delight to behold
With their lovely bright green
And rich red, yellow and gold.

Your neat little Churches
Render service to man
And brotherhood reigns
Regardless of race, creed or clan.

Yes, Haliburton
You're well known abroad
As that beautiful village
Nestled deep in the hills of God. (Elsie Moore, *Haliburton Echo and
    Minden Recorder*, 21 March 1984)

Poet Elsie Moore, like countless others across Ontario, writes of her
immediate and best known world – her own community. She proudly
displays her vision of her town's finest qualities: its commerce, its
educational achievements, its attractive landscape, and its strong moral
outlook. This is a utopian vision, stressing only what is valuable and
good.

We often find such verse in a poetry column or on the editorial
page, but sometimes it is simply inserted anywhere in the paper as
filler. Among a host of other topics it may describe a local hockey
team's success against its rival from a nearby community, commem-
orate the death of a neighbour, or solicit funds for building a new
hospital. The same poems, or ones like them, can be read or recited
at a Women's Institute meeting, a church concert, a community shower,
or some other public event. Like Elsie Moore's verse about Haliburton,
they refer to what seem at first glance to be only the most local,
mundane matters. Many display their writers' lack of interest in the
technical aspects of literature. But their most socially significant feature
is their concern with what the community considers to be appropriate
activity and behaviour, and in order to explore this cultural territory
they appropriate the symbolic or "semiotic"[1] resources available to
the community.

As I've just used it, the word "appropriate" has two senses. The
first, according to the *Oxford English Dictionary*, refers to what is
proper, "specially fitted or suitable"; the second means ownership,
"attached or belonging as an attribute, quality or right; peculiar to,
own." These notions are related, especially in the cultural-materialist
perspective that only that which is indeed appropriate (proper) is
appropriated (made one's property), and vice versa. In its first sense
appropriate seems more passive, referring to what may appear to be
inherent; in its second the word concerns an active production or
teasing out of a certain quality. Both concepts have implications for

Ontario culture and for the place of vernacular or folk poetry in it because what is fitting and proper in traditional Ontario communities is often most fittingly and properly expressed in verse form. Locally composed folk poetry celebrates people, events, and (like "Haliburton" above) scenes that versemakers consider especially appropriate. Folk poets can criticize what they see as inapposite, and sometimes they can even take foreign cultural material – a poem by a nineteenth century American author, for example – and transform it, or "appropriate" it into their own works. In these ways folk poetry imparts and expresses aspects of Ontario culture; it praises what is valued by some Ontarians or condemns what they ideally should avoid.

The perspective of this study is that of the folklorist. My basic assumption is that human behaviour centres on collective symbolic communication. This applies not only to expressive cultural forms like art, literature, and music but to politics, economics, and history as well. In the folklorist's view, what a group of people think is happening is just as significant as what is actually taking place. Vernacular poetry may not be classifiable as literature or have a meaningful existence beyond its cultural context; rather, it is part of a complex of sociocultural interactions. My explanation of folk poetry, then, extends beyond formal characteristics and reaches into the poets' intentions and the uses they make of their works in their communities.

In some perspectives, however, vernacular poetry seems highly inappropriate. Many writers belittle or scorn it. In *The Four Jameses* (1927), for example, William Arthur Deacon conducts a satirical critique of a number of vernacular poets. One James McIntyre (1827–1906), a furniture manufacturer in Ingersoll, Ontario, is subjected to a mock stylistic analysis:

His frequent device of double rhyme is clear proof of conscious artifice:

> For they must be clad in fur well,
> For it blows cold in Burwell;

And when he ventured into the triple rhymed structures the happier specimens of his ingenuity are beyond praise:

> Other lakes seem inferior
> In size to great Superior.

In so complicated a construction, he is not always up to the mark of the lines just quoted. For instance, I do not care nearly as much for:

'Mong choicest fruits you ramble on
From Niagara to Hamilton,

and, while all will agree that Killicrankie is a much harder word to rhyme
than Timbuctoo, which Sir William Gilbert could only match with "hymn-
book too," McIntyre's attempt was more courageous than wise:

And historians will rank the
Chief highland victory of Killicrankie.   (79)

Like other critics of folk poetry, Deacon mocks the poets' topics as
much as their styles. He discusses one of McIntyre's everyday subjects
thus:

Whenever cows come on the scene, be it noted, the poet grows particularly
tender. Perhaps what he meant to convey in that last passage was the
need the West would soon feel for mixed farming, and a fear which
modern scientific agriculturalists confirm. There is also to be taken into
account the difference between thought and emotion. He understood the
greatness awaiting other districts, but his own he loved.

Some see no beauties near to home,
   But do admire the distant far.
Each one doth know it is not wise,
   Though our songs may not be vocal,
Chants of our home for to despise,
   But to prize them 'cause they're local.   (85)

Some writers are not content merely to deride actual folk poets.
Humourist Paul Hiebert, for instance, is famous for creating the "Sweet
Songstress of Saskatchewan," the fictional Sarah Binks. He wrote both
Binks's biography and poetry, though, with a thorough understanding
of content and context as well as style. For example, Binks publishes
in the *Horsebreeder's Gazette* and *Swine and Kine* (locally distributed
special-interest periodicals) in addition to her privately printed books.
Her subjects, too, are familiar ones in vernacular poetry; farming, the
seasons, her dog, and other everyday matters (Hiebert 1964).
   Similarly, performer Randy Woods invented the vernacular poet
Peter Paul van Camp, employed this persona for public readings and
recitations, and published *The Better Poems of Peter Paul van Camp*.
This volume includes recommendations and appreciations from fictitious community members, who are also Woods's personae, and "Questions for Study" (1978).

In the Deacon, Hiebert, and Woods perspectives, it is not only vernacular poems that are disparaged. These critics evidently expect their self-consciously sophisticated audiences to feel superior to such poets, real or fictitious, and to see their verse as representing backward sentimentality, poor education, and other negative stereotypes of rural life. They ignore or downplay the true significance of this poetry to its creators and their audiences. The sympathetic reader, from the community or beyond it, is implicitly scorned along with the poets, their verse, and their milieux.

But literary academics, humourists, and their sophisticated audiences are not the only ones who reject vernacular poetry. Folklorists, too, have been unwilling to consider its merits, partly because it lacks the broad inherent interest of other kinds of traditional texts. The appreciation for a traditional ballad like "Barbara Allen" (Child 1885),[2] for instance, is relatively widespread and certainly not limited to the culture areas in which it is still sung. "Barbara Allen" deals with love and betrayal, a theme readily translated from culture to culture and between groups in society. In contrast, a local song lyric enumerating all the members of a church choir or a poem about the need for a new highway bridge in some small town is not particularly absorbing outside its immediate context, group, and milieu.

Yet people in cultural groups where this less universal, decidedly particularistic folk poetry actively functions find its significance unquestionable. This was made very clear when I attended a Women's Institute meeting to collect and document this group's use of folk verse. Asked to explain my presence there, I said that I was studying poetry in Ontario because it was important and did not deserve to be overlooked. My justification wasn't very satisfying to the membership, who already understood that this poetry was significant. Their meeting's roll-call exhortation, "Tell a story or say a poem," indicated that, contrary to my view, folk poetry wasn't being neglected. The reaction of urban Ontarians was quite different when I asserted folk poetry's value. Among this group the verse was disdained, and at best my ideas met with scepticism.

APPROPRIATENESS AND
FOLK CULTURE

Before I proceed further, the meaning and use of "appropriateness" needs clarification. Things are right and proper only when they fit their context. Take clothing, for example: what is appropriate to the beach may be odd or even shocking in the boardroom, and vice versa. Likewise, a folk poem in an urban, sophisticated context looks like doggerel. Divorced from its context, apart from its intended place in the culture, it has little interest. Ontario folk poems are tied intimately to their particular circumstances, and they lack qualities that might lend them a more universal appeal. Dismissing them, however, eliminates one avenue to understanding Ontario's pluralistic culture. This is not only because Ontario folk poetry discusses ideals – what some Ontarians find appropriate and inappropriate – but because folk poetry is a significant medium for grassroots participation in and contestation of cultural change.[3] Folk poetry enables us to discern how local communities perceive the sociocultural disjunction that threatens their status quo, and often how they expect to resist or alleviate the threat.

Ontario is currently experiencing rapid and drastic development. In its southern region especially, rural areas and small towns are urbanizing, and many are flanked by subdivisions. More and more of the province's residents live in bedroom communities and commute to work in far-removed urban agglomerations. As Ontario's population becomes more mobile, residents of any locale – rural and urban alike – are increasingly strangers to one another or mere acquaintances, not family or friends. People can no longer take for granted that their neighbours will share their worldview and ethos.[4] The society is characterized by a profound cultural pluralism. Appropriate behaviour, activities, and perceptions must, then, be brought to the community's attention in order to be commonly understood. In the forum of the local newspaper or community gathering, folk poetry is a medium to express these subjects and feelings. This will be discussed in chapter 3.

Apart from its sociocultural significance, vernacular poetry is a valuable example of the prodigious creativity that human beings display in their everyday lives. Despite limitations of time, energy, and materials, people with no formal training and with little thought of material reward consistently produce new objects and texts that explain, elaborate, or criticize their lives and cultures. Assuming meaning, purpose, and usefulness for most creative endeavours, and presupposing the heterogeneity of the human mind, it seems safe to assume that its products are similarly complex. In dealing with issues of concern in community cultures and in resolving them in specific ways, Ontario folk poetry can be enigmatic, and it requires sympathetic and informed attention.

But if Ontario folk poetry is so significant, why do most urban Ontarians know so little about it? This is partly because of the trend in modern Western society for folklore forms to retrench, to retreat from the public sphere and return to private areas. The most prevalent forms of folkloric expression in Canada – personal-experience narratives and family photography, for instance – belong to fairly intimate collectivities like families, work groups, or small communities. Very little folklore pertains to such broadly based cultural entities as the nation, or even an entire province. Nevertheless, the significance of some aspects of folk traditions transcends their local origins and milieux. For instance, the Terry Fox poetry and songs discussed in chapter 5 strive to create a national culture hero and to identify, assert, and in some cases even reconcile diverse cultural values. These works present what is appropriate about Fox as an individual and what makes him, though he is a *national* public figure, nevertheless symbolically one with and part of the *local* community. Despite the parochial nature of individual pieces of Ontario folk verse, it has much to contribute to recurring, problematic questions of national and regional identity.

In addition to its significance to the community and to an understanding of local culture, vernacular verse is a genuine and unique aspect of Canadian folk culture. Not understanding the subtleties of tradition, Canadians frequently assume that our folksong repertoire or colourful ritual and ceremonial practices are mere facsimiles of immigrant origin and that there is no truly Canadian folk culture. At best, they may say, Canada has a very rudimentary indigenous heritage – an echo of the truism that "we are a young country." They feel that only material found exclusively in Canada or something that is the cultural property of every Canadian can be designated as our folklore. They fail to recognize the essential pluralism of our traditional and popular culture.

Ironically, this fallacious view has been echoed by the distinguished American folklorist Richard Dorson. He suggests that Canadian culture – in contrast to its American counterpart – is not indigenously developed but is instead a fusion of distinct, transplanted European cultures and inheritance from the native peoples (Dorson 1959). This opinion reflects a weak knowledge of Canadian culture as well as a deficient understanding of cultural dynamics. The influence of native culture on Anglo Canada has, in fact, been extensively filtered through European notions of the noble savage; actual aboriginal societies have had infinitely less effect than have archetypes from popular culture. For example, a sign at the entrance to the property of Ontario folk artist Lawrence McGuire names it "Laughing Waters," and, as this suggests, his spectacular outdoor tableau of an "Indian village" reflects Longfellow more than the actual cultural history of the native peoples who once inhabited his region (Greenhill 1985a).

Even recent European immigrant traditions have been significantly transformed in both form and meaning despite relatively brief histories in Canada. The erection of tile (*azulejos*) pictures of popular saints on Portuguese houses in Toronto's Kensington Market area is very different from their use in the home country. The introduction of images of the Holy Family, an unlikely subject for such representations in Portugal, is part of an attempt to remedy the effect of contact with a modern urbanized worldview on the traditional concept of the family. The Holy Family as a symbolic referent serves to mediate the modern Canadian and traditional Portuguese views of child-rearing and the place of children in the family (Greenhill 1982).

Canada does possess distinctive traditional and popular culture, however little awareness there is of its existence. Its uniqueness has developed despite the country's historical domination by other cultures, initially Great Britain and more recently the United States. The current proximity and availability of American culture has undeniably and profoundly affected Canada, but its influence has produced no carbon copies. As the vernacular poetry discussed in chapter 4 shows, a distinctive aggregate emerges from the confrontation of Canadian sensibilities with American cultural texts.

In fact, Ontario folk poetry displays an implicitly contestative force against American cultural domination. Rather than accepting the total repertoire of imported and sometimes imposed texts (historically, there has been strong American content in our popular literature and periodicals, and even in our public school textbooks), Ontario poets and performers select only appropriate texts and influences. If the material they choose includes content inappropriate to local use, it is discarded or more radically adapted into something more suitable – American Mary Dow Brine's "Somebody's Mother" becomes Ontarian William Dyer's "An Act of Kindness," for instance (see chapter 4), or "The Yellow Rose of Texas" becomes Edward Miller's "Haliburton Highlands," and so on. In choosing and transforming the materials available to them, Ontario folk poets and presenters develop, extend, and maintain indigenous control over an emerging and changing oeuvre.

CATEGORIES AND TERMINOLOGY

This discussion so far has introduced the terms folk poetry, popular poetry, local poetry, and vernacular poetry, and it is time to clarify the relationships among them. Folk poetry is the most general category, referring to any indigenous verse directed to a group or community of peers. Most of it is local in origin and vernacular in language. Popular poetry is somewhat different. Much of it is imposed material of non-indigenous origin, such as school reader verse. It is important in Ontario because it is appropriated both by poets who use its structures as models for their own verse and by presenters who see an apposite quality in an individual text and re-present it to their community.

Folk poetry as a recognized genre of folklore has grown far beyond its original scholarly boundaries. Until recently most folklorists would consider only the lyrics of folksongs, "largely traditional, anonymously created, orally disseminated, and widely popular" (Renwick 1980, 2), as a legitimate folkloric verse form. But within the last thirty years or so folklorists have begun to include local song and local poetry because of their similar histories, performance contexts, and texts. Local song differs from folksong in having more concrete and topical subject matter, less formulaic and predictable content and language, and relatively little variation from singer to singer. Local poetry differs from both because it is "for reading and recitation, not singing" (ibid., 4).

These three together – folksong, local song, and local poetry – share the features of all forms of folklore; "the thread linking these three major genres of act and expression within the same field is their delimited, publicly performed, and socially relevant content, ethos, and pragmatic" (ibid., 7). Though they may lack some traditional textual and textural qualities of folksong, local song and poetry, like other folklore forms, are "artistic communication in small groups" (Ben-Amos 1971, 13). All folk poetry is symbolic, appropriate, and traditional.

Nowadays, most Ontario folk poetry is not sung. Historically, however, folksongs were performed at house parties, at hotel taverns, and in the lumberwoods. Traditional singing was associated with entertainment and with passing leisure hours, though the songs' topics – from love and death to emigration – were often serious. Nowadays there are "better" ways to be entertained – by professional entertainers and in escapist forms like television, recordings, and movies. Contemporary local poetry, though it may be light or amusing in tone, tends to be more didactic and serious in subject than folksong. At a wedding reception, for instance, the poem is incorporated among the speeches and toasts to the central participants and usually deals with morality, fertility, and other serious topics. It belongs to the "work" aspect of the event, though it may be its playful part. In contrast, the disc jockey provides "entertainment"; the dance is the "play" part of the evening, when less social pressure is placed on the principals and their formal duties are few.

Ontario folksong has historically paralleled other forms of folk poetry. For many years folksong was associated primarily with the winter lumbercamps where, fostered by the camps' isolation, it provided entertainment to the shantyboys (see Fowke and Cazden 1970). However, lumbering conditions have changed, and Edith Fowke found in her research that her informants were recalling songs they had not sung for twenty, forty, or even sixty years. She concluded in 1963 (134) that folksinging was not a living tradition in Ontario.

It is still possible to hear traditional song and singing in Ontario. However, one may find extensive influence from mass media and popular culture. For example, folk poet and traditional singer Edward Miller of Haliburton, a former shantyboy, learned his version of "Barbara Allen" from a Vernon Dalhart recording,[5] and "his" song in the lumberwoods was Wilf Carter's "Escape from the Moose River Gold Mine."[6] Miller has had a number of his folksong-inspired compositions published in the local newspaper, but he is the only individual I have found so far whose textual influences from folksong are so obvious and traceable.

Local song has a history in Ontario as lengthy as that of folksong, and some early compositions have entered tradition. For instance, a song about the drowning of Bill Dunbar in 1883 (Fowke and Cazden 1970, 143–5) is known across the Peterborough and Haliburton regions and was heard in the lumbercamps in the 1920s and 1930s. Over time, local song received diminishing influence from traditional song but increasing influence, in the later nineteenth century, from popular, non-indigenous poetry.

An equally long history pertains to newspaper and privately printed local poetry, which has been published in Ontario since shortly after the arrival of the first United Empire Loyalists. John S. Moir's *Rhymes of Rebellion* (1965) shows that such poetry was flourishing by 1837. But collections like Moir's raise more questions than they answer about the historical tradition of folk poetry in Canada. It is often difficult to distinguish between local songs and written or recited poetry. Many of Moir's examples, culled from contemporary newspapers, have a suggested tune – perhaps "God Save the King" or "Yankee Doodle" – to which the verses could be sung. Yet they seem in practice unsingable, and it is clear that the prototype served primarily as a model for the new poem's structure. Fowke and Mills's *Canada's Story in Song* (1960) contains a number of such "songs" whose actual currency in singing tradition is questionable, such as "The Scarborough Settler's Lament." This blending and confusing of newspaper poetry and folksong takes place most often when writers and compilers need material from Ontario, because relatively little of its song tradition has been collected, especially in comparison with the Atlantic provinces and Quebec.

FOLK POETRY AND FOLKLORE

The definition of folk poetry is broadening partly because of the development of a newer dialectical interpretation of folklore.[7] On the one hand folklore is traditional, appearing in contexts that are historically known and understood in a community and taking forms that are familiar and even conservative. On the other hand it is emergent, adapted, by those who present it, to their own needs and to those of their audiences at individual performances in temporally and spatially unique situations. The same folkloric event or text can never be experienced more than once. By the time a song has been re-sung or a tale retold, the total circumstances have changed, either slightly or drastically.

Modern approaches to the study of folklore seek a balanced view of the folklore text itself and the context in which it is presented, and an elucidation of their mutual influence. Thus we find an emphasis on folklore as situated performance and as communicative event. For instance, Barbara Kirshenblatt-Gimblett's "A Parable in Context" (1975) demonstrates both the appropriateness of the performer's choice of story and the resolution of implicit conflict that its use provides. Text and context are presented as interlinked factors with mutual effects; neither one is given analytical primacy.

For the contemporary folklorist folk poetry is best described as a form of symbolic communication. According to anthropologist Marshall Sahlins, culture itself is symbolic. Its decisive quality is not its material constraints but conformity to them of a symbolic schema that is only one of many possible such schemas (Sahlins 1976, vii). Thus symbolism provides the basis for choosing, for example, "edible" food and "fashionable" clothing. Because folk poetry consistently highlights certain aspects of its topics and equally consistently ignores others, it encourages a symbolic perspective on culture. It confirms that though people share their environment and human needs, they may choose to assent to the community's notion of appropriateness by acting within or outside the agreed boundaries. Alternatively, they may attempt to change shared notions of appropriateness. For example, a poet may write a verse in which she points out appropriate and inappropriate activities for an older woman, or she may write a verse that questions traditional notions of appropriateness and inappropriateness in that area of social relations.

Another anthropologist, Sherry Ortner, suggests that there are two kinds of key symbols. "Summarizing" symbols are primarily sacred, emotional, and non-reflective, while "elaborating" symbols are analytical vehicles for sorting out the complex and the undifferentiated. Elaborating symbols, she contends, can take two subforms: "root metaphors" are conceptual and "key scenarios" are action oriented (Ortner 1973). Consistent with Ortner's notion that "societies ... contain their own interpretations" (453), we can view folk poetic texts as more or less systematically expanding and commenting upon a series of elaborating symbols. These may refer to root metaphors – as do poems on spring or Mother's Day – or to explorations and extensions of key scenarios – like poems about wedding anniversaries or hockey games. To understand Ontario folk poetry, then, we must not only translate or uncover the meanings of its key scenarios and root metaphors (these symbols are usually the topics and often the titles of the poems), but also consider just what topics are apposite as key scenarios and root metaphors.

Folk poetry is symbolic particularly in expressing the "relation between 'words' and the 'world'" (Rosaldo 1980, 20). It is not overtly tropic: its language is most often descriptive, realistic, and concrete. Metaphor, metonymy, synecdoche, and irony are rare. The semiotic activity of Ontario folk poetry occurs at the level of choosing topics and methods of elaborating them. Ontario folk verse evaluates and manipulates the known; it does not deal abstractly with concepts.

However, as Clifford Geertz emphasizes, "art forms generate and regenerate the very subjectivity they pretend only to display" (1973, 451). Hence, folk poetry is an active force for change in culture as well as its reflective expression. Poets or performers use verse interpretatively not by opening up the world but by attempting cultural closure. They attempt to have the last, summarizing word on a topic or to resolve the situation spurring the poem's composition and/or presentation. This happens regardless of whether the poetry's meaning is negotiated in oral or in written performance.

In order to understand this poetry we must first identify the communicative system in which it is created. Texts, performers, audiences, performance occasions, sociocultural contexts, and finally the total ecosystem are all relevant to folklore's production and use. All are mutually influential. In any oral performance, for instance, both the performer's intentions and the audience's reactions (as he or she interprets them) affect the text; for example, he or she may shorten a song if the audience seems restless. The performer's choice of a specific verse is constrained by the nature of the performance occasion (whether it is a community shower or a Women's Institute meeting, for instance). This in turn is influenced by the kinds of contexts felt to be appropriate for poetry in that society, by more general cultural meanings and uses of verse, by the behaviour expected of women and men, and so on. And all of these conditions are affected by constraints placed upon the culture by its physical environment.

FORMAL LEVELS

Within folk poetic texts, we can usefully distinguish four formal levels. Though they are interrelated, we can sort out collectively shared folkloric aspects of poems from more individualized ones. First, some textual content is present because the work is a poem – that is, it exhibits such features as rhyming words and division into lines and verses. Second, the poem reflects its particular type. Poetry celebrating, for example, an individual's life-passages has a structure specific to that type of verse. And third, the poem typically comprises material particular to a topic. For instance, many life-passages verses list family members' names and the circumstances of a couple's meeting.

These first three levels are of greatest interest to folklorists who are concerned with textual reproduction and transmission. Poetry cannot be a complete intersemiotic translation between experience and language, and it is not meant to be so. However, given cultural expectation and an understood tradition, any two poems about the same individual, incident, or phenomenon will have substantial textual similarities, reflecting their common form. As we will see in chapter 5, poets writing about a similar topic are likely to choose related concepts, much the same wording, and comparable symbolism.

The fourth level pertains to authorial concerns. Any poem is an intersection of the individual poet's knowledge, experience, skill, and understanding on the one hand with his or her culturally patterned material on the other. Sometimes a poet speaks for the entire group; no member of her community would argue with Bonnie Hind's "Dover Flood of 1979," which asks for assistance to flood victims. But more commonly, as in Mae McGuire's "Women's Liberation," which upholds a traditional role for her sex, the personal element is central, *yet always in dialogue with the community*. Folk poetry is not an automatized, knee-jerk reaction to cultural problematics, nor does it express a unified or monolithic culture; it is purposeful, aware, and sometimes even consciously analytical.

To make their commentary worthy of attention, poet/performers must share many aspects of their identities with their intended audience. Most verse-makers are recognized by their communities for their ability to compose poetry, just as others may be known as gardeners or wood carvers. But their primary identities, like those of their neighbours, derive from their occupational, kinship, and other local connections. Mae McGuire, for example, presents her identity as a

McGuire and a farm wife as being more significant than the fact that she is a poet. The majority of Ontario poets are non-professionals, deriving neither income nor occupational identity from their verse, though a few have some entrepreneurial interest in selling broadsides, books, and recordings.

Folk poetry functions to interpret rather than just to entertain. In vernacular language and usually in fairly concrete style it approaches realistic subjects of common, collective experience. Folk poetry in Ontario, both indigenous and imported, concerns culturally problematic areas: aging, the effects of natural disasters, death, and so on. A poem may refer to its topic on a number of levels and may offer either a reflection on the problem or a suggestion for resolving it.

Likewise, the subjects of folk poetry may range through a series of levels of cultural significance. Transitional seasons of the year – spring and autumn – are inherently less socially disruptive than a community member's death. However, both topics share an equation of physical liminality[8] (the melting of snow in spring echoes a physical passage from one state to another) with one of potential danger to the community (the resultant flooding and economic disruption of spring is like the grief and cultural disruption of death). Such poetry may be said to concern actual or potential inappropriateness. Other verse, praising a community or lauding mothers, for example, concerns the assertion of a particular and special appropriateness. Subjects need not come from within the community. Cancer victim and marathon runner Terry Fox, who was of national and even international interest, was extensively celebrated by folk poets. Similarly, the national conversion to the metric system or nuclear war, though external to the community proper, have potential repercussions for it, and they are as suitable as more local topics.

Though all folk poetry describes, (re)generates, and evaluates culture, it is a particular kind of active force. The poet who argues for a traditional view of women's roles is clearly trying to produce (or forestall) a change, however effective or ineffective such an attempt may prove to be, as well as to express her generation's view to another. The expression itself is not primary, but the endeavour to change the views of others is. Folk poets often seem to be striving to glue together what they see as the ragged edges of culture. They are concerned with ordering aspects of social life that are messy, uncertain, changeable, and/or problematic – that is, with appropriating them and making them appropriate.

Even outside Ontario, folk poetry as a genre is confrontation sensitive and problem oriented. English folk poets Martha Bairstow and Emma Kittredge, poetry about the Lofthouse Colliery Disaster (Renwick

1976 and 1980), and Greek laments (Caraveli Chaves 1980), for example, contest or minimalize points of sociocultural conflict. In Ontario, where confrontation, change, and problematic situations are rife, folk poetry is an important everyday genre for expression. Most communities periodically rely on it to express, contest, assert and generally deal with ongoing cultural dynamics.

SOURCES AND TRADITIONS

Folk poetry in the province comprises not only what's *made* in Ontario but also what is *used* here, regardless of whether it was originally indigenous or imported. Non-local popular poetry is found in similar contexts, applies to comparable subjects, and can function interchangeably with indigenous verse. For instance, "Somebody's Mother," by nineteenth century American children's author Mary Dow Brine, should be included as Ontario folk verse; like local poems, it has been used as a recitation and published in local newspapers. It differs from local verse mainly in being popular over a wider geographic area and a greater span of time.

Most popular poetry found in Ontario is not Canadian in origin. It comes from Britain or America, two countries that have culturally colonized Canada throughout its history. This means that Mary Dow Brine's verse is better known than that of Edna Jaques (an early twentieth century Canadian who published much sentimental poetry about prairie life). Foreign poets have been imposed upon Ontarians by hegemonic forces like provincial school textbooks ("Somebody's Mother" appeared in three readers used in Ontario from 1883 to roughly 1950) or American popular magazines like the *Saturday Evening Post* and *Reader's Digest*. Even the *Family Herald and Weekly Star*, published in Montreal as "Canada's National Farm Magazine" (well remembered by the Ontarians to whom I talked, most of whose families subscribed to it) contained very little Canadian fiction. For most Ontarians Canadian poetry was simply much less accessible than American or British material.

Nevertheless, not all imported verse becomes popular; performers and presenters of folk poetry in Ontario select only relevant and apposite works. Because of their appropriate semantic fit with the genre and with other cultural expectations, the same poems – "Somebody's Mother," "The World is Mine," "A Little Mixed Up," and others – appear again and again in community newspapers and other local contexts. These and other examples of popular verse will be discussed in some detail in chapter 4.

It can be difficult to demonstrate that individual Ontario folk poetic texts are traditional, yet their genre is, because folk poets are likely to employ certain conventionalized models (the structural aspect of tradition) and because forms like popular poetry are passed around from hand to hand within a community and beyond, thus undergoing localizing and conventionalizing change (the temporal aspect of tradition). In employing the structural tradition a poet may choose identifiably traditional folksong models, as when Edward Miller of Haliburton refers to the Irish broadside ballad in his

Now come all you young maidens
About to choose a man
Forget those boys on the dry side
And pick a green side man. (T84–24)[9]

However, Miller borrows from a more popular tradition when he writes verses to the tune of "The Yellow Rose of Texas." In both cases he works from his immediate repertoire of cultural resources, a base that widened through his life as the mass media, his neighbours, and his experiences made more material available to him. As I have suggested, indigenous local and imported popular varieties of Ontario folk poetry share formal qualities, ranging from poetic structure (four-line stanzas, iambic meter, *abcb* rhyme schemes, and so on) through sequential and compositional structures to underlying symbolic concerns.

Only a limited amount of Ontario folk poetry is traditional in the sense that is has been known and used for generations. Though popular works can often be applied to a variety of situations, locally composed folk poetry is usually topical and relevant only in limited circumstances. It is used in ways that emphasize how it applies to a particular current problem, and its text usually refers specifically to that situation. Most local works are intended for use only once and are not passed around like traditional folksongs. In general, folk poetry in contemporary Ontario is timely rather than timeless.

Of course, the tradition of Ontario folk poetry pertains to its sources and to its transmission as well as to the continuity, variation, and selection (Halpert 1951) evident in its texts. It is presented in and received from contexts where its appropriateness is expected and understood. These contexts are aspects of folk poetry's symbolic appropriateness as well as of its tradition. Folk poetry in Ontario is useful, and it functions in particular ways: that is, it deals with problematic areas of culture. Despite vernacular poetry's quotidian presence and wide range of media and presentation milieux, it is specific and fundamentally limited; it is constrained with respect to its topics, subjects, and settings for presentation. The world it shows is an ordered and limited one. The appropriate use of verse achieves a cultural closure or wholeness not obtainable in another genre, though there seems to be no situation where a poem's use is mandatory. But what is its sociocultural milieu, and where does it fit therein? The answer requires an examination of Ontario community life, worldview, and ethos – the subject of the next chapter.

CHAPTER TWO

The Appropriateness
of Community

What does it mean to belong to a community? As I use the term "community" here, it means more than a grouping of individuals in a physical space; it assumes some sense of common interests or mutual concerns among residents. In small towns and villages the community may constitute a political unit, but cities are made up of neighbourhood communities with a less formal existence. Community does not presuppose a single identity for all members but an implicitly agreed association, based in a shared locality.

Certain patterns are evident in how Ontarians see their communities, and they are the concern of this chapter. Yet it is important to recognize the pluralism of perspective that occurs among Ontarians; all the generalizations about Ontario communities that follow should be qualified by place, time, and individual. However, if common perceptions of community do not emerge from what follows, shared understandings of the problems of community do. Anthropologist Isabel Emmett suggests that "to live in a community is to know a more complex meaning in each social encounter than could be known elsewhere" (1982, 209). Residents are familiar with one another's histories, backgrounds, positions, affiliations, and day-to-day activities. But Ontarians' perception of community is also based on a sense of difference; what sets "outsiders" apart is their social unfamiliarity. Faced with a large influx of outsiders (a condition typical in much of southern Ontario since the Second World War), a community must somehow adapt to its new circumstances. Folk poetry is one method that Ontarians who feel they represent the traditional community use to acquaint newcomers with and persuade them of appropriate knowledge and values, and to express their apprehension of what is – and what is not – right and proper.

Many urbanites lack the experience of being historically based members of any community in Emmett's sense. Instead they live in areas where a sense of alienation from place and neighbours is more common than a feeling of belonging. With this comes an ignorance of the experience of community culture. Middle-class urban Ontarians – this writer included – are to a surprising degree culturally isolated and generally unaware of the sheer quantity of folk poetry in the province. This verse is not directed to outsiders such as ourselves, and we do not participate in its communication. Like other aspects of Ontario's folk culture, folk poetry is displayed and its meaning negotiated in the esoteric contexts of ethnic group, social club, work group, religious or voluntary organization, family, and so on. But among insiders like the Women's Institute group mentioned in the previous chapter, folk poetry's presence and significance is taken for granted. For them, it does not need to be publicly reaffirmed because everyone already knows where to find it and how important it is.

Urban Ontarians do not have much of a sense of identity. Just as they would deny having any folklore, most anglophone residents of the province fail to recognize that they have a distinctive culture. But their sense of having an indefinable, or at best nondescript social character is not shared by the other regions of Canada. Newfoundlanders, westerners, and Maritimers, for example, see Ontarians as distinguished by an undue sense of superiority; in their eyes Ontario is the wealthy province and "Upper Canadians"[1] are cold and impersonal. The capital, Toronto, epitomizes these qualities, as the following comment from a Ukrainian Manitoban who has lived in Newfoundland indicates: "People from Toronto think they're greater than anyplace else in the country ... They think they're really sophisticated and they're not ... The far west and east of the country get the short end of the stick and there's a lot of resentment about that ... We're always being told we're just a bunch of farmers" (Valdine Ciwko, N 11 May 1985).

Ontario is indeed one of the country's more wealthy and urbanized provinces. Not only do urban districts encroach more and more upon farmland but the density of their population has increased. Expanding suburbanization, transforming the regions around Toronto, Hamilton, London, Kingston, and Ottawa into dormitory sectors, has changed the character of many towns and villages. And although Ontario's population was in the past mainly of British origin, immigration has recently brought new ethnic groups to the major cities and their near margins. One obvious index of this change is the fact that in some areas one is now as likely to hear Portuguese, Italian, Chinese, or West Indian patois as English.

Though the province's borders are political, they are also to some

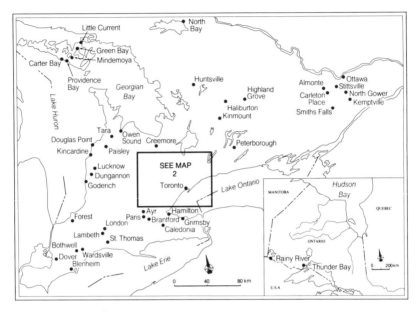

Map 1   Ontario communities in *True Poetry*.

extent natural and social. The Great Lakes and the St Lawrence River provide most of the southern and part of the western boundaries. Ontario's northern region, sparsely populated and with an economy based on forestry and mining, is geographically and culturally unlike the primarily agricultural and industrial southern region in which my study is based. The northwestern boundary is shared with the province of Manitoba, and the northern extremities are on Hudson Bay and James Bay. In the southern region the northern boundary is the Ottawa River, and to the east lies the francophone province of Quebec.

Ontario's other main cultural boundary divides it from the United States. Indiana, Wisconsin, Michigan, Ohio, Pennsylvania, and New York border directly, or indirectly through various bodies of water, on Ontario. Though most Ontarians live close to the American border and few can identify variations between American culture and their own, significant differences do exist. For example, the Ontario (and Canadian) interest in "peace, order, and good government," expressed in the British North America Act, which established Canadian confederation in 1867, contrasts with the American constitution's invocation of "life, liberty, and the pursuit of happiness." And as soon as one crosses the border in either direction,   there are obvious dialect differences. The province is more physically and culturally isolated than might at first appear.

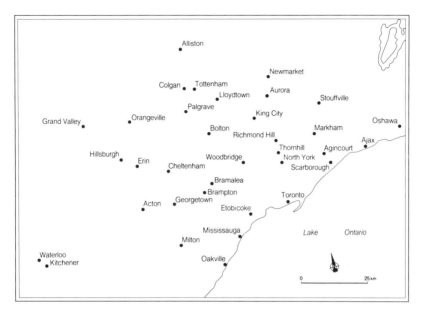

Map 2 Detail from Map 1.

PERCEPTIONS OF COMMUNITY

My analysis of community life in Ontario derives from written accounts or from discussions with the Ontario residents who were my informants. Despite their divergent backgrounds and collective experiences that span eighty-odd years, they are nearly unanimous in their view of one aspect of life in the province: they all see the pervasive presence of some kind of rift or disjunction within their own communities. They express it as a historical break between the old Ontario rural life and modern times, or as a contemporary barrier between traditional residents whose families come from the area and newcomers who come from the cities. Many locate the rift at the end of the Second World War. This may be an arbitrary point to mark the beginning of dramatically increased mobility for Ontarians, but it is also the most recent event in which substantial and identifiable groups, including but not restricted to the young men who fought in the war, left their home communities.

In other areas my sources differ. Some see the historic, homogeneous community – the kind defined by Emmett – as having stability and meaning while the modern, socially heterogeneous way of life is characterized by alienation. Others are more encouraged by modernity and see benefits as well as drawbacks to it. Any consideration of communities in Ontario must recognize the complexity and difficulty of the problems they face. The residents themselves are acutely aware of and involved in the dialogue concerning the province's changing political economy. For example, Tottenham resident Gerry Eagan suggests: "Our town and township have more to offer, but the old days when you knew everyone are gone. This is noticed especially by former residents back for a visit and not finding many familiar faces. The new and the old have many different viewpoints which often surface at election time as we have a large commuter population. I feel most newcomers are an asset to the community but feel our town and township have enough people now. More growth would destroy our rural atmosphere" (L 29 May 1988).

In times of crisis, social cleavages in Ontario communities are most clearly displayed. For instance, in late October 1984 two children were found strangled in their schoolyard in Orangeville, a bedroom community and rural centre of fourteen thousand people north of Toronto. A strong current of public opinion held that a newcomer to the area, the karate instructor of one of the children, was responsible. These suspicions led to harassment and rumours of potential vigilante action against this innocent individual. Further, the suburbanites (whom he evidently represented) were blamed for producing an atmosphere that encouraged the tragedy. Said one resident: "Are the commuters doing anything to make this town better? ... They eat and sleep and work, that's all. I don't think they contribute much" (*Globe and Mail*, 6 December 1984).

Though "commuters" have an obvious economic impact on the areas in which they reside, most have little connection with, and place meagre value on, the forces and hallmarks tying the traditional community together: the Women's Institute, the volunteer firemen's association, the co-op, the church, the concession line, the fall fair committee, and so on. Their impact on the traditional community and the hostility with which they are viewed by some of its members are indicated in the Orangeville incident, and in a more benign fashion in folk poetry.

Folk poets and performers share with their fellow Ontarians a worldview that is a symbolic expression of the objective reality. How residents perceive their society's transformation is integral to an understanding of folk poetry in Ontario.

THE IDEALIZED ONTARIO COMMUNITY

Many of the individuals whose descriptions of Ontario community life appear here are recalling times they now see as being better than present circumstances. Much of what they say is the result of selective memory: some have foregrounded the appropriate and more or less forgotten the inappropriate. Accordingly, several of these descriptions reflect an ideal rather than objective historical circumstances. Whether or not these views are a result of the "escalator" perspective in which, according to culture theorist Raymond Williams, each generation idealizes its past as particularly harmonious or pure, "a well-known habit of using the past, the 'good old days,' as a stick to beat the present" (1973, 12), change is now the status quo in Ontario. While few Ontarians wish to give up the benefits of modern life, many mourn the loss of a community feeling generated as much by hard times as by good ones. Thus we find in these memories a pervasive concern with difficulties – limited travel, fire hazards, poor medical conditions, and so on – as well as with proximity, kinship, and institutional association as creators of community.

What do Ontarians see as characterizing their traditional community? For most people, it was rural. Its central place included a general store, "which means they sold everything from shoes to corsets to dry goods to feed, flour, and gasoline" (Jeanne Greenhill, T84–30); a church; often a public or private assembly hall; a post office; and other service functions as well as residences. Beyond the town there were working farms and the homes of non-farmers who delivered mail, performed handyman tasks, drove milk trucks, and so on. Farming was the predominant occupation, but many men supplemented their income with winter work in the lumberwoods.

Changes to this picture have taken place throughout the southern portion of the province but probably began in the area immediately around Toronto. For example, during the post–Second World War boom speculators bought up the mainly dairy and mixed farming land. As the countryside northwest of the city was transformed from a farming economy and given over to industrial, residential, and service uses, the central town of Brampton increasingly became a suburban dormitory for the growing metropolis. Since local factories are not labour intensive and the town cannot employ its own population, most Brampton residents now work in Toronto and commute daily by car or commuter train. Margaret Laycock, who grew up in the late 1950s on a farm now part of the suburban dormitory of Bramalea, says: "I don't think that I saw an awful lot of traditional rural Ontario. I think I saw it as changing into whatever form it has now ... Certainly people who are ten, fifteen years older than my parents still identify with the small church they went to, even though it hasn't been open for twenty years; their friends are from there ... I don't know if that's going to continue with people who are, say, ten years younger than my parents. I think that they were just at

the tail end of that old rural tradition." But some of these transformations weren't restricted to rural areas: "Even for my mother who
grew up in Toronto, her street was a community. She still is in contact
with a lot of those people. It was a time when you lived on your
street for years and years; people weren't as mobile" (T84–33).

MOBILITY

What has happened in Brampton is paralleled throughout most of
southern Ontario. The mobility of families and individuals has contributed to the breakdown of the traditional community. Newcomers
arrive and former residents leave. Once people depart from the community, they usually no longer belong to the group. For instance,
when Mac Swackhammer of Little Current, on Manitoulin Island,
heard a neighbour talk about her daughter, his impression was that
she had moved far away – to Alberta or California, perhaps. He soon
discovered that she had married someone in Mindemoya, twenty-eight
miles away. The distance was immaterial. It is appropriate to ask
after a former resident, but the history and activities of someone who
has left cease to be central or significant to the community as a whole.

Traditionally, most travel for a farm resident consisted of going,
perhaps once a week, to the nearest town for supplies. Such a place
was almost as familiar as home, and might become home if in later
life a person chose to give up the farm: "They'd buy a new house,
which was something special to get, and retire quite happily. But
they were probably a maximum of ten miles from the rest of their
family and their old community. Making the switch from living on
the farm to living in Brampton was no big move because everyone
had always socialized to a large extent in Brampton, and done their
shopping there, and it was the centre that they considered that they
belonged to" (Margaret Laycock, T84–33). This group still constitutes
a large portion of Brampton's population. Though it maintains close
ties with former farm neighbours, the loss of the rural area on which
the traditional community relied to suburbs means that the group
will not survive its current members.

Before efficient snow removal and air travel, mobility in Ontario
was severely restricted, especially in winter. A Lucknow area resident
describes typical difficulties encountered before snow-ploughing equipment was introduced in the late 1930s: "In the late fall we would
begin to fight the snow and ice with shovels, tire chains which needed
constant repair, and a box of sand in the car trunk, the weight of
which gave traction to the rear wheels; we used to sprinkle the sand
in front of the wheels when stalled on ice. We always carried a heavy

logging chain in the event we needed a pull from a passing team of horses ... Then around the tenth of December we gave up the struggle between snow and car and jacked the latter up on blocks in the garage. From then on we used the horse and cutter" (Johnston 1972, 56). In some areas the only method of travel in winter was by rail. Though winter can still inhibit mobility, even in Ontario's cities, the isolation known before municipal road clearing services and technological improvements came to the scene is now almost unthinkable.

Not only in winter was transportation difficult; roads were impassable in spring, "pretty much until they dried up. Because of frost coming out there would be great potholes. And these were dirt roads, of course, they weren't paved. They weren't even tarred. And they were single track" (Jeanne Greenhill, T84-30). In communities not able to support a resident minister, church services were held only from early spring to late fall, when an itinerant preacher could travel. Recently, however, small churches often have consolidated, thus limiting the cost of maintaining buildings. The congregation, rather than the minister, must commute to worship.

Now, not only is travel outside the community more feasible for its traditional residents but there is also a considerable influx of outsiders. Gerry Eagan of Tottenham says: "Quite a few people have come from down east. My wife is a Newfoundlander, and Dunns from the banks of the Miramichi [in New Brunswick] came in here and rented a place up the road and eventually he started his own carpenter business and has done quite well, and four out of five of the family are living locally. But a lot of people have moved here, sometimes because of the proximity to a school; some want the country life – there's always the love of the land; and some of them will buy ten acres and then find it's quite a problem looking after it, see" (T84–39).

Outsiders who want to become part of the community, as these remarks suggest, are less disruptive than those who move from the city with an idyllic and unrealistic view of country life. A resident from nearby King township referred to the social disruption that resulted when a couple bought and renovated an old farmhouse, praising the area's peace and quiet, only to move back to Toronto five years later because they missed the excitement of city life. The long-time residents find such instability in the community difficult. And more seriously, the village of Cheltenham has boiled over into open disagreement between traditional residents who want the old brickworks reopened because it will provide job opportunities, and newcomers who oppose such a move. Bill and Millie Wilkinson, whose roots in the area go back some hundred years, explain:

Millie: [The newcomers] were worried about pollution and trucks on the road ...

Bill: Well now, at the meeting they had over at the brickyard, just to tell you how foolish they are, there was one fellow there from Erin which is twelve miles farther north. And he got up and made a spiel. And somebody said to him, "What's your beef about? You live up there." Well he says "I have to drive down past here every day to go to work. If I get behind a brick truck I'm going to be twenty minutes late for work." Well gee [laughs], it's just plain craziness.

Millie: It's funny; it's the people who have lived here all their lives or most of their lives who are not protesting against it, and it's all the ones who have moved into the area within the last few years that are protesting against it. (T84–65)

This is often the case; representatives of the traditional community are active supporters of industry moving into the area. Gerry Eagan suggests that "our new factories – Honda, F.&P., etc. – have enabled many locals to get jobs and slowed down the exodus to the city" (L 29 May 1988). He sees these developments as supporting the traditional community and rural values, while the commuters often oppose them because they fear further destruction of the rural ambiance. Interestingly, the ultimate purpose of maintaining rural culture is shared, but perceptions of how this might be done are directly opposed. As Millie Wilkinson of Cheltenham contends: "The outsiders' ... only drawback is that they often do not participate in rural community life. They also do not like to see a change in the rural scene, even though they themselves have created such a change" (L 8 April 1988).

Newcomers are often acutely aware of their situation as outsiders to the traditional community. John Moss, who moved to a small hamlet near Kingston, comments: "The village is split half and half between newcomers and people who have been there for generations, related to one another three times over ... generally reserved, polite if circumstances demand, drawn easily into conversation only by tragedy or scandal" (1983, 31).

To the newcomer, there is often a clear sense of not belonging and of not being accepted, as Mac Swackhammer of Little Current explains:

We are the people who have come there. We were not born there. No matter how long we live there, we will be not "Billy Ferguson"; we will be "That Bee Keeper." My friend Dan is "the Bee Keeper" and he's been there, hard working as a farmer, for a long long time. People still do not call him by name.

The newspaper editor has owned the paper for fifteen years and [has been] a permanent resident for eleven years. He knows more about the island, has had as much effect on it, as any single individual. He would never be considered a member of that community and that hurts him, actually, quite a lot. They may call him up at three o'clock in the morning to come and take pictures of the curling championships, but they would never invite him to the wedding of their daughter. (T84–41)

Newcomers often feel that they are not wanted at such events as community showers (supper dances held to raise money for couples about to marry), which bring the traditional community together. Says Swackhammer, "Commonly a notice is put in the paper 'Please take this as your invitation.' But they aren't open, because nobody who didn't know those people would go. I would read that, but I'd never think it would be at all proper of me to go to it. You know to whom you are addressing this; you don't expect half the town to come out" (T84–40).

Economically and professionally as well as socially, a clear break exists in most communities between established residents and newcomers. This is especially true when the latter are numerous enough to be perceived as a group; where they can be approached as individuals, they can be more easily integrated into the community. For example, Betty Burton, a local weekly newspaper columnist, came to Palgrave about twenty years ago. She now considers herself part of the local "we" and the people in the subdivisions "they." She describes the transition: "They think we're such doddering idiots up here; it's the truth. When I came up I felt the same too. Good Lord, you go to the store to buy something and fifteen minutes later you're still talking to the six people around the cash register about all the people and things that have been going on. But after you've been here a few years – if you can't hack it, you leave – you gradually find out you're one of the worst ones ... When we shop around here, it's not a thing that you have to do, it's a social occasion. I love it" (T83–34).

Gerry Eagan agrees that this is possible. As long as the newcomers can be seen as individuals, not as representatives of outsiders as a sociocultural group, they can in some senses be incorporated: "In the '40s, '50s, and '60s, new residents moving into our area or coming to our church was a sort of novelty; it happened so seldom. There was a real curiosity to find out more about them and an effort made by many to welcome them. Some people readily accepted newcomers while others adopted a sort of 'wait and see' attitude. The more outgoing new residents soon became community-involved, while others kept more to themselves" (L 29 May 1988).

Earlier in this century it was much more unusual for anyone to move into a small community. For instance, no family moved into the area of Highland Grove from around 1920, when Jeanne Greenhill's parents arrived to take over what was formerly her maternal grandfather's general store, until they retired to Peterborough during the Second World War. Only one role, the schoolteacher's, required or expected mobility. But the teacher usually found she could "belong" by getting married, or because of her unique position as an educated woman with responsibilities extending beyond her pupils. Helen Campbell, a young woman who taught school in several communities around Frontenac county in the early twentieth century, tells us that "the small, often isolated school in a farming community was the centre of that community" (Campbell 1975, 21). The teacher, like her students, had to be a working part of the rural system: "The farm unit required the labour of every member of the family. All children had their assigned tasks to perform – both before and after school. There were no complaints – it was simply their job. Total involvement did not come easily to some rural teachers, but 'Could you spend the weekend with us? We have to go to town on Saturday' or 'How are you on quilting?' were more than a kindly invitation to participate: it was a responsibility tendered on the generous tray of genuine friendship" (ibid.). Accepted in the community as experts, teachers were often plunged into very unfamiliar circumstances, as Campbell suggests:

A serious lack of teachers early in the century cast many a High School graduate, with no teacher training, into the profession ... Then because we had received more "book learning" than themselves, parents elevated us to the pedestal of possessing superior knowledge in every field. Some of us failed them badly. Pitchforked into a small farming community, I was unbelievably and disappointingly ignorant ... The first time I was asked to assist at a "birthing," I wondered seriously just what was my role in the community. Although I understood the need, I resented, at first, this intrusion into my private world ... Very soon I recognised and was grateful for the compliment. (Ibid., 22)

The immigration of new, socially unknown people into traditional communities is not the only disruption in contemporary rural Ontario; out-migration, more common now than ever before, is also a problem. In 1984, for instance, Tottenham celebrated its centennial. Resident Gerry Eagan comments: "We're looking at school pictures, and it's amazing how few [residents] have remained. They will move away where the action is. Say, take in our family. There's seven kids. My brother there is in Ottawa. I've another one in BC and one in Toronto, a sister in Fort Frances, and three of us live locally. And sometimes you won't even have that high a percentage. There'll be one might

stay on the family farm and the rest move on to other things"
(T84–42). This exodus of family members has made it necessary for
farmers to be more autonomous than was previously the case. They
can no longer call on a relative when they are ill or behind with
work; "you are getting more independent, perhaps too independent,
really" (David Laycock, T84–42).

FAMILY

In the traditional community, the extended family was an integral
part of everyday social and economic existence. Margaret Laycock
saw the importance of such a network of assistance because her own
family lacked one: "My mother had been raised in Toronto and so
came to the farm when she married my father when she was in her
late twenties. My father's family was unusual in that only one of
them out of six brothers and sisters, other than my father, got married.
And he left the farm and didn't live in that area at all. And my
mother would always complain that she had none of that group that
everyone else had" (T84–33). Primogeniture was the rule in most
families, but children other than the first son were also provided for:
"At the turn of the century, a farmer deeded a portion of his farm
to his son – as a marriage dower. Or if there were several sons, the
father bought land nearby, and all members of the family helped each
other to build solid homes and stables. Also, all work was shared"
(Campbell 1975, 37). Three generations of one family might live in
one, or possibly two houses on the same property: "It varied from
family to family. I knew of one family where the grandmother lived
with them. In a lot of families, though, they would have two farm-
houses. Either they had bought another farm so the younger family
might move into that farmhouse, or there may have been occasions
where the parents retired to Brampton and passed the farm on to
their sons" (Margaret Laycock, T84–33).

Of course, it was not merely family connections that created a sense
of community in Ontario. As one resident of a small hamlet informed
Helen Campbell, "We always look after our own" (Campbell 1975,
21). Such belonging involved, in addition to residency, the affiliation
with a common church, school, concession line, and so on.

COMMUNAL ACTIVITY

The loss of the co-operative spirit generated by proximity, kinship,
institutional association, and need is frequently lamented by Ontarians
like Gerry Eagan:

You used to know everyone that lived in town and on these sideroads. Well, I'm interested in people, but you can't keep track of all of them now. So you lose some of the community spirit. The old-timers, well, they were naturally all interested in what the neighbours were doing. And then there's threshing bees, where you would go around and help each other ... There used to be a group of six neighbours had a threshing machine here. We didn't have a share in it, but we traded work with all of them, and they would go around to the different areas, and they were great for the community spirit and getting the work done (T84–38). You still have good neighbours, but it's more set up that you're maybe trading with one person, say my brother down the road. The numbers are still there, but you're not as close as you were, just due to the fact that you're not involved with them as much. (T84–39)

The one activity that evokes traditional Ontario's community spirit, to insiders and outsiders alike, is the barn-raising bee. William Johnston remembered one that took place around 1900 in the Dungannon area:

It was a mass onslaught of one hundred or more neighbours. In one afternoon they put together the beam framework of a sixty-by-eighty foot building. Once this framework was up, the work could be finished at a leisurely pace by a small crew of professional carpenters. The day ended with a rousing contest between two teams chosen by captains. Each team undertook to put up the rafter framework of half the roof, racing to be the first to finish. With the noisy shouting of orders, and men climbing wildly over the framework as they tossed pieces of lumber about with abandon, it was a miracle that no one was injured. The winning team eventually swung nimbly to the ground, privileged to be the first to sample the food from rows of heavily laden tables under the orchard apple trees. And what a spread! Roast chicken and roast beef, home-made bread and rolls, dozens of cakes and pies, jugs of milk, buttermilk, and lemonade. There may have been some apple cider or a stronger beverage hidden somewhere about, but I didn't see any. (Johnston 1972, 10)

The barn-raising bee offered both work and play, and it involved women, men, and children alike as participants and spectators. Much other economic activity was traditionally performed communally – quilting,[2] threshing, maple sugaring, and so on.

Community events were not exclusively functional, though. There was also a regular sequence of entertainments. Euchre (card game) clubs, tea meetings, and garden parties took place in the spring and summer: "There was always time after seeding, a couple of weeks or maybe three weeks when things are a little slack, and then there's the time between haying and harvest where there might be a little slide; you'd have a garden party or something" (David Laycock, T84–42). Fowl suppers took place in the fall, and square dances in the winter, and "the people of Lucknow entered enthusiastically into their fall fairs, public auctions, ... church festivals, family reunions, and even their funerals" (Johnston 1972, 25).

In this milieu, some activities, like church dinners and Christmas concerts, were for the entire family, while many others were for specific ages and sexes. Women had Women's Institutes and organizations like the United Church Women or Ladies' Aid, which met to exchange information or perform charitable works. For younger people there were 4–H, Junior Farmers' Association, and church groups. Men had partisan political organizations like the Orange Order, but the latter's association with religious unrest was muted by the turn of the century. A Lloydtown woman related a local legend about Paddy, the only piper in town and a Catholic, who on one drunken occasion played "The Wearin' o' the Green" on an "Orange Walk" to celebrate 12 July, without any violent consequences. There were also service clubs and economic associations like the co-op.

Some of these organizations remain vital today. The Cheltenham Volunteer Firemen's Association exemplifies the wide range of activities supported by such institutions:

All the guys belong to the volunteer fire department. It's a social outing for them. I mean, they do actually respond to the fires when they happen and I think they do very well. They're all trained and know what they're supposed to do when there's a fire. I think they have saved buildings and animals, and I guess they've had to save people, but it's a fun thing to do. It's like another club because they have parties – not when they're supposed to be being stand-by firemen – but they have all sorts of parties and dances and they go out and do things and hold events for other people, barbecues and what not ... I think they had a shower for my brother – he's a volunteer fireman in Cheltenham – and Karen, the bride. (Margaret Wilkinson, T84–63)

Periodic events and meetings were important, but much community togetherness was reinforced on an everyday basis. For instance, "no neighbour ever left a farm home without a friendly cup of tea" (Campbell 1975, 79). The kitchen was the focus of sociability: "It was the only living room we knew – a haven, homey and warm – and safe. The country parlour was kept exclusively for Christmas Day, the minister's quarterly visit, or for wakes or weddings. We did not use it in the summer – it must be kept scrupulously clean. We could not use it in the winter – we might freeze to death" (ibid., 103).

ADVERSITY

Adversity as well as pleasure brought the traditional community together. Especially in rural areas, the middle of winter was a dangerous time. Stove pipes were likely to overheat and cause a fire, and the chance of help arriving in time to save a house would be small. In one case, Jeanne Greenhill remembers, a family "lost their house, the whole thing. Everything they had was in the house, and that was it. So there was a great rallying around of everybody to provide clothing and boots and places for them to stay because there were so many – nine children, I think, as well as the mother and father – and they couldn't all be put up at one place" (T84–31).

Even if residents had a sense of belonging to a co-operating community, life in pre-war Ontario was hardly idyllic, especially from the doctor's perspective: "In my day, a rural and small-town doctor like myself was interviewing from Sunday to Sunday about two hundred people ... He met all the emotions, from fright to lust. The average rural doctor had about twenty-five deaths a year and about twice as many births. He dealt with countless colds, much indigestion, many anemias, chronic bronchitis, and urinary infections. He was presented with an occasional suicide and abortion, a little madness, and much personal misery from worry and anxiety" (Johnston 1972, 4). Then as now, rivalry and gossip created problems. However, the community ethos supported co-operation, and minor rivalries were not supposed to be allowed to grow into major ones. As Jeanne Greenhill suggests, "If you didn't like them, you were supposed to be kinder than you felt like being, so you tried, I guess" (T84–30).

With minimal differences between community members in levels of education, wealth, and so on, the traditional community's pecking order was often established on other bases. In Brampton, for instance, "there were a couple of United Churches. One was sort of the establishment church and one was – it was all right, but there was a rivalry between the two of them. Premier Davis's[3] family went to our church, and the mayor of Brampton went to our church, and the MP went to our church" (Margaret Laycock, T84–33). To be associated with this church and in contact with its high-ranking members offered conspicuous advantages. One woman who came to Ontario in the 1950s with her husband comments: "Do you know what was said to me when I came to Canada? This man said 'If you want to get ahead in Canada, you must join a church.' That's exactly what he said ... I thought you joined a church because of your religious convictions. I didn't think it was because of getting ahead, or it would be advantageous in any way except a spiritual one" (Dorothy Herridge, T83–21).

It is obvious from the foregoing that there was not always a consensus of opinion among community members. Yet most of the descriptions I have seen of life in Ontario in the past concentrate on the positive aspects, primarily on the sense of shared community.

COMMUNITIES IN TRANSITION

Much of this spirit of co-operation is transformed by the physical and social interactional changes of modern times. The economic base of many communities has changed, and this has pervasive effects. As John Moss comments: "A century ago there were six operating mills and a cheese factory. There was a school, now used for euchre nights in winter and an annual pot-luck supper. The church has been duplexed. One mill remains ... The kids are hauled great distances by bus to district schools" (1983, 29–31). The expansion of most of Ontario's rural school districts into regional areas in the past few decades has meant not only a transformation of the landscape – old schools are being turned into houses, outbuildings, and stores – but also wide-ranging social changes. Traditionally, school trustees "living in the community and knowing the problems of their neighbours ... administered justly and wisely ... Their chief function seemed to be to save money and to maintain the 'status quo'" (Campbell 1975, 27). Most now administer much wider areas and have less individual and personal involvement with any particular community in their jurisdiction. Students who live too far to walk travel to school by bus. This can foster misunderstanding, as Margaret Laycock suggests: "When I went on the school bus, we also picked up kids for the separate school in Malton. And most of the Catholic kids came from families that weren't farming; they just happened to rent a bit of land and a house. And they always had more kids than the farm families that I knew, and their clothes weren't quite as nice, and they would talk about how they had to share rooms with so many brothers and sisters. So I just thought, well, the two must go together ... And I always thought Catholics were poor, and my parents didn't set me straight" (Margaret Laycock, T84–33). In this case, the pluralism of the Ontario community has extended to the generations. Margaret Laycock's parents could not correct a false conclusion that they did not know she had drawn. This kind of misunderstanding would have been much more difficult where the home and the school were located in the same community.

Rivalries and individual differences are often in the foreground of activities in Ontario communities today. Mac Swackhammer trenchantly observes: "If you chose to do anything there would always be somebody against it. The town worked very hard at getting grants and support for building a new hockey rink. Some of the people worked their can off, thinking that was the greatest thing in the world. Half the community thought it was the most sinful waste of crap and they wouldn't darken the door … If they put sewer and water [services] in the town, half the town objects" (T84–30). Swackhammer, a newcomer to his community, attributes such rivalries to a "tradition of bitchiness," but he also suggests that demographic changes have deepened its effects. With fewer individuals to support the family or group point of view – a result of out-migration – everybody now feels obliged to be more vocal and to compromise less. Whether or not Swackhammer's analysis is accurate, the checks against "traditions of bitchiness" may operate less successfully now than in the past. Rivalry between communities, though, has always been encouraged. Swackhammer offers a characteristically pungent description: "Providence Bay and Mindemoya are two little towns that are eight miles apart. They both have piss poor hockey arenas in their community because they could not and would not agree to put one good hockey arena between the two of them" (T84–40).

Many people sense the working of change in Ontario and feel that the complete destruction of the community spirit may be inevitable. Areas like Cheltenham, once zoned to prevent suburbanization and industrialization and to maintain valuable farmland, may soon go the way of other communities near Toronto: "I think it's just taken longer. I think it's happening now. There seems to be a fight now about some of the farmland in that area … Because it's a little village, they still had things like the volunteer fire department; the church is still a social centre; the Women's Institute had their own little building. I think things have just lingered there a little longer, though Cheltenham's changing a lot … About fifteen or twenty years ago a country club went up there, predominantly for riding, so you had a lot of city types moving in, and now the suburbanization is taking place; a lot of people are moving there who don't farm" (Margaret Laycock, T84–34).

Inevitable or not, the changes, transitions, and disjunctions in Ontario life in the past few generations are obvious. Most poet/performers represent the older families and the traditional communities, whether they live in a rural or urban area. Their poetry may be critical, addressing the kinds of problems raised by change, transition, and disjunction: the loss of kinship connections and community spirit, the sense of placelessness for the old, and so on. Or verse may be affirmative, celebrating traditional community values and often indicating ways in which appropriateness is mirrored, paralleled, or preserved.

ONTARIO'S FOLK POETS

Folk poets in Ontario are not specially chosen individuals with a valued role that is everywhere recognized; they select themselves. They do not apprentice to other poets or seek recognition as people who possess any special talents or skills. They are not personally accountable for their poems as works of art and hence for themselves as poets. They are accountable, instead, for the poem's expressive content as a symbolic rendering of appropriate feelings, ideas, and judgments.

It is important to realize that Ontario folk poets are cultural spokespersons, but they do not speak with the unanimous and consensual voice of the entire community; this is unthinkable in a complex and pluralistic region like Ontario. Like other local people, they express opinions that are of interest to those with whom they interact every day. Their use of poetry rather than another communicative genre says something about the kinds of opinions they express and the kinds of topics they discuss, but their roles as poets and the fact that their comments are in verse do not make their statements any more or less valuable, interesting, or special to most others in the community. In fact, unlike an academic poet, a folk poet's words are valued in a community in so far as he or she has roles, values, and worldviews in common with others in it, not in so far as he or she is different.

Ontario folk poets come from widely varying backgrounds and have different occupations and roles apart from their common one as poets. Of the versemakers I contacted, the ratio of males to females was almost two to one. I suspect that the actual ratio is more balanced, but male poets were easier to find because they publish in newspapers more frequently and consistently than their female counterparts. Several of the women I located had never published; only one man had never done so.

The poets spanned the generations from the teens to the nineties. The teenagers were girls and their poems were about Terry Fox. These were not composed for school assignments, to please a teacher, or as an exercise to fulfil class requirements but to communicate their ideas with their families, friends, and community and to express a widely held ethos. But it is from the older generations – those over fifty years of age – that most Ontario folk poets come.

This does not mean that folk poetry in Ontario is a dying tradition. Nearly a quarter of my sample of poets was under fifty. But writing poetry is something that requires time, an understanding of the community, and perhaps some boldness. As evidence of the need for the latter, for example, only one of the teenaged poets submitted her work to a newspaper on her own initiative; the rest did so at the request of an editor or some other adult. But for the majority of poets, available leisure time, and often a loss of a near relative or some other major change in their lives, provided the spur to versifying. Time is the prerequisite most often cited by the poets themselves, and most did not begin verse-making until their late fifties. Laurena Wright of North Gower said that before then she was too busy working and raising her children; Anne Boyes of Aurora started when she was forced to retire from being a real-estate agent because of ill health.

However, verse-making also flows naturally from the kinds of instrumental and expressive roles taken on by a community's more mature members. They are held to be more knowledgeable about the group and thus more capable of the cultural stock-taking that goes on in folk poetry. They have experienced more sociocultural change and thus may see a greater disjunction between the appropriate and inappropriate. Older people have also developed extensive intergenerational ties with young adults, their own peers, and their seniors. Thus poet Gerry Eagan of Tottenham writes for events involving participants from several different generations. His wedding-shower verse celebrates his children's age group, and his retirement and anniversary verse reflects his own.

Educational levels vary widely among folk poets. To a certain extent this variation corresponds to generational differences; it was certainly more common for people to stop their schooling at grade eight in pre–Second World War Ontario than it is today, especially in rural areas where there were few high schools. For Ontario folk poets higher education is clearly neither a prerequisite for good verse nor essential to successful communication in other forms, spoken or written. But the university-educated among those surveyed in this study are distinctive in other ways: several are immigrants to Canada, including the only two with a first language other than English.

Variety extends to the occupations of folk poets as well. Two women in my sample were exclusively homemakers, but most worked in a service field – medical, secretarial, educational, or sales – or combined homemaking with raising children. The male service workers included a medical technician, a tailor, and a businessman. The rest were farmers, professional entertainers, industrial workers, or jacks-of-all-trades.

Both rural and urban residents write folk poetry. However, many of the urban poets – from Toronto, London, and Ottawa – formerly lived in a rural area and now reside in a suburb that has some sense of community, or write for a particular ethnic, occupational, or social-recreational group. Eric Parker of Scarborough, for example, writes verse directed to his fellow expatriate English amateur theatre players or his co-workers. His poetry offers subtle suggestions for possible improvements in their behaviour or comments on their foibles.

The characteristics outlined above are general. Most interesting, perhaps, is that Ontario folk poets seem to fall into three categories. The first is composed of those who have written only one poem in their lives. All were willing to talk to me, but because they in no way perceived themselves as poets, they were sure that they could not be helpful. Their verses were always highly topical and dealt with a subject for which the poet felt a strong personal and emotional involvement. Astrida Reader of Paris wrote "It Is about Us" to urge parents to join the home and school association, of which she was then membership secretary. She had been invited back to visit Newfoundland to assist in the formation of a home and school association there. Because of her strong positive emotional attachment to that province, where her family had moved from Europe when she was a teenager, she was especially flattered by the offer. Reader used the poem in her recruiting speech and also submitted it to her local newspaper, the *Paris Star*.

The majority of folk poets, though, write on occasion or on demand. Their poems, like those of the first group, are invariably topical. Their works may be written as a response to some problematic situation or at the request of a friend or relative. Some of these versemakers felt that the designation "poet" was mine, not their community's; others, like Gerry Eagan, the "Bard of Tecumseth," obviously have local recognition. Lynn Allison of Paris exemplifies many of this group's qualities. He wrote "Break Zero Four" as a memorial to a young girl, "Shortcake," with whom he and a number of other commuters from Paris to Toronto communicated on their citizens' band radios. The poem was copied and passed around to this group. Allison has also written verse invitations to his family's reunions and was asked by his wife to do the same for hers.

The final group includes the self-styled, self-defined poets. Although these people were sometimes surprised that a Torontonian like myself had managed to locate them, they were not at all uncomfortable with the idea that I wanted to talk to them as poets. They wrote numerous verses; some produced as many as two or three a day. Although most of their works were topical and communicative, the relation between topic and poem was often quite tenuous, or the problem the verse addressed might seem relatively insignificant to the community. Other verse seemed, in contradiction of the ethos of folk poetry, inherently personal and self-directed rather than other-directed. Even this super- ficially less functional poetry would often be sent to the local news- paper. Perhaps it is written because the community expects a poet to write a great deal of verse, even when truly appropriate topical material is unavailable.

One such poet, Bob Raymes, the "Poet Laureate of Palgrave," began versemaking when he moved to Palgrave in the 1950s and was asked to write for community showers and other events. He soon sent works to local newspapers and is now a regular weekly contributor to Betty Burton's "Palgrave Patter" column. He can write two or three poems a week when he wants to, he says, but does not because the paper cannot accommodate such high production.

Some of Raymes's verse concerns extremely significant local prob- lems, like a rash of convenience store hold-ups in the summer of 1983. Raymes expresses the community's outrage over one case, which took place nearby, in "Do We Pamper Our Criminals":

A little girl worked in a milk store
Just giving service of need
Three scoundrels came in and shot her
Oh what a dastardly deed.

However, he also writes poems on subjects with much less cultural import, like "March":

The first part of March
Has been snowy and cold,
But now old man winter
Is losing his hold. (Raymes collection)

In a socially and culturally diverse area like Ontario no single individual genuinely represents the entire community (see Mark 1984). Most poets questioned on this matter suggested, perhaps from modesty, that their poetry was self-expressive rather than community-expressive. However, their audiences may not agree. When asked if she felt that Bob Raymes spoke for the traditional side of the community, Betty Burton said, "Yeah, I do. Probably not consciously; he just speaks from the heart" (T83–34).

Yet Ontario folk poets are not unconscious producers of spontaneous works; they are quite aware of their audience. Tottenham's Gerry Eagan says that he has not tried to branch out into different kinds of poetry or to send his poems beyond his immediate community: "The facts involved aren't of that much interest to someone else [from outside the community]. Because for perfect poetry and rhyming and all that, I'm sure in some cases it leaves quite a bit to be desired" (T84–38). Other poets do send their work to national or international poetry contests, choosing not only their "best" work but that which has the fewest local references and which they feel would have the widest appeal.

Almost every poet agreed that a versemaker needed nothing more than interest. The shared identity of a significant other – a fellow community resident – rather than individual technical skill as a versemaker was paramount. The question of a poet's individuality becomes almost irrelevant; it is as important – and as unimportant – as that of any other resident. What is most significant to these poets as well as to their community is that they speak to it: "I don't think poetry should be a place where you try to display your knowledge of big words or anything like that. I like it simple; it's easier to read, easier to understand, and in most cases more interesting because if you put the accent on all the big words, you lose the down-to-earth" (Gerry Eagan, T84–38).

Yet Ontario folk poets share a self-conscious or externalized difference from the rest of their community. They are informal ethnographers as well as members of their own society. Only a very few are problematic personalities like Newfoundland songmaker Paul E. Hall,[4] but they are nevertheless different. Some personal experience allows them to separate themselves from and objectify their worldview and ethos. This may result from biculturality, such as being Catholic in a mainly Protestant area, foreign-born among Canadians, or country-born in the city; from some physiologically related problem, perhaps a speech impediment or childhood injury; or from a sense of placelessness or curiosity that results from being an adopted child or having an unusually great interest in history and the past. Their difference allows them not only to experience what happens in their community but also to stand apart from it and offer a comment on its appropriateness or inappropriateness.

THE FOLK POET'S FOIL: THE NEWSPAPER EDITOR

If poets generally represent the community and appropriateness, local newspaper editors usually exemplify the opposite. They are often outsiders who do not share local values. Yet they are the most influential audience for newspaper poetry since they determine whether or not an item will be published: "[Editor] M.B., he was the guy that put all that stuff in the paper. And he wanted me to – he wanted all [the poems] I could get and so I kept giving them to him ... Cause he wanted all he could get from Haliburton. And then he went out west. The [other] editor came back. So he only put two of mine in ... and he put the other [poets' verses] in. So I don't bother with them [now]" (Ed Miller, T84–24).

As outsiders, whether or not they are trained journalists, editors see the functional and semantic place of poetry very differently from poets. Editor John Slykhuis of Bradford, a trained journalist, receives two or three poems a week – almost as many as letters to the editor. He comments:

We like to offer readers a forum for not only poems but for stories, letters, whatever they want to submit. I think that's an important part of a community newspaper, to cover all aspects of human activity in that community, and that includes that type of thing. And we don't run Poetry Corner every week; we don't have room for it every week. We run it when we can.

The majority of poems we do get aren't particularly good, I think. I don't particularly like them, but that doesn't make them any less legitimate. That's not really a criterion I use for using a poem or not using a poem. Like I say, if people had enough interest to write it then certainly we'll do our best to publish it. (T83–44)

Slykhuis, and poet-editors Jim Merriam of Tara and Bob Shrier of Goderich, were the only editors out of about ten I contacted who consented to be interviewed on the subject of local poetry. Obviously, they are unusually sympathetic to it. Most editors commented that they published the poems they received when there was space between the ads, and otherwise they threw them away. Several said that they did not publish much verse for fear of being sent more that they would then be obliged to use. Considering this pervasive negative attitude, that local poetry is published at all testifies to its great symbolic significance.

It is not surprising that the local newspaper is a difficult medium for publication. Publishers and editors see the local newspaper first as a money-making enterprise, a view reflected in its contents:

Layout starts with ads, which tells you how big the paper will be. Sixty-six per cent ads is about paying, and it could go as low as fifty per cent or as high as seventy per cent. And [the number of pages] has to be in multiples of four because of printing. Let's say you have twenty-two pages at sixty-six per cent, so you have a big choice. What have you got this week? Oh God, there was a skating carnival. A full page of skating carnival pictures and we could run a house ad if we have to; or God, I have all this backlog of something or other, so you run twenty-four pages. If nothing bloody happened that week, you'd run twenty pages, so you put the same number of ads, fewer pages. (Mac Swackhammer, T84–41)

Thus, to editors, poetry's most useful role is as filler:

It's three o'clock in the morning. You're doing layout and you've got this goddamned hole where there's supposed to be a letter and a letter didn't come in. You go to E.R.'s file, and there may be fifteen or twenty poems in that sucker.

We never discouraged anybody because if you discourage somebody, anybody, you're in trouble. If someone brings in something, my God, you just welcome it with open arms. And you find some way, usually because you've committed yourself and you don't want to make E. mad, to use it in one form or another. (Ibid.)

Editors are often concerned about aspects of the works they print that are quite unimportant to the poets themselves. "They seem to think that's – it's the easiest form of expression, although it's pretty apparent that it's the most difficult to do' well. But you can see that in the quality of the poems. Most think they can throw down a bunch of rhyming couplets and 'I've got a poem,'" (John Slykhuis, T83–44). Clearly, to Slykhuis, the technical rather than the social and communicative aspects are paramount criteria for judging the poetry he publishes. Readers from the traditional community, however, judge it more important that a poem is by a neighbour or about a familiar experience than whether it fits conventional expectations for poetic style and form. For them a beautiful poem is one asserting appropriate sentiments, not necessarily one displaying elegant expression.

Editors understand that printing a poem encourages its writer – and others – to send in more material. John Slykhuis comments, "You can tell when you're getting through to particular poets because they keep submitting poems. We've got several people in there that have – they might send in one a month or so and they just keep writing them and keep sending them in. So certainly seeing their poem in print obviously acts as a spur to them doing more, and I doubt if they would if they sent something in that didn't get published. I'm sure that would put a damper on their enthusiasm. It would be discouraging. And certainly sending poems to newspapers has got to be the most difficult way of getting something into print, because most editors aren't too sympathetic to poetry" (ibid.). Having a work published is not only encouragement to write more and have those poems printed also, but it provides personal validation, as a positive comment from a neighbour would: "Well I'm sure that when they write them, they think it's good enough for publication. They want some – I guess it gives it legitimacy when they see it in print. 'Yeah, that really was good enough to be published, that really was good.' Although it isn't necessarily so" (ibid.). In addition, publisher Bob Shrier suggests, "You never know what one thing like that will do. The person could go on to be a great poet, just be the sheer encouragement of seeing their name in print, or their stuff in print. I think that's very important" (T83–54).

How do the poets themselves view the editorial function? Their perspective on the role of their works in the newspaper is evident in their comments, letters, and actions. Letters they send to newspapers accompanying their submissions show that versemakers see literary merit, reader interest, almost anything but economics as the prime forces determining whether or not an item will be included. One poet wrote: "Am enclosing a poem which you might find appropriate for this time of year. Hope you like it enough to print it."[5] Poets also suggest that the newspaper publish their poem as a favour, as in: "Here is a submission for your poetry section. I sincerely hope you'll publish it for me."

If a poem is not published promptly, the person who submits it usually complains. As Palgrave's Betty Burton commented, "It's a little bit upsetting if you do something and then week after week it isn't in. Especially if it's timely – if it's on rain and [when it's published] we're in the middle of a drought. If they don't go in within the week, people say, well, 'What's he talking about?' It's a little bit of a blow to their ego, too, you know" (T83–33). For the poets/presenters, it is not ego alone but a sense of the immediacy of their verse's significance that makes them agitated when their work is not published. Their self-image as community members speaking purposefully to other community members suggests that meaning, not economic importance, should determine an item's place in the paper. As Burton has noted, the worth of their poetic commentary can be attenuated over time as its benefit to the community – though not its value as filler for the newspaper – is reduced. Poets see their work as meaningful in a timely context and are understandably upset when it is reduced to near nonsense because it has lost that currency.

Mac Swackhammer told me that local poet E.R. used to bring

pressure through her friends to have her verse published and that "when her poems aren't printed, she will come in and ask for them back so that she can send them to the other newspaper" (T84–41). Other poets try to add some incentive for publication when they submit their works, such as "I have enjoyed seeing my poems in your paper and it is certainly rewarding to be told by people who have read them that they too are enjoying them."

As far as the readers' interests are concerned, editors' and poets' perspectives merge. John Slykhuis says, "I guess it may act as a catalyst to get other people to say, 'Hey, maybe I can write a poem too'" (T83–44). Editors hope that a published poet will be a more attentive audience for the paper and may encourage others to read or subscribe to it. Poets hope that their audience will read and respond to the expression. But both editors and poets (though with different ends in mind) assume that a major reason poetry is published in a newspaper is that the readers want it there.

FOLK POETRY AS "EQUIPMENTS FOR LIVING"

Critic Kenneth Burke suggests that forms of literature are "equipments for living" (1967, 103), and folk poetry is no exception to this. But what are appropriate uses for it in Ontario, and what can folk poetry as a genre accomplish? What particular events, scenes, or persons are valid subjects for a poem? How does poetry produce an effect on the situation of its presentation that might not be realized in another communicative folkloric genre? In seeking to provide some possible answers to these various queries, we might use the distinction between descriptive and hortatory folk poetry as a point of departure. Descriptive texts have a benign, passive aspect, as in:

I grew up in the country
Went to a one room school
And took with me a scribbler
A pencil and a rule. (Gordon Winters, *Grand Valley Star and Vidette*, 28 April 1982)

Hortatory poetry, on the other hand, is active in intention, and concerns the need to rectify an inappropriate situation:

So let's go out and do our part
And show these folks we care
And help in any way we can
To bring their lives repair. (Hind 1981, 9)

Some poems are almost exclusively active and hortatory, like "Before
It Is Too Late":

> If you have a tender message,
> Or a loving word to say,
> Do not wait till you forget it,
> But whisper it today.
> The tender word unspoken
> The letter never sent,
> The long-forgotten messages,
> The wealth of love unspent –
> For these some hearts are breaking,
> For these some loved ones wait;
> So show them that you care for them
> Before it is too late. (Frank Herbert Sweet, *Alliston Herald*,
>   3 August, 1983)

But few descriptive poems lack any hortatory element. Even verse
celebrating everyday life in a particular locale does so in implicit
contrast to life in the city or in other regions. When a poem idealizes
the activities and concerns of traditional communities, it is implicitly
suggesting that the status quo can and should be maintained, even
in the face of incursions by newcomers and the appurtenances of
modernity. Insiders, moreover, understand that a number of poems
that appear to be textually descriptive are in fact critical. For example,
in Bonnie Hind's "Dear Dad" a young boy berates himself for not
playing hockey well enough to make his father proud. The verse
implicitly condemns the father for taking the game too seriously and
for being angry at his son without a valid reason.

In addition to the descriptive-hortatory features of folk poetry,
Aristotle's distinction between deliberative, forensic, and demonstrative
rhetoric usefully suggests what poems can do, to whom, in what
ways, and for what reasons. Deliberative rhetoric is directed to future
activity and attempts to sway the audience on matters of public policy,
as in the following:

> If everyone who takes the wheel would say a little prayer
> And keep in mind those in the car depending on his car[e],
> And make a vow and pledge himself to never take a chance
> A great crusade for safety would suddenly advance. (author
>   unknown, *Forest Standard*, 24 November 1982)

Forensic rhetoric refers to the past, as when a lawyer attempts to
persuade a jury of an individual's innocence or guilt;

I guess it's hard to tell what happened so how can we decide
We are sure the driver did his best, and we look at him with pride.
(Bill Crewson, *Agincourt News*, 10 December 1980)

Demonstrative rhetoric can involve either praise or blame, is oriented towards the present, and deals with general virtues:[6]

Love your country and abide
By all the rules that's set aside
They'll be rewards for you my friend
When you take that ride around the bend. (Leon Robbins, *Smiths Falls News Record News*, 14 December 1983)

This division of rhetorical forms concerns not only whether the poem's view is directed towards past, present, or future but also the kinds of issues referred to and the mode in which they are considered. The rare examples of deliberative and forensic rhetoric in Ontario folk poetry have narrative content. For instance, before Bonnie Hind's "Dover Flood of 1979" deliberatively suggests that the community provide assistance to victims, it describes the sequence of events that led to the flood. Similarly, Bill Crewson's "Disaster at the Crossroads 1975" gives an account of a train and bus accident and then submits forensically that the driver was not to blame for what happened.

Most current Ontario folk poetry is demonstrative either by stating explicitly appropriate morality and behaviour or by implying them. Most texts have a minimal narrative content, but they could by no means be called strictly lyrical either, as this example, concerning an attempt to start a local theatre, shows:

Although discouraged you must seem
You are one step closer to your dream
Of owning your theater someday
We know there surely is a way.
This community should be proud of you
Who have showed again what you can do
And given of your very best
Now surely we can do the rest.
To support our youth who had this dream
And work together as a team
That someday in the sands of time
Their footprints they will leave behind. (author unknown, *Grand Valley Star and Vidette*, 19 May 1982)

When a demonstrative work discusses an event, it usually does so perfunctorily; the poet apparently assumes that readers will know the facts. What is significant to both the poet and the community is the message transmitted in the work; dramatic aspects of the event, which might detract from this message, are played down in favour of a drier, descriptive mode.

Whatever rhetorical strategy it uses, all folk poetry in Ontario bears on some kind of perceived cultural appropriateness or inappropriateness. The latter may stem from an overt problem. For instance, when a young female employee of a small town convenience store was crippled during a robbery and the men who injured her were let out on bail, poet Bob Raymes saw a situation in which it was clear that both the moral rule that evil-doers should be punished and the moral and pragmatic rules that the public must be protected from dangerous criminals were violated. He expressed his concern in a poem in order to condense local opinion into a succinct, evocative form and to unify the community in opposing antisocial behaviour.

Alternatively, the social rifts or disjunctions considered in folk poetry may be ethnographically more familiar than these day-to-day social problems of Ontarians. A wedding, for instance, creates a community disjunction (see Van Gennep 1960); two individuals who previously held different status and belonged to different households sever old kinship relationships and begin new ones with each another and with their families. Simultaneously, they begin new social relationships with other groups in their community. Folk poetry about weddings indicates the necessity of re-situating the couple within their local and kinship groups. As presented at a community shower or public event, a poem works partly to mediate or negotiate the rift created by a marriage. Similarly, memorial poetry situates a deceased person in the social body and acknowledges the gap created by his or her death, while attempting some kind of resolution – remembrance of good deeds, the prospect of heavenly rewards, and so on.

At any time, however, folk poetry may assert or support appropriateness. Laudatory expressions in a poem celebrating community life or family relationships, for example, serve periodically to reaffirm community ties and strengthen common bonds between individuals. Such periodic affirmations raise the level of community interaction from the ordinary to the level of the special and marked. Without such affirmations the ties of consensual morality might be gradually attenuated.

Disjunction or inappropriateness is approached differently when imposed from the outside rather than generated within the community. For instance, Bob Raymes's poem referred to above situates the source of a rift both in the robbers' criminal act and in the judge's decision to free them on bail. These individuals are all outsiders, and Raymes overtly condemns their actions. However, if a problem's root lies inside the community, the poet cannot uphold shared morality by naming names and finding specific faults, and thus must approach it in a roundabout way. Accordingly, in Bonnie Hind's "Out of the Mouths of Babes," a wise child's confrontation of her father's possible infidelity and certain neglect of her mother is portrayed as a fictitious, hypothetical situation.

The aim to blame or to praise may seem fairly simple, but in much Ontario folk poetry it is not so. Commendation and denunciation here apply not to the specific content of the poems but to their function in the society. Obviously, verse that tells of "10 little drivers cruising down the line, one had a heavy foot and then there were nine" (*Manitoulin Expositor*, 26 January 1983) is blaming individuals who drive at excessive speeds for traffic fatalities. It even includes a "moral" at the end, "Speed limits are set for your safety," and is headlined "A parable ... for careless drivers." Yet within the text itself, expression of blame is implied rather than stated.

Other poems explicitly praise their subject:

O Canada, fair Canada, you've given us so much
The maple tree and the willow trees and evergreens and such
We love you through the summer's heat
And even winter's cold
And in the lovely springtime fresh
And autumn's red and gold. (Ada Bertram, *Alliston Herald*,
    6 July 1983)

In contrast, a poem that textually lauds some valued trait or characteristic may be contextually intended to blame someone for not living up to this ideal. Again the source of the rift becomes significant. Poems that are concerned with problems within a community are couched hypothetically – "If everyone who drives a car would lie a month in bed" and connotatively – "If everyone could stand beside the bed of some close friend / And hear the doctor say 'No hope,' before the end" – (author unknown, *Forest Standard*, 24 November 1982). Such verse suggests rather than states the source of the problem. In this example the guilt of the driver and the sorrow of friends are implied in a fictitious mode; although the poem refers to a realistic situation, the poem does not identify a literal event.

The hypothetical, connotative, and fictitious mode contrasts with that of poems about inappropriateness from outside the community. The latter are usually situated and realistic, as in "The New Stamp":

The cheapest thing I bought last week
Was barely an inch square
Paper-thin, of quality poor,
True value wasn't there. (Eva E. Coles, *Caledonia Grand River
Sachem*, 23 February 1983)

They can also be explicit and denotative:

It's true we do need postage stamps,
For business, as well as to keep in touch,
With our families and our friends,
But this 32 cent one is just too much. (Ibid.)

Again, it is most unusual for poetry that seeks to place blame
within a community to be textually explicit about a problem's source.
This important feature is a function of poetry's usual context for
public presentation, the newspaper. That medium is not used for the
expression of intracommunity criticism but for opinion. Most contention occurs around matters in the public sphere, such as whether to
build a new hockey arena, and thus is public knowledge anyway.
Otherwise, rivalries are hushed up or placed in the background, as
when children are told to be especially nice to someone they do not
like.

Especially where a specific individual is involved, local residents
deem it neither safe nor acceptable to be explicitly critical. Ed Miller's
reaction to his satirical song's inadvertently going public was to resolve
never to write another:

That was back when I was a kid. I wrote one about B.L. He was an
awful torment in the [lumber]camp. Stout lad ... he was a good lad,
good fellow you know, but – he was a neighbour of ours and I used to
go in there and borrow the lantern and everything – but he was always
tormenting us young fellows, you know. And A.L. and I went for a walk
on Sunday in the camp ... and we made one [song] up on B. And A.
came and sang it to him. And boys that – it got out in the town, and
on Saturday night in the town the kids were singing it [laughing] to him.
I felt sorry for him. And it was a nasty song, you know [laughs]. And
I have to laugh. I never would make anything up bad about anybody
[laughs], take off on anybody, nobody, after that [laughs]. No way would
I do that. So I always kept pretty careful after that. (T84–24)

Though the song was taken up by the "kids," the unruly element of
the town, their performance apparently caused no permanent problems

for the songmakers or their community. However, public presentation of critical material dealing with internal problems violates both the ethos of neighbourliness and folk poetry's ethos of social harmony. Miller suggests that since critical verse is inappropriate for public consumption yet its distribution is more or less uncontrollable, the only alternative is self-censorship.

Because such works can set up animosities that are difficult to diffuse, a poet wanting to criticize personal behaviour must do so in hypothetical, almost parable form. By using poetry, the performer invokes an ethos of togetherness that suggests that there is no substantial disagreement on the issue. The matter is raised as one of shared morality rather than one of contention. Take, for example, Bonnie Hind's "Out of the Mouths of Babes," the poem cited earlier about marital inattention (or infidelity). Hind wishes to denounce certain activities, but as they are problems within the community she cannot do so explicitly. We cannot tell if the poet intends a particular case, and this ambiguity is essential to her poem's effectiveness.

"Out of the Mouths of Babes" is mainly a monologue by a wise child who instructs her father, a form and style familiar in Victorian popular ballads (see Ellis 1978). The speaker describes the situation at home when the father is away. Hind uses demonstrative rhetoric; she portrays the hard working, the selflessness, and other fine qualities of the mother:

There's lots of things we just can't do
So she does it alone
Like when she does the dishes while
I'm talking on the phone. (Hind 1981, 31)

The situation is finally resolved in three verses, narrated in the third person, in which the father cancels his assignations for the evening, embraces his wife, and resolves to lead a more virtuous life.

Very few poems seem to deal with intracommunity problems in a tone of censure, even if the issue is a public one. An exception is KB's "Lamentation for a Golden Dream," which was submitted to the Bradford-based weekly Topic but not published. The poem is very explicit and concrete about the individual and situation it criticizes:

There once was a Mayor named Ripper
Who loved baseball, hockey and so –
He dispised all the rest
Of the arts and detest-ed
The players of theatre, you know!

By presenting it only under his or her initials, the author refused to acknowledge the work. It was rejected as inappropriate by an editor who in comparison with others in his position is unusually sympathetic to poetry.

Within a community, if praise is involved, either the hypothetical-connotative mode of expression or the situational-denotative one is possible. A local resident can be lauded for exemplifying ideal community morality:

> Joe Vanderpaelt's that kind of guy
> And everywhere he goes
> He'll always stop to lend a hand
> To everyone he knows. (Hind 1981, 10)

Since praise is her main intention, Hind can explicitly describe her subject and the characteristics she particularly likes, again using demonstrative, present-oriented rhetoric and considering her subject's general character rather than citing some specific act.

However, poets often employ a hypothetical mode when praising a community event or activity. For instance, Doreen Young's poem about the Paris Block Parents' Association redresses a lack of publicity for that organization. Modelled on Clement Moore's "A Visit from St Nicholas," it describes a Christmas night when Rudolph's nose light went out:

> What did Santa look for that dark foggy night
> Why a Block Parent sign; could they fix Rudolph's light.

Santa Claus obtains a Christmas tree light for the purpose from the Block Parent home, and:

> A short minute later she saw Rudolph's new light
> All of the reindeer leapt back into the sky. (*Paris Star*,
>   23 December 1981)

Young uses the parable both to impart the information that Block Parents can be available sources of aid to anyone, not only to children, as well as more generally to draw public attention to the organization.

Situations where disjunction comes from outside the community need not be dealt with so delicately and carefully, even if blame is involved. Some editorializing poems explicitly indicate their topics, such as the introduction of the metric system:

Please bring back the weights and measures,
The ones in by-gone days we knew,
As I for one do not agree,
With the Federal Government's view. (Eva E. Coles, *Caledonia Grand
River Sachem*, 16 February 1983)

The issue may be a significant one affecting everyday life, but it is
not as potentially divisive as one involving local personalities, even
in the unlikely event that other local people are metric supporters.

When something outside the community is to be criticized, folk
poets can do so implicitly, though this is inevitably less effective since
they run the risk of being misunderstood. Consider, for instance, Mae
McGuire's highly connotative and symbolic anti-war poem:

We will not march to your trumpets,
Nor suffer and die to your drums
Don't tell us to place our glory
In the grave where the white cross stood
For we know they are covered in shellholes
In slime and sewage and blood. (*Woodbridge Vaughan Times*,
16 December 1981)

This poem is as generically appropriate as any more specific one, and
its demonstrative rhetoric is effective. Here, the poem's strong symbolism makes its message fairly clear, but the work certainly cannot
be described as realistic or situational.

When folk poets praise outsiders, they are almost always explicit.
Given the prevailing attitude about the outside world implied, for
instance, in poems about towns, we may be surprised that aspects
of life beyond the community could merit any praise. However, a
few outside scenes, people, and events become prototypical for local
poetry. Cancer victim Terry Fox, for instance, who ran a marathon
race through the Atlantic provinces, Quebec, and Ontario to raise
money for cancer research, obviously indexed personally many com-
munity-valued moral qualities, which were outlined in scores of poems
and songs about him. All of these favour an explicit mode, as exem-
plified in this one:

Go, Terry, go
You can do it. We all know that you can.
The miles were long and the pavement hard,
But you won many hearts as you ran. (Grant Filson, *Education
Insight*, 5 January 1981)

We have seen that folk poetry, unlike some other traditional genres, emphasizes the benign aspects of the community: cultural consensus rather than the culturally questionable. To characterize folk poetry as "social glue" is perhaps simplistic. However, the common rhetorical uses of verse take advantage of this unifying function, especially where praise is involved but sometimes even in cases where blame is laid. Ontario's folk poetry, whether presented in oral or written contexts, has sociocultural work to accomplish. We have looked at its rhetorical strategies; now we turn to its special proficiency in its tasks and its methods of undertaking them.

CHAPTER THREE

Ontario Folk Poetry and Its Appropriate Contexts

In Ontario the most important single medium for the public presentation of folk poetry is the weekly newspaper. Nearly every community, urban and rural alike, has one, and almost every one prints verse periodically, at least half a dozen times a year. Some have regular poetry columns to which contributors send their favourite works, but the majority include poems on an ad hoc basis. The broad distribution of these weeklies – *Manitoulin Expositor* reporter and photographer Mac Swackhammer suggests that every household on Manitoulin Island subscribes to a local paper – means that this is the medium through which a versemaker or verse-presenter's works reach their largest possible appropriate audience.

The community newspaper's content is distinctive. Beginning editors and reporters, fresh from university or college journalism, may try to implement a concept based on urban dailies or national newspapers, but they inevitably meet considerable resistance from those who have a better understanding of the medium. Swackhammer comments:

There was lots of news which we identified as news happening all around us; there was a lot of news happening around us which we did not identify as proper news ... We would write all these news stories and sometimes your stories in the front would be too long and you have to run them into the back. Out goes the Green Bay News – the Green Bay News is "Mr and Mrs Carl Skippen motored to see Mr and Mrs Rene Skippen Sunday afternoon" – and in goes this news story about shady land deals at Carter Bay.

Mrs B., our community contact, goes "Look at this! There's thousands of people all over the world who get the *Manitoulin Expositor*. They don't care about this thing in Carter Bay. This is Green Bay News; this is a letter from home." And she'd say every week, "This is a letter from home." She said that so much that I made up a house ad about it. (T84-41)

This means that the community newspaper's contents will little resemble those of an urban daily. In the *Bothwell Times* of 4 May 1983, for example, headlines on the front page included "Rodeo Postponed," "Fire Area Board Meets," "School Board Requisitions Up," and "Spring Pansies." The report from the local member of Parliament and "From the Early Times: Items from Past Issues" were on the second page, with local columns from community correspondents – "St. Ignatius School News" and "Talk of the Towns" – and advertisements taking up the final eighteen pages.

Local newspapers are currently undergoing change, along with the communities they serve. Conglomerates like Metroland (which owns some twenty papers in the Toronto area)[1] are buying up weeklies that were once local family businesses. Such papers are immediately identifiable by the full-colour pictures displayed on their front pages. Others cannot afford such extravagance. The Metroland papers' contents reflect the impersonality of the transformed modern Ontario community: "They don't have the same feeling for the people. You know, it's a big corporation, so it's controlled more or less by the people in Metroland who give orders to the editor" (Betty Burton, T83–33). Rival editor John Slykhuis says: "People out there have this idea that there's this giant corporate octopus that is more or less dictating their home town news to them. I don't think they like that. I think they like a paper that is locally owned and locally operated and has the local sympathies at heart and knows what's going on in the community" (T83–44).

Metroland papers are not only glossier and more impersonal than other community weeklies; they are also larger and are obviously modelled on urban dailies. For instance, the *Mississauga News* of 9 May 1984 (published by Metroland) had one hundred pages and six sections. In order of appearance, these were a front portion including a business section; Sports and Entertainment; Real Estate; Community; More Community; and Classifieds. Page-one stories were political and dealt with issues that extended in substance beyond local concerns, such as "Drunk Driving Killed Teen, Inquest Told" or "Environment Waste Group Gets Off To Disappointing Start." There were editorials, on page six, on these kinds of issues, but the first letter to the editor concerned local Rotary Club activities. The Sports and Entertainment section had both district news and material of broader interest on the front page, but there was more of the latter than the former inside. In contrast, the two community sections looked much like any other local newspaper, with front-page headlines like "Pocock Students Win Annual Math Bowl" or "Church Seeks Vendors For Garage Sale." It is ironic, but very telling for the sociocultural situation, that Real Estate appeared before Community in the paper. Metroland tries to appeal to the ex-urban newcomers – their advertisers' market – rather than to the traditional community.

Betty Burton is a paid columnist and correspondent for one of the many rival privately owned newspapers that were started as competition for Metroland or that pre-dated it. She outlines some of the changes apparent in her local paper after its takeover by that company:

The tone of the paper's different now. They used to go after community news all the time, and now it doesn't seem to have the same thing. They've got little bits from Woodbridge, and I mean, who the heck knows anybody over there? ... It's a long way [about 20 miles] from here. And things that happen right in the area they don't seem to pay much attention to, or they kind of qualify it, "Well, gee, is it going to be ok?" You know, before, you could phone and say "Hey, come on, the scouts are doing this" or "There's somebody down the road having a party" and they'd be right there. So what happens now when you send things in they usually don't have room for it. (T83–33)

The *Gananoque Reporter* of 9 May 1984 represents the most common format for weeklies. It lies somewhere between the purely local concerns of the *Bothwell Times* and the aspirations of the *Mississauga News*. It had twenty-eight pages and two sections, otherwise undifferentiated. Page-one news included an article about the local representative to the national Liberal party leadership convention. The pages following contained an editorial on local politics, columns from contributors, and sports, all of which was local, such as "Legion Ladies Bowling League Ends Season." On page six the first wedding announcements and obituaries appeared, and the last two pages of classifieds included "thank yous" and "in memoriams."[2]

Local newspapers, including the community sections of the Metroland papers, are the major medium for publishing items of very immediate and local social and cultural concern. To the resident who reads about the Legion Ladies' Bowling League or the activities of the Skippens, some but by no means all of the material may actually be news and not already familiar knowledge. However, an important function of the local newspaper is to verify the significance of quotidian ritual activities, from house visits to Women's Institute meetings, that take place in a community. In words and in pictures the articles take an inventory of community members as active agents in local life, and the emphasis on "good news" indicates the self-presentational ethos intended. Betty Burton maintains, "If you want to be uplifted, buy a community newspaper. I mean, you know, how many got killed today, how many got raped, you wouldn't see that in the paper, not around here. It wouldn't be acceptable. I don't write about accidents or fires or stuff like that, but things I know that people want to read about like a community shower. I know that people are going to read it because that's what they're always asking me about. That's what they talk about" (T83–34).

Local newspapers provide one sure venue for the performance of folk poetry in Ontario, but not the only one. Verse can also be performed orally. Historically, the church concert and the school concert were extremely popular contexts for song and verse presentations. Jack Miner's autobiography tells of a Methodist lawn social in the 1880s where he and his brother sang two highly moralistic, sentimental songs about filial duty, or lack thereof, and parental death: "Poor Old Dad" and "A Flower from my Angel Mother's Grave" (1969, 99–102). More recently, for a church concert sponsored and performed by the "Mr and Mrs Club," Pansy Allison of Ayr composed a four part dramatic recitation in verse about a prototypical, sentimentalized life-cycle.

The public contexts where Ontario folk poetry is performed orally, like those where it is presented in written form, are themselves indicators of change and its accompanying disjunction within a community. Changes may be active and obvious, such as those marked by celebrations of future marriages or individuals' departures from the area, when social relations are permanently altered. Or they may be more subtle, such as those signified in wedding anniversary parties or at meetings of associations like the Women's Institute or senior citizens' clubs, where individuals are temporarily separated from the community and symbolically incorporated into a group.

Ontario folk poetry can appropriately appear publicly in either oral or written form. The latter is most prominent, of course, in the local newspaper. Oral contexts are a bit more diverse than written ones, as well as being considerably less common. However, verse serves much the same functions in either medium, in most cases with identical styles of expression and to similar effect. In Ontario, vernacular poetry concerns issues of (in)appropriateness and affects them by appropriating material from the cultural milieu.

But why is poetry used rather than some other genre? What does a poem achieve that another textual genre cannot? These questions bring us to the pragmatics of folk poetry: how it is actually used and its relationship to its users, both performers and audiences.

Folk poetry is special because it allows its performer to say things that cannot be otherwise expressed. This dictum is true in two respects. First, using a particular genre changes the nature of performers' accountability for their material; for example, a joke-teller may deny cultural prejudice while telling "Newfie" Jokes, or a liberal male revival folksinger may say he is no misogynist despite the fact that he performs anti-female blues. Implicit arguments that "it's only a joke" or "that's not me, that's the tradition" – though underlying currents of ethnocentrism and misogyny are undoubtedly present – allow the teller or singer to use the genre to deny immediate, normal accountability for content that could be taken quite differently if it were said in everyday conversation. Furthermore, any genre carries tacit meanings peculiar to it that are part of a community member's knowledge and understanding. Thus, some concepts inherent to a genre are literally inexpressible in another; Ontario folk poetry has a particular symbolic language that makes assertions an audience could interpret wrongly, or fail to make any sense of, in another genre. And the two aspects of the dictum are not totally unrelated. The mitigating quality associated with folk verse is partly the result of this special language, and conversely, its unique idiom is partly directed towards assigning proper accountability.

In Ontario culture vernacular poetry affirms appropriateness or changes culturally problematic situations by retroactively re-evaluating and reconstituting their circumstances. In other words, folk poetry makes an issue appropriate by appropriating it. The outcome desired most often is to reduce disjunction, or to minimize the effects of change. This result must be for the most part retroactive, a marked difference from the Aristotelian one: "The poet's function is to describe not the thing that has happened, but a kind of thing that might happen, i.e., what is possible as being probable and necessary. The distinction between historian and poet is not the one writing prose and the other verse; ... it consists really in this, that the one describes the thing that has been, and the other a kind of thing that might be" (McKeon 1947, 635–6).

Ontario folk poetry accomplishes its sociocultural work primarily through analogy and mediation, and occasionally through inversion and reversal. Its juxtaposition of symbolic elements – the signifiers – allows the analogy, mediation, reversal, or inversion to try actually to change the community's perception – the signified – of an event, a scene, or an individual, as well as sometimes to elicit action by the audience. In semiotic terms, the signifier has an active relationship to its signified.

The symbolic function most frequently employed is the construction of analogical relationships between phenomena in order to elevate a local subject. For instance, when versemaker Bonnie Hind calls the 1979 flood in her area a "tragedy," she elevates and intensifies it from an incident of everyday life (which it undoubtedly is) to an event that is marked, highly significant, and merits attention even from those not directly affected by it (which it also is). Specifically, her analogies between the ice that dammed the river and a giant army tank on the one hand and between the floodwaters and a cobra on the other reflect the momentousness of the actual alteration of the familiar, safe, and life-supporting river to the unfamiliar, life-threatening, and decidedly dangerous flood.

An analogy like Hind's serves to exaggerate rather than to minimize its topic, and this method of elevating the local signifier is clearly preferred in contemporary Ontario folk poetry. Though no poem of which I am aware attempts to diminish an issue rhetorically, this is common in some other vernacular and local genres, such as the letter to the editor. Ontario folk poems achieve their effects by stressing the great symbolic size, weight, and general import of their concerns. In these works people are lions, not fleas, events are disasters of great importance, not minor issues, and scenes have magnificent qualities.

Alternatively, folk-poetic symbolism can work through mediation, in which an apparently opposing pair of signifiers finds a middle point that makes light of their differences. This is the most acceptable way in Ontario folk poetry of achieving the effect possible in a minimizing analogy. Thus, in order to realize the desired result in her poem about a young hockey player, Bonnie Hind could have drawn an analogy between the game and some fortuitous, insignificant event – a shopping trip, perhaps – and between the father's behaviour and that of some ill-reputed animal, like a skunk. Instead, to make her point that fathers should not berate their sons for lack of success in what is, after all, "only a stupid game," she creates an opposition between the young hockey player's father, whose over-involvement in the game causes him to shout, "Well it's about time that you did / Something right for a change," and the father's own father, whose lack of involvement was total: "He just stayed away." The point of mediation is hinted in "You said it was just for fun / And at first it was too." The boy says that despite his own lack of interest in the game, he hopes to match his father's over-involvement by making the National Hockey League, finally affirming "But I'll keep trying just for you / Because I love you Dad." Thus, Hind maintains that both over-involvement and under-involvement with children's hockey are inconsistent with fun (the object of the game) as well as with love (the expression intended). She suggests that the boy's love can be matched only by a mediation in the extremes of involvement. This solution is present in the poem's text, implicit in the exaggeration and extremes of behaviour it portrays.

Of less importance generically but occasionally found in Ontario folk poetry are two other forms of symbolic opposition: inversion and reversal. These are employed infrequently, with the aims of mediation or elevation, as discussed above. Using symbolism to increase differences between signifiers of real people, events, or scenes is inconsistent with Ontario folk poetry's "social-glue" or appropriation functions.

Folk poetry that deals with local events, scenes, and individuals is particularly useful in mending rifts that have been created in communities as a result of local change. Verse is uniquely fitted to this task, partly because of its special extra-textual association, which emerges in its everyday presentation. No one who reads or hears a poem expects it to be contentious. Thus, its audience reads or hears and then interprets verse in a way that emphasizes its benign qualities. A poem about a named community member may criticize, but it must do so humorously. A reproach expressed in verse is understood as a joke. The special language and symbolism of folk poetry can be perceived in terms of mediating and elevating analogies only because its audience already understands that it has such qualities. These symbolic functions are not always as clearly and plainly present in the text as they are in the Hind flood example.

We can best understand folk poetry's symbolic functions by considering them in practice. Accordingly, two oral and two written performances of poetry are presented here, with emphasis on the aims and methods of the poets and presenters.

BRAMPTON EAST WOMEN'S INSTITUTE

The first example is from Brampton, the central city of an area that has experienced rapid, intense change in the past thirty years. Brampton East Women's Institute branch, where this verse was presented, is a kind of microcosm of the region's transformations. It shows the community's split between traditional residents and newcomers.

At the branch's meeting in May 1984, all but four – one of whom was myself – of the twenty-seven women attending were over fifty years of age. The majority were over seventy. My contact, Mrs Shirley Laycock, suggested that the branch was moribund, having great difficulty maintaining its membership because most young women were uninterested in joining. One exception, Mrs W.R.D., with whom I discussed this problem, is a nurse at the local hospital who joined at the urging of a co-worker, the group's chairwoman. Mrs D. commented that most women her age are employed during the day and thus cannot attend afternoon meetings. Yet about half the group's sessions are scheduled at that time, both to accommodate older members who do not keep late hours and to adhere to the traditional time for such events. Mrs D. further suggested that the branch's membership was composed mainly of women from "the old farm families" of what is now suburban Bramalea and that they had little in common with many of her age group, most of whom were newcomers to the area.

The rift in the Brampton East W.I., though perceived by the membership as separating young and old members, spans lines familiar all over modern Ontario. Traditional residents and newcomers, farmers and suburbanites, are placed in open conflict. Further, Brampton East W.I. has few individuals in the structural or personal position of being mediators. They include Mrs Laycock, who is somewhat younger than most other members and a former city resident who retired from the farm more than twenty years ago, and Mrs W.W., whose role as chairwoman requires that she see all points of view. It was clear at the "Grandmother's Meeting" I attended that the bent of the group was not towards changing the schedule or otherwise accommodating younger members. Compromise was reached only very uneasily. For instance, when the group attempted to decide on an activity for the next month's meeting, one younger member suggested a tour around the new police station. After much hesitant but strongly stated discussion, this was vetoed as being beyond the physical capacity of most of the older women. Though a dinner was tentatively scheduled at the time, I learned that the group later decided on a trip to the race track.

The poetry performed at the May meeting, and its traditional place in the sequence of activities, show how folk verse is used to affect its situation of performance. Though superficially it avoids confronting the issues at hand, it closely concerns them.

The group shares hosting responsibilities, and this meeting was held in the living room of a member's apartment. The place was crowded. Though most women found chairs, a few had to stand. Before the gathering began officially, with the chairwoman, Mrs W.W., ringing a bell and calling the group to order, there was casual greeting and discussion of recent events. Mrs W.W. welcomed everyone and then, as is customary, she read a poem appropriate to the day's theme, "Grandmothers":

Grandmothers have magic. How else would they know
The out of way places where buttercups grow;
The pond in the meadow where pollywogs dwell;
The gossip the breezes are anxious to tell?
Or how can they tell by the tracks on the ground
Where hideaway rabbits and squirrels can be found?
And why do they hug you with eyes all aglow
And tell you the secrets you're longing to know?
Grandmothers have magic. Or do they recall
The things that were magic when they were quite small?

The members then recited by memory or read from their meeting books the "Institute Ode":

A goodly thing it is to meet
In friendship's circle bright,
Where nothing stains the pleasure sweet
Nor dims the radiant light.

No unkind words our lips shall pass,
No envy sour the mind,
But each shall seek the common weal
The good of all mankind.

This was followed by a collective recitation of the Protestant version of the Lord's Prayer. The chairwoman renewed her welcome; then the secretary, Mrs B.V., conducted the roll-call. In this part of the meeting she addressed the women formally, as Mrs John Smith or Mrs J. Smith, yet at all other times the members used each other's given names. At another meeting the roll might be answered by paying annual membership dues or gathering donations for some worthy cause, but at this one, as previously arranged, members responded by "telling a funny story or poem." Although a few simply said "present," ten women told stories or jokes, four delivered poems or short verses, and two gave both. (Several others arrived late and were not included.)

Notice how the roll-call's artistic content brings to the foreground the conflicts in the Brampton East Women's Institute, and in Ontario society in general:[3]

Secretary: ... Mrs H.G.
Mrs H.G.: Well, this isn't my own, but I'm going to read it. The American

cleric Henry Ward Beecher was handed a note one Sunday morning before the service. It contained a single word, "Fool." Mr. Beecher described the note to his congregation. "I have known many instances of a man writing a letter and forgetting to sign his name," he said, "but this is the first case I've ever known of a man signing his name and forgetting to write the letter."

Secretary: Mrs G.H.

Mrs. G.H.: Well I'll have to tell you a story.

Chairwoman: Come out here, Mrs H.; we can't hear you back there.

Mrs G.H.: I can hear, I can tell you, there [laughter from the listeners].

it was when men wore hats to church
and this poor chap
his hat was getting wore out
and he couldn't go to church
well he um he thought
the minister was going to [?] him
and he didn't know what to do
so
finally he went to the minister and told him
he said
he looked at hats but they were all too dear for him
and there was only one hat would suit him
so at last he bought the hat
he thought he could do with a little less meat and a little less
    sports and so
he got his hat
so he went out and he told the minister "I got my hat"
and he said "I'll be into church now" so the minister was glad
    to hear this
so it was he didn't show up again
and he'd lost his hat [laughs]
so the minister he knew the minister would [be angry] and he
    was just about frantic
so he went to the minister
and the minister thought well "I've got to do something"
he said ah
he knew the man was just going off the deep end
cause he was just beside himself he couldn't afford another hat
so he got the ah
the minister thought well "The ten commandments never let me
    down before I'll
try the ten commandments" [laughs]
so when he started he explained each commandment

and he said to the minister ah
the minister said to him
he got as far as "Thou shalt not steal"
and the man looked so dreadful he thought
it was going to let him down
so he got to "Thou shalt not kill"
and the man looked terrible
so when he got down to
and he explained every commandment as he went along so
    he got to "Thou shalt
not commit adultery"
the minis – the man was smiling
and he thought "The queer thing
Maybe it's working"
so he ah
when it was all over he said "Do you feel better you smiled" and
    he said "Yes"
he said "I am smiling and I feel a lot better"
well he said "Would you tell me
When I got to 'Thou shalt not steal' you looked terrible
And you looked worse when I'm telling
'Thou shalt not kill'
But you were smiling when I got
Near the end"
well he said "It was like this Reverend" he said
"When you said 'Thou shalt not steal'
I could have murdered that man [who stole my hat] [laughs]
When he said
They should
Thou shalt not
um
Kill
I could have strangled him with my bare hands
But when you got to [laughs]
'Thou shalt not commit adultery' I just remembered where I left
    my hat"
[laughter and comments: "She's getting this on tape!" etc.].
Secretary: Mrs D.L.
Mrs D.L.: Well, when ordering checks for a joint household checking
account, the teller asked Mrs Jones, "Do you want the plain blank checks
or the scenic type?" "The plain type," she answered. "I write the checks
and Mr Jones creates the scenes later" [laughter].
Secretary: Mrs M.I.

Mrs M.I.: Well, I was dumbfounded tonight, so I asked my daughter if she knew any jokes that were, you know, good enough to say here. So anyway she said, "What do you call a cow with no legs? Ground beef" [laughter].

Secretary: Mrs F.N.

Mrs F.N.: The young housewife was complaining. "These eggs are very small," she said as she stood in front of the egg counter at the grocery store. "They are straight from the farm this morning, madam," said the grocer. "That's the trouble with those farmers," she replied. "They're so anxious to sell their eggs,   they take them off the nest too soon" [laughter].

Secretary: Mrs J.A.R.

Mrs J.A.R.: I think those are a little bit hard to follow but I've got one. My mother aged seventy-eight refused to answer a vital question when a hospital intern came to take her medical history. "Young man," she snapped, "you can tell by my appearance that I am not a young woman. If I told you how old I am you would say my complaints are all due to old age. I know I'm old, but I want to find out what else is wrong with me."

Secretary: Mrs. J.S.

Mrs J.S.: When my nephew Bobby, a grade one pupil, became sick of school just before lunch, the teacher took him home during the noon hour break. Bobby had to give her the directions. After covering quite a distance and backtracking according to his instruction, the teacher became suspicious. "Bobby, are you sure this is right?" she asked. "Oh yes, the school bus does this every day" [laughter].

Secretary: Mrs B.V. Well. Being today was a grandmother's meeting and [laughs] me being a grandma not too long, I got a card in the mail and it said

> For you, Grandma, on Mother's Day.
> Nobody anywhere all the world through
> Could have a more wonderful grandma than you.
> Happy Mother's Day, love and kisses from Jennifer. [laughter,
>   comments: "Ah"]

But I also answered the second part of it too. I didn't take it as "or"; I took it as "and." But it was just a short little joke in here. "How did you know you were going only fifteen miles an hour?" the judge asked the driver accused of speeding. "I was on my way to the dentist."

Secretary: Mrs B.W.

Mrs B.W.: I really didn't have one. I just picked up this *News Appeal* and

Molly Rayner had submitted this in the last *News Appeal* at the hospital. An elderly man said to his wife, "You have always been with me. When I broke my leg you were there. During the Depression you were there. When I joined the army you joined as a nurse. When I was wounded you were there. When our house burned you were there. Now I'm sick in bed and you are here. You know, I think you are bad luck" [laughter].

Secretary: Mrs C.C.

Mrs C.C.: Well, it's too hard to get up but [laughter] but this being Grandmother's Meeting, this is called "Grandma's Gone."

In the dim and distant past
When life's tempo wasn't fast
Grandma used to rock and knit,
Tat, crochet, and babysit.

When the kids were in a jam,
They could always count on Gram.
In an age of gracious living
Grandma was the gal for giving.

Grandma now is at the gym
Exercising to keep slim;
She's off touring with the bunch;
Taking clients out to lunch.

Driving north to ski and curl,
All her days are in a whirl.
Nothing seems to stop or block her
Now that Grandma's off her rocker. [laughter]

And I have a little joke here too. It's a young mother invited the minister to dinner but she was worried because her two sons had picked up a few choice words that seemed to slip out now and then. "Tell you what," the mother said. "If you don't swear once tonight, I'll give you a fresh apple pie. If you do swear, I'll make the pie for the minister." The meal was uneventful. Before the minister left, he said to the boys, "Remember. By God we live and by God we die." And one of the boys chirped out, "Yes, and by God you lost the apple pie" [great laughter]. That was out of a church calendar [even more laughter].

Secretary: Mrs W.R.D.

Mrs W.R.D.: This is a little verse on a bookmark that's my favourite.

Not till the loom is silent
And the shuttles cease to fly
Shall God unroll the canvas
And explain the reason why
The dark threads are as needful
In the weaver's skilful hand
As the threads of gold and silver
In the pattern he has planned.

Secretary: Mrs N.S.
Mrs N.S.: Just a small verse from John Milton in Paradise Lost after he
went blind in 1858 in England [sic].

You may have health – You may have wealth, you may have health,
You may have thoughts as light as air,
But more than happiness, more than wealth
Is a merry heart that laughs at care.

Secretary: Mrs W.W.
Mrs W.W.: This is one from a paper back in 1976 and because of our
Grandmother's Meeting I thought it was rather fitting. It's a little bit sad,
but I thought the words were quite lovely. And it's entitled "Grandmother's
Letters."

"Go up to the attic, my darling," she said
"And there in an old oaken [chest]
You'll find a bundle of letters
Tied with a white shoelace.

"Bring them and read them to me, child,
Don't mind if my eyes fill with tears,
For the dear ones that sent them to me
Have been gone for many years.

"Yet they still bear the sweetest message.
There's still music in every word
Stirring my heart's emotion
Like the flutter of a little bird.

"Child when you're lonely – Child when you're alone and lonely,
And waiting seems far too long,
May you have some lovely letters
To comfort your heart like a song."

Then she took my hand and she whispered
"If ever you cannot see
May you have an angel of mercy
To do what you've done for me.

"Now come and kiss me goodnight, dear,"
And she told me to pray every day,
And while I was sleeping and dreaming,
The angels took Grandma away.

Secretary: Mrs B.W.
Mrs B.W.: This is just a saying on my – from the calendar.

May every port you enter
Bring pleasures ever new.
May good health be your steward
And good friends be your crew.

Secretary: Now that's all the ladies that's on the membership list. As you know, last month was our month to pay our fees so there's a few ladies that ...
Chairwoman: Any ladies, Doris do you have anything?
Doris: Oh yes, being I'm a grandma, you know, and kind of proud of it cause they're all three – and you know and I wasn't here the last night to pay, last month to pay my dues. Um, Stacy is the oldest and she's three and I don't phone up too often and so I didn't think she'd recognize my voice. So I phoned up one day and it rang for the third time and I knew what I was going to get. Little voice, picks up the phone, and she says "Hello." And I thought I better tell her who I am. I said, "Hi Stacy, it's Grandma." She says, "Uh huh, I know it's you Grandma" [laughter]. That can just put you right in your place.
Chairwoman: Anybody else? Mabel, have you anything to read?
Mabel: Yes I have.
Chairwoman: Good.
Mabel: A few years ago when Phyllis first left home to assume a teaching position near Chatham, and Marshall was away at college, Margaret turned to her husband Bruce and said tearfully, "You're all I have left now." "Darling," he replied consolingly, "I'm all you had to start with" [laughter].
Secretary: Mrs M.
Mrs M.: Well a young girl clerk was working for the Hudson Bay Company and a very obnoxious lady customer came in and the young girl was trying her best to please her this way and that way. And finally the customer said to her, "Are there no smarter clerks around than you?"

And she said, "Oh no, ma'am, they all ducked when they saw you coming" [laughter].

After the roll-call, the minutes of the last meeting were read and accepted, a collection taken up, correspondence read, and next meeting's program discussed. This business being complete – and taking about one hour – the activities began. One member read a paper on herbal healing; another conducted a silent auction; a third organized a puzzle contest complete with prizes; and another read a story about Mother's Day. A spelling bee was planned but was shelved for lack of time. After this the hostess, aided by a few others, served a "lunch" consisting of tea or coffee and sandwiches. The meeting closed with a member "doing the courtesies," thanking everyone who had presented activities at the meeting, and with the "Mary Stewart Collect," a group prose recitation from the meeting book. The gathering ended around 11:15 p.m., about three and one-quarter hours after it began.

The themes of the roll-call poems and stories reflect the most important levels of conflict among group members and within the community as a whole: young versus old, farmer versus urbanite, and newcomer versus traditional resident. The two genres, however, are used differently; poetry for the most part minimizes the rifts between the groups, whereas the jokes and stories generally emphasize those same gaps.

Poetry is always part of the chairwoman's first official welcome. It belongs to the moment when the group is formally convened – or re-formed – for the monthly meeting. Its place in the total event, as much as its content, evokes the mediating, unifying function of poetry. Like the rest of the welcome, it emphasizes the commonalities of the gathered individuals; they are fellow Brampton East W.I. members.

The poem that the chairwoman chose for the Grandmother's Meeting textually reinforces this message. It rhetorically closes the gap between the old and the young. Told from a child's point of view, it concerns grandmothers' unusual capacity for understanding their grandchildren. It shows the young and the old as having shared qualities, in implied or understood contrast with each one's relationship with the intervening generation. Grandmothers' ability to appreciate children is presented as a magical one, perhaps because such a close relationship between any other generations – parents and children for example – is inconceivable in the poem's world.

The Institute Ode and the Lord's Prayer, which immediately follow the chairwoman's welcome and are spoken collectively, are obvious poetic appeals for togetherness. They are textually mediatory and/or collectivizing, traditional, and are repeated at every W.I. meeting.

In contrast, the roll-call material is generally partisan. Of the "funny stories" especially, few are more or less neutral. The opening three, by Mrs G.H., Mrs H.G., and Mrs D.L., for example, set up a male-versus-female ethos, which I assume is cross-generational. However, the next two stories, by Mrs M.S. and Mrs F.N., ridicule the younger, newcomer generation's lack of knowledge about farming and farm animals. The young women in the Brampton East W.I. have non-agricultural occupations like nursing. Their ignorance of farming activities, though exaggerated in the stories, is evidently perceived by older members as a lack of basic cultural knowledge. The next two stories deal overtly with the young-versus-old question; in Mrs J.A.R.'s story, the old woman wins the verbal battle by making a clever retort, and Mrs J.S.'s anecdote shows the stupidity of a young person as well as incidentally invoking the school bus, which is an index of community breakdown in modern rural life.

The poem that follows these two stories implicitly tries to integrate the two groups. Though Mrs B.V. celebrates grandmothers in her poem, she introduces it as a message from a young person. Her joke appears to be neutral, as does the next story, by Mrs B.W., which is similar to the third.

Mrs C.C., who offered the humorous "Grandma's Gone," is well known as a performer of stories and poems at W.I. meetings. In asserting common ground for the generational groups, her poem is the most integrative in the entire roll. It shows that the modern grandmother is as up to date as members of the younger generation. Her activities are almost identical with theirs, and the commonalities between the two – the result of the grandmother's adjustment to modern life – are greater than their differences. The poem is especially conciliatory in these particular circumstances because of its suggestion that it is the older not the younger generation's responsibility to adjust. However, Mrs C.C.'s joke deals with intergenerational conflict between parents and children. It received the most enthusiastic and positive audience response of all the selections, perhaps partly because of its contrast with her previous selection.

Mrs W.R.D.'s bookmark poem is collective and integrative, as is Mrs N.S.'s, which follows it, though they do not directly address the issue in conflict. Mrs W.W.'s "Grandmother's Letters," like her opening verse, deals directly and positively with intergenerational contact. It urges the young to value the old, as the old value the young, for their potentially symbiotic relationship and especially because the older generation may be gone before it is appreciated. The younger Mrs B.W.'s calendar poem is general and collectivizing. Doris's telephone story concerns conflict, with the younger generation in the socially unacceptable position of putting the older generation in its place.

Mabel's husband story alludes to some of the problems of older people. The final, clerk story is the only one in which a younger person, though clearly an underdog, is the sympathetic favourite.

The poetry consistently emphasizes or tries to induce harmonious feeling within the group. When it deals with the immediate problems – the Grandmother's Meeting and intergenerational conflict – it does not point to the differences between old and young; instead, it shows their common qualities. The folk verse approaches local rift and disjunction by attempting to minimize it or to draw the individuals involved together on common appropriate ground.

COLGAN COMMUNITY SHOWER

My second example is from a community shower in Colgan. At these kinds of celebrations the poetry refers to the coming marriage that will permanently change the socially recognized relationship between the future bride and groom and between them and the community at large. In all cultures, weddings include ceremonies that mark that transition for the community and (re)incorporate the couple into it (Van Gennep 1960). In Ontario, community showers are part of a complex of events with this end – the actual wedding ceremony, the reception that follows it, and in many localities also a "shivaree" and/or presentation.[4]

At the Women's Institute meeting the poetry emphasized the commonalities within the group and, by implication, their difference from outsiders: poetry was part of an attempt to close rifts between W.I. members. At the community shower, in contrast, poetry makes and marks a rift and helps to separate two individuals from the rest of the community. It may do so by elevation, by ridicule, or, as in the verse below, by both. The change considered in this type of poetry is one that the community encourages and approves, and so the poetic texts themselves are specific, concrete, colloquial, and informal.

In Colgan Catholic parish the community shower is organized by a family member or by a friend of the bride and groom, who begins preparations over a month in advance. He or she arranges for use of the hall (most often the shower is held in a local school hall that can be obtained free of charge), applies for a liquor licence, places an advertisement in the local paper that invites everyone in the community to attend, and begins to collect money for the presentation.

The shower itself is usually held on a Saturday evening and begins around nine o'clock. Most people, as they enter, place a donation for the couple in a box by the door. Celebrants choose a chair at one of the tables placed around the three walls of the hall – there are none along the immediate edge of the stage where the disc jockey sets up his equipment, leaving a dance floor – and begin quietly to greet and socialize with those at their own and neighbouring tables. Some save places for friends who will arrive later. Just outside the hall itself, where the donations box is set up, people buy tickets for liquor, the profits from which go to the couple. At a table on the opposite side of the stage from the entrance door, people choose their drinks.

Nearly all the tables are filled by ten o'clock. Shortly after, the fêted couple arrives. In the hall, which was dark before, the lights are suddenly and rapidly flashed several times, and the disc jockey plays the first tune. The entire assembly stands until the couple has found seats, which they do only after greeting their parents and the others at their tables. Things calm down again fairly quickly. The lights are turned off again, except on the stage, and people begin dancing to the now continuous music. By half past eleven most people have had a few drinks, and the noise and hilarity have increased accordingly. The music stops, the lights are turned on, and the master of ceremonies takes the microphone and calls the couple up to the stage. The two sit uncomfortably on their chairs while the MC makes remarks about their upcoming wedding. A friend or relative then takes the microphone to read a poem written for and about them by local poet Gerry Eagan.

At the Cooney-Finn shower the master of ceremonies, a friend of the bride's family, began by ostentatiously wiping with a white handkerchief the chairs to be used by the groom and the bride-to-be. Then, he took the microphone:

MC [to Gerry Eagan]: Gerry, Gerry would you turn the lights on please? Good evening, ladies and gentlemen. So nice to see everyone here again. Um, I think before we start we should have our guests of honour here. [To the bride] Mary, the time has come. Please bring John up. Hey, up. [Everyone claps as the couple starts up to the stage. When they are on stage and seated, everyone claps again.] Yeah, please sit down. [Everyone laughs heartily.] Are you both comfortable? Yeah? That's good. I hope so. Well, it's referred to as the hot seat. But anyway, we have here our guests of honour. We've got Mary and John. [A few people clap.] Yes, that's two friends that you have. [Everybody laughs.] And they also have brought John's brother along and his name is Paul. Paul, will you please stand up. [Everyone claps.] And we're just missing one, one sister here and her name is Candy. And with a name like Candy she must be very sweet [laughter and one "Boo!"]. But anyway, Gord and Barbara and John [the groom and his parents], ah Cathy has been through these – ah, Mary, has been through these many times [laughter]. And, ah, I know for the

Finns, this is your first time to be involved in a community shower in our area, but they historically have been a way for all the friends and neighbours and relatives to express their appreciation and love for their, ah, young people who are stepping out on a big step. But, um, you know John, ah, I don't know how much you know of your background, the history that you're getting into, because it's really something [laughter]. You are truly marrying a young lady by the name of Cooney, but that's just one side. You're basically marrying into the Burton clan [laughter]. And out there tonight we have an awful lot of Burtons. Is that not true? How many Burtons out there? [Some people clap. Someone calls out "Get that one off the floor!" in reference to Gerry Eagan who is taking photographs of the event.] That is Tottenham's Karsh [laughter]. But anyway, one way, ah, one thing I'd like you to know of is that, ah, John we know we have a very very talented person in our community and his name is Gerry Eagan. And Gerry, thank heaven, has been very very generous with his talents in writing poems. And once again, I understand, he has taken his pen in hand and he has come up with a beautiful poem. Now we've got a – quite a lady here to read it. I'd like to call on Barbara Partland [another friend of the Cooney family; great applause]. The first time she came here, it was ginger ale [referring to her drink].

B.P.: Yes. [There is a big laugh from one person in the audience.] It's just a sip of [?]. [At this point there is about ten seconds' worth of banter between Mrs Partland and the MC that did not record clearly. The MC then left the stage.] Well, it's my pleasure again to read the Bard of Tecumseth's poem.[5]

It seems like only yesterday
That Cathy Cooney went
Up the aisle at St James Church
To meet a guy named Brent.

Fr. Paul was waiting
The knot was quickly tied
They promised to be faithful
Right till the day they died.

Her attendant Sister Mary
Was a young attractive lass
Who had trouble waiting
Until the end of Mass! [some laughter]

She had spied the best man
And been thinking to herself

I wonder if he could be coaxed
To take me off the shelf! [much laughter, some clapping]

When they signed the register
She found he was John Finn
And devoted all her efforts
In her plans to snare him in.

Before the night was over
Her plan was going well
Cause Mary's dancing is divine
And she *intermissions* well! [much laughter]

Poppa Jim was watching
He could see Mary's plan
He knew it would cost money
The day she caught her man. [much laughter]

He thought he'd better tell her
To travel sort of slow
Another wedding just might break him
With the price of corn so low! [laughter]

But Doctor Dot [the bride's mother, who is a nurse]
   was watching too
And making her own plans
She wasn't going to miss a chance
To get Mary off her hands ... [laughter]

She had a chat with Mary
And told her with a laugh
"If Donkey Jim is short of cash
I think I could pay half"!! [laughter]

Meanwhile I will be checking
As the wedding day draws nigh
John must meet the Cooney standards
Which are always very high.

She found that little Johnnie Finn
Was born to Gord and Barb
And as a boy he used to play
Down at the *railroad yard*.

It seems he was arrested
For walking on the tracks [some laughter]
And had to pay a 10 buck fine
He never got it back. [laughter]

His first job was paper boy
Which lasted just two days
He said "to make my fortune,
There must be better ways." [laughter]

He has an older brother Paul
With whom he used to fight
We're glad to hear they now are friends
And he is here tonight!

His younger sister Cathy
Worked on her Math each night
Brother John was not too patient
When he tried to set her right ...

As a young and busy goalie
John rose to early fame
Sometimes it was a problem
To get him in a game.

His equipment was so heavy
That it threw his skating off
His playmates carried him to the goal
And later carried him off! [laughter]

As a happy Loblaws [grocery store] parcel boy
John was known miles around
He went to Leaside High School
And to College at George Brown.

To the Toronto Maple Leafs
John is a loyal fan
He knows that next year they will win
It's in Harold Ballard's plans. [laughter]

John is a careful shopper
And before he buys a thing
He checks out all the specials
He is called "the coupon king."

[At this point, totally embarrassed, John hid his face in his hands. Everyone in the audience laughed uproariously and applauded. This was obviously a highlight of the evening.]

If Mary picks a place to dine
John sometimes will desist
"I must remind you honey
They're not on my coupon list." [laughter]

John is a neat and tidy lad
Who cleans his car each day
We hope he will be patient
With Mary Cooney's ways. [laughter and guffaws: "Ho ho ho"]

Dorothy found that Johnnie Finn
Was really quite a catch
If Mary could just land him
T'would be a perfect match.

In Leaside Barbara Finn
Was watching John each day
She wondered if this country girl
Would lead her boy astray.

She too did some checking
And a history did unfurl
In school at work and socially
Mary was a busy girl.

Mary is a lively lass
With a million things to do
She had a lot of fun in school
But had a problem too.

Each day about 8:20
When the bus stopped at the lane
Poppa's donkeys were on hand
To serenade again! [laughter]

Mary was embarrassed
And she sometimes said to paw
"Someday I'll shoot that Rachel
When she gives that loud 'Hee Haw.'" [laughter]

With her friends Brenda and Vicki
Mary liked to raise some hell
But when exam time came along
She always did quite well.

There was a time when Mary tried
To be a baseball star
Coaches Frank and Tim soon told her
"We'll see how good you are."

Mary wound up for a pitch
She was a sight to see
But when the ball had come to rest
It was up in a tree! [laughter]

When the playoffs came around
Mary's pride got quite a wrench
The coaches thought that she and Peg
Would help most on the bench ... [laughter]

When she reached the age 16
Mary thought she'd drive the car
With Doctor Dot as teacher
She went driving near and far.

Everything was going fine
Till Mary took her test
The inspector took her driving
But he wasn't too impressed ... [laughter]

Back to the car for practice
With momma Dot again
When she had her second test
Results were still the same ... [laughter]

This called for desperate measures
Mary's eyes turned red
She fired her *teacher Dorothy*
And went to driver's ed. [much laughter]

Next test was successful
And in her new Dodge car

Mary travels round the country
Checking out boutiques and bars!!

After Banting graduation
Mary said "I could do worse
Than follow Dot and Theresa
I will train to be a nurse."

When she finished nurse's training
Jobs were very hard to find
Paul the plumber said "I'll hire you
I need a nurse at times." [laughter]

Next stop was Scarborough General
Scrubbing backs and dumping pans [laughter]
Mary started looking round
To find some rich young man.

Mary and her good friend Lloy
Had a chat one night
"For young attractive girls like us
The streets aren't safe at night."

In the Star they saw an ad
For all defenceless girls
Come join our new karate club
Mary said "We'll give it a whirl." [laughter]

She won white, orange and brown belts
A very dangerous lass
Don't let that big smile fool you
And don't dare make a pass!

So John we'd better warn you
With Mary you don't fool
She has a wicked back kick [laughter]
That's worse than *poppa's mule*!!

Mary likes to holiday
And with buddies Peg and Lloy
She travelled all around the west
A trip they all enjoyed.

At Banff our Mary got a job
As a busy chambermaid
By this time she'd have owned the place
If only she had stayed. [laughter]

But the girls were very lonesome
For those lively weekend nights
They missed *"Maw's home cooking"*
And the *"Loretto Tavern lights."* [(laughter]

John there is something else
We feel that you should know
Mary likes to gamble
Be it win, place, or show ...

When you get the morning paper
Don't let her see the stocks
She always picks a hot one
And in two weeks it drops! [laughter]

After sister Cathy's wedding
John Finn was often near
But he wouldn't ask the question
Which Mary longed to hear.

John took Mary for a drive
In the fall of 83 [John looks embarrassed again, and there is
  laughter at this.]
To a cottage up in Beaverton
He wanted her to see.

They took a stroll along the beach
The night was clear and bright
As Mary sat down on a rock
John's nerves were all uptight. [laughter]

"I really love you Mary
Here, have a sip of wine
I'll give you all my coupons
If you promise to be mine!!" [much laughter, applause]

Mary said "Okay, I guess
I've turned down lots you know

If you cook and make the beds
All the garden I will hoe."

John said "alright it is a deal"
And warmly shook her hand
"Perhaps you could ask your dad
For a little plot of land." [much laughter]

Next weekend Mary C went home
Jim met her at the door
His smile seemed to be wider
Than she'd ever seen before.

"Better grab that fellow Mary
He's the best one I have seen
I can afford a wedding now
I've made a pile on beans!!" [much laughter]

Mary phoned up Johnny Finn
"I have great news for you
June the second is the day
Cause poppa has come through." [some laughter]

So it seems this handsome lad
Is the lucky man who wins
This young and pretty daughter
Of the Cooneys Dorothy and Jim.

Mary we are very pleased
To have a chance to say
We appreciate your friendship
And your cheery thoughtful ways.

John we're glad to meet you
And we want you both to know
You always will be welcome here
No matter where you go.

For your June 2nd wedding
We wish you perfect weather
And hope that day will be the start
Of fifty years together.

[To the sound of much enthusiastic applause Mrs Partland quickly leaves the stage, and another woman takes the microphone.]

Woman: A bunch of the ladies got together and dug in their purses and here's something for you and Mary. [Someone calls from the audience, "Coupons!" and there is much laughter at this. John then stands up and takes the microphone.]

J.F.: If you think my face is red now, wait till you see my tie next week [laughter]. They told me to keep this to last about ten minutes so I figured that's no problem, just read it fifty times [laughter]. I'd just like to thank everybody for coming out tonight. We're like – we're in tough competition with the, ah, Schomberg Fair and the Loretto House [laughter]. It's not too often you get to have a tractor pull, a demolition derby, and have Mary Cooney married off in all the same week [much laughter and applause]. I'd like to thank Gerry Eagan for that beautiful poem and, ah, Barb Partland for reading it, and now I'm sure Mary has a few words she'd like to say [much laughter and applause].

Mary C.: I'd like to thank everyone for coming. I really appreciate, well we really appreciate it [laughter]. And the kitchen committee, and everybody, and the bartenders [laughter] and everyone. Thank you very much. That's all [much laughter and applause].

At this point a friend of the family led the assembly in "For They Are Jolly Good Fellows," and three cheers for the bride and groom. The MC returned and made additional presentations to members of the audience: a couple who was expecting a child, and the mother of the bride. John shook hands with the MC, the couple left the stage, and the MC announced, "I understand that the ladies are now going to serve lunch. Thank you." Lunch was followed by more dancing to music provided by the disc jockey. People began leaving about half past twelve, but the celebration did not conclude until about three a.m.

Gerry Eagan's poem contains humorous references and descriptions that have culturally conventional associations with weddings. For instance, the bride is the ensnarer, plotting in collusion with her relatives, who are eager to get her off their hands. Associated with community shower poetry as a genre is the convention that the bride and groom are both remembered and celebrated for their quirks in childhood and early youth. In the verses about the interaction of these two principals – a local young woman and her fiancé from the city – things become topsy-turvy. Gender roles are reversed; John will "cook and make the beds" and Mary will hoe the garden. The two behave with humorous inappropriateness; for instance, they shake hands to seal their engagement. Social expectations are violated; John asks Mary if her father will give her a plot of land. Since it is usual for land to be passed through the male line, the joke is that in traditional Ontario society a man without land, like city-dweller John, would be without means of subsistence. He would thus be reduced to such improprieties if he wanted to marry.

The topsy-turvydom here is an occasion for laughter. The fact that these two individuals are appropriately choosing to marry and to place their relationship publicly and formally under community control – by, among other things, attending their own community shower – reduces to a joke what might otherwise be a threat. The poem humorously describes the now inappropriate pre-marriage state; in it Mary and John are depicted as individuals who lack basic cultural knowledge. Implicitly the poem suggests that this differentness will be appropriately alleviated by their approaching role as a married couple.

In addition and in contrast to being ridiculed, Mary and John are elevated. They are physically raised on a stage above the shower celebrants; they are thus made the centre of collective attention; and they receive the community's compliments and good wishes at the poem's conclusion. This is the obverse, rather than the true opposite, of the ridicule in Eagan's verse. Within a community, individuals are set apart and elevated in this way only for the collective benefit. Since this is so, their temporarily raised status must be mitigated. Local people cannot be praised without some reminder that on a day-to-day basis, beyond the special circumstances in which they may find themselves at the moment, they are peers of the rest of the community. To be fully integrated into their new status as a married couple, John and Mary must be taught to see themselves as being just like everyone else. Thus, in the community wedding shower they are simultaneously or alternately set apart and elevated – shown that they are *different* from others in the community – and ridiculed – shown that they are the *same*.

POETRY REDEFINES:
"THE BRIDGE"

Several poets clarified for me their view of poetry's special qualities by commenting on its differences from other genres of expression. Most contrasted verse with history. Gerry Eagan, who writes both folk poetry and local historical prose, likes to combine their contents. Of poetry he says: "I try to work in [the subjects'] history as much as I can – or the parts you can make, well, sort of funny. But people aren't interested in the whole statement of facts if that's all that's involved" (T83–39). Eagan's poetry always has humour, while in his historical writing it is not essential, though funny anecdotes can be included. As a poet Eagan feels he has licence to stretch aspects of the truth somewhat in order to achieve an effect. Such methods are anathema to history, the exactness of which Eagan always verifies. However, poetry must be much more than simply factually correct; it must incorporate emotional validity. On Remembrance Day poetry, for instance, Betty Burton commented: "Some of these November the eleventh ones don't grab me, and I think the reason why is the people that write them have never had anything to do with the War. Like, my father was in the First World War, and my cousins were in the Second World War. And some of them were killed, and some of them were maimed for life, so, well, I feel I have a bit of an insight into it, OK? These people are writing about something they don't really know anything about, I think" (T83–33). The poets Burton criticizes lack an emotional understanding of the issues to counterbalance their information. She suggests that such insight comes largely from experience; mere facts cannot suffice.

However, in Ontario it is not history that offers a generic antithesis of poetry but the letter to the editor, which manifests qualities that are opposed to the ethos of folk verse. Though the two have superficial similarities, their structures and functions are quite different. Letters to the editor and poetry can appear on the same page,[6] and both are written and presented by local residents about issues of community interest. Yet letters to the editor are almost exclusively contentious and/or overtly hortatory. Poems may be social glue, attempting to heal rifts and to (re)establish the traditional perspective through the mediation, analogy, reversal, and inversion that redefine reality or suggest appropriate attitudes. But letters to the editor aim to point out, and sometimes even to exaggerate, current rifts, situations where the prevailing ethos and worldview are challenged or need buttressing.

The following examples clarify this opposition by illustrating the contrast between a folk poem's symbolic and rhetorical content and that of two letters to the editor that discuss the same issue. All three texts[7] are by Bob Raymes of Palgrave. The letters to the editor are about the need for a new bridge crossing the Humber River at Palgrave: the earlier is undated; the later is dated 11 December 1958. The poem, published 14 February 1961, announces and applauds, finally, the building of the bridge. Obviously, Raymes employs the two genres at different times in the sequence. The letters bring the matter to the attention of the newspaper's readers, with strongly partisan commentary by a community member; the poem, in contrast, marks the problem's resolution.

Raymes's first letter apparently begins discussion on a local issue that has been previously unconsidered, or perhaps reopens an earlier debate. It urges action in the near future:

It would appear that the residents of North Peel are the poor cousins of the rest of Ontario. The other sections seem to get highways, speedways, and a half dozen other ways, but we cannot even get a decent bridge to span the Humber on Highway 50 at Palgrave. What we have now is just a glorified cow path, not even a good horse and buggy bridge. In fact it would go further back than the ox cart days.

We noticed that the Township of Albion had two bridges got out at the corner of 25 sideroad and the 6th line of Albion. What happened – brand new bridges in short order. We are very sure that the residents of Albion Township would not have tolerated such an obsolete monstrosity as has been pawned off on the residents of North Peel.

When this bridge was first erected we expected it would be a temporary bridge for 6 weeks or 2 months at the outside. That was several years ago and there seems to be no movement afoot to do anything about it. Some have excused the Highways Dept. by saying that the course of the road was to be changed. This we know to be true as we have seen the plans which leave the present highway about 100 yds. north of 25 sideroad and goes around the pond the opposite side to what it is at the present time. This may take place in 1 year, 5 years, or 25 years. Who knows? But in the meantime with the increasing amount of traffic on Highway 50 it would appear the time is long past due for a new bridge.

If the road does by-pass Palgrave are the residents of Palgrave not entitled to a road north. The old adage that the squeaking wheel gets the grease would lead us to believe the squeaking has been very silent, if any. So how about a little "bally hoo" on behalf of the residents of North Peel.

- PALGRAVE FOREVER

In the 1950s and perhaps later Raymes used the above pseudonym. It affirms his sympathies and allegiance but is not intended to disguise his identity.

In the first paragraph, Raymes draws a series of denigratory analogies. The residents of North Peel are described as "poor cousins"; the road is a "glorified cow path," not a "highway, speedway, and half a dozen other ways." The negative evaluation of the problem is heightened by this comparison. The writer ranks a series of textual and understood signifiers (shown in parentheses below) according to their historical association, from the modern to the obsolete, and by the appropriateness of vehicle to roadway. Thus, though the most apposite association is (modern conveyances) are to horse and buggy or oxcart as highway/speedway is to horse and buggy bridge or glorified cow path, the decidedly inappropriate linking suggested in Raymes's letter is (modern conveyance) to glorified cow path and (modern conveyance) to horse and buggy bridge. This sets up a symbolic imbalance and exaggerates the bridge's old-fashionedness in order to suggest the need for a new one.

Having characterized the need for a new bridge and road, Raymes goes on to employ less metaphorical language to bring another imbalance into the community's view. He compares the treatment that North Peel region receives, described in his previous paragraph, with that of Albion Township in a similar situation. Because of inter-community rivalry, drawing attention to inequalities in government attention or services should incite North Peelers to act. Imbalances of this sort cannot be locally tolerated. Here too Raymes uses tropic language. North Albion's bridge is "brand new"; Palgrave's is an "obsolete monstrosity." This dramatizes the bridge's drawbacks, adding to the charge that the bridge is old-fashioned.

The third paragraph narrates a sequence of events pertaining to the existing bridge that re-emphasize the need for a new one. Raymes demonstrates his understanding of the situation by quoting dates, locations, and time-frames previously discussed by officials and planners. This special knowledge underscores his qualifications to comment on the issue. In addition, he shows that there has been an unfulfilled expectation for improvement within a reasonable span of time. The comparison of time-periods follows the narrative frame: what the officials said was temporary – what was supposed to take six weeks to two months – has been extended to a couple of years. Raymes suggests that this could be further increased to twenty-five years. Again, a time-sequence is exaggerated to indicate the urgency of the need for a resolution to the problem at hand. However, Raymes departs in this paragraph from what is expected of criticism in Ontario regional culture. He deflects blame for this unsatisfactory state from an outsider institution, the Highway Department, which he sees as the distant source of the problem, to his fellow residents ("Some have excused"), who through their inactivity have allowed an unfavourable situation to continue.

The fourth paragraph asks two questions, neither of which is labelled with a question mark. The first rhetorically affirms that Palgrave is entitled to a road north. The second invokes folkloric wisdom as an admonition to effort. Raymes asserts an analogy between the traditional squeaking wheels and grease and "bally hoo" by the people of Palgrave on the one hand and the action of getting the bridge built and the road improved on the other. This is no simple analogy. The signifiers and their referents are part of a particular kind of common relationship. That is, in both situations the noise enables a response only by showing – repeatedly and graphically – a need for it.

Raymes's second letter, dated 11 December 1958, extends his previous one, adding new material and taking a different rhetorical and symbolic stance:

A couple of weeks ago we mentioned the crying need for a new bridge crossing the Humber at Palgrave. This matter seems to have been completely overlooked by the Ontario Department of Highways.

Maybe when they get to Palgrave they act like an ostrich and stick their heads in the sand. On second thought that would not be possible as you need all of your five senses to navigate this so called bridge and come out with a whole skin.

This past week a pick-up truck was not quite so fortunate as the road being slippery and he trying to stop, managed to hit the abutments and goodness it is not hard to do as you are only inches from oblivion when the roads are in good condition.

They are talking about raising the speed limits on the highways but we feel anything faster than the speed of a tortoise would be disastrous in this area.

We hear that there is likely to be a bye-election in Peel soon as the former minister has resigned. Maybe this would be a good time to send a few letters to the would be replacements as they always like to make a few promises of what they would do if elected. The new planks in their platform could be well used in a new bridge for Palgrave for goodness knows the ones that are in it now seem to be getting mighty sloppy. We must revert back to our old slogan of "The wheel that does the squeaking gets the grease." So if they got 25 squeaks in the form of letters I am sure we would have action.

PALGRAVE FOREVER

Rather than formulating completely new arguments, this letter restates the previous ones more appropriately. Raymes employs newly available real-life signifiers and situates blame for the problem outside the community. In general this argument seems more likely to be successful in swaying local public opinion.

This letter opens with a reference to the previous one but immediately corrects its inappropriate aspect by emphasizing that the source of the problem as well as the reasons for it originate outside the community. The Ontario Department of Highways, not the passive local residents, as in Raymes's first letter, is responsible. Having thus established outsiders as the continuing cause of the problem, Raymes can still argue that local residents should be more forward in voicing their grievances. However, he does not risk offending those whose opinions and actions he hopes to sway.

The second paragraph uses an analogy that diminishes its referent (recall that this type of analogy is rarely seen in Ontario folk poetry): the Department of Highways is compared to an ostrich with its head in the sand. Raymes enjoys some play with his analogy, suggesting that the department's behaviour is unsafe when employed by a driver; though an ostrich might not need all five senses, the successful navigator of the road does. The negative qualities thus associated with the department are stupidity and blindness to obvious local need.

In the third paragraph a real event is held to signify all the problems Raymes has previously raised, showing that the road and bridge are outdated and generally unsafe. The event is recent and so is particularly apropos. The bridge has been demonstrated to be unsafe; it was in such poor repair that a driver had difficulty stopping. In addition, its condition will have deteriorated further as a result of this accident; the driver was forced to stop by hitting an abutment. The fourth paragraph presents another denigratory analogy. As in paragraph one of the first letter, an underlying appropriate series of associations is proposed. The semantic domain is speed of travel, rather than time. It should be tortoise speed is to car speed as current road conditions are to (proper road conditions), yet car speed and current road conditions are an inappropriate match. The predicted increase in the speed limit will make this pair even more inappropriate.

The closing paragraph returns to the final analogy of the previous letter, presented in a more subtle yet still effective manner. Raymes points out to his audience that they have an unprecedented opportunity to affect outsiders – politicians – by voting. The figurative "planks" of the election "platform" are metaphorically changed into the actual wooden planks that will be used to construct the needed bridge. Here, Raymes affirms symbolic action's real effectiveness. Election speeches and promises – prompted by the words of local people who bring the problem to the candidates' attention – can prompt a material response. This rhetoric transforms what was in the other letter an internally critical commentary into an acceptable and persuasive call for community action against threatening outside forces.

Clearly, the language of the two letters differs. The first contends with insiders and the second with outsiders. The first uses symbolic language – exaggeration, and the creation of a time frame – in culturally anomalous or even inappropriate ways. The second, more effectively, combines convincing realistic examples with denigratory metaphorical description and prescribes action in a more persuasive manner.

"The Bridge" was published just over two years after the previous letter:

A brand new bridge we're going to have
With pillars all shiny and white,
A dandy bridge she is going to be
For in Palgrave it must be right.

The piles they are far too long
Or that's the way they look,
They'll drive them down into the mud
To span our little brook.

The boys are working in the cold
To get the job complete,
They have to keep right on the jump
Or they would freeze their feet.

Allan has a diesel now
To chop the farmer's grain,
It's just as well, the water's low
We need a lot of rain.

Yes! We are going to have a bridge
To keep us up to date;
The only trouble I can see
It's twenty years too late.

Raymes signed this work with his own name. He nowhere refers to his previous concern with the bridge problem but writes as if he were entering for the first time into commentary on the subject. Only at the end does he allude to the contents of his letters to the editor. Overall, Raymes uses the poem to redefine the bridge's symbolic association for the community and his stance on the issue.

The poem begins with a description of the bridge; it is "brand new," "shiny," "white," and "dandy." These are realistic adjectives; there is no more metaphorical horse and buggy bridge, and no glorified cow path instead of a road. Finally, Palgrave has an actual, appropriate, modern bridge. Palgraveites have also changed; no longer are North Peelers the apathetic poor cousins of Albion residents. They are not willing to settle for what they are given, no matter how inadequate.

The bridge has all its positive qualities because "In Palgrave it must be right." This has two possible interpretations, on which Raymes plays. First, Palgrave people will not tolerate inappropriateness. But second, simply being in Palgrave makes the bridge "right." Both interpretations are clearly complimentary to Palgrave and to its people and evoke the kind of PALGRAVE FOREVER sympathy and allegiance that is never really explicit in the letters.

The second stanza continues the inventory of the building of the bridge and its components. The first line's exaggeration is immediately mitigated in the second line and clearly stated to be illusory. The poem magnifies the positive qualities of the bridge. (Compare, for instance, the result had Raymes said that the piles looked too short instead of too long.) The vertical movement of driving the piles into the mud in the third line allows the spanning of the little brook in the fourth.

The river, unnamed in the poem, is described in the letters as a danger to human life because the bridge's going out in Albion is clearly the result of flooding and because "you are only inches from oblivion" crossing it. In the poem it is a "little brook," evidently benign, friendly, and even the subject of diminutive affection. This is a realistic description of the Humber at the time of the poem's publication, in early spring before the snow melts and flooding commences.

The third stanza praises the bridge's construction workers, referring to them familiarly as "the boys." They are toiling at great speed to finish the job. They work against a natural obstacle, cold, but like the bridge itself in the previous verse, they are not defeated by nature. Rather, the weather humorously and playfully spurs them on to greater and speedier production. Now that the Highway Department, adversary of the second letter, has conceded, a new adversary, the natural elements, which like the Highway Department can be manipulated by local people to their own advantage, has taken its place.

In much Ontario folk poetry, reflecting Ontario culture's symbolic oppositions, *nature* receives positive valence, since it is associated with human fertility, while *culture* is perceived as something negative because it is implicitly linked with what outsider suburbanites bring into the community.[8] But in "The Bridge" production, manufacture, machinery, and modernity are objects of praise. This symbolic reversal of the usual evaluation is the reason for the otherwise anomalous, apparently unrelated fourth stanza of Raymes's poem. An outsider might ask what farm machinery, crops, low water, rain, and grain have to do with the construction of a new highway bridge. The poet includes them as signifiers because he must show that the bridge, a technological advance that might otherwise be seen as community-threatening, is a reasonable object for praise. He does so by directly associating the bridge and its advantages with (collective) farm fertility. He juxtaposes the two and sets up an analogy between them. In the context of the poem the current improvements in highway transportation parallel modern advances in agriculture. These increase the efficiency of grain chopping and are poetically associated with the prodigious rain and thus with greater fertility. The result, then, is a larger crop that will need to be processed for marketing.

This association is by no means mystical or unrealistic. Because the river will be more efficiently bridged, it can rise and accommodate the amount of rain that farmers need to produce abundant crops without endangering the bridge or those who cross it. The farmer does not need to restrain his joy at copious spring rain and its positive effects on his crop from fear that he and his family will be injured crossing the bridge into town, where their grain is chopped and eventually sold and where they buy provisions. Because of the new bridge, spring, rather than being a negative time of dangerous flooding, becomes a positive indicator of fertility to come. Allan prepares for this by matching technology with technology and buying a diesel chopping machine, which can accommodate the farmers' larger grain crop. Raymes clearly indicates that this benefit will be collective and will introduce no threat to the community. It will not increase the wealth of a single individual; the entire community will become more affluent.

Thus, this section of Raymes's poem explicitly links the farmland to the town – as the bridge itself actually does – so that a material link, an economic link, and a symbolic link are poetically reaffirmed. A stanza that initially seems anomalous and unrelated is in fact central to understanding the poem.

The final verse is the only one that directly addresses the issues raised in the letters to the editor. The imbalance asserted in the first and second letters between the bridge's suggested temporal association – old-fashioned – and the need for one that is up to date has been explicitly redressed. However, Raymes says that there would have been even more cause for praise had this occurred at an opportune time. Again, he employs exaggeration. Comparing the time periods suggested in both letters and in the poem, a maximum of about six or seven years has passed since the temporary bridge was erected. Calling it "twenty years too late," then, is a considerable overstatement. But nowhere in his poem does Raymes place direct blame for this tardiness. Neither the residents, as in the first letter to the editor, nor the Highway Department, as in the second, is castigated. As is most appropriate for poems about local events and scenes, the tone is generally celebratory and congratulatory.

In the letters Raymes makes points with a series of comparisons between situations in North Peel and Albion, tropes in an analogy, time-frames, and even proverbial elements. In all these comparisons the local referents – Palgrave, North Peel, local residents, now, the current road, and the extant bridge – are described as inadequate or deficient. The only realistic, concretely specific signifier in either letter is the incident with the pick-up truck. This is employed, as it would be in a poem, to suggest the actual, real, and present gravity of the situation that Raymes is calling to the readers' attention.

Though we might expect the opposite, metaphors and other tropes are more obvious in the letters to the editor than in the poem. The letters are contentious, and their tropes alert the community to unacceptable aspects of the situation. They indicate that the bridge is unrealistically old, unsafe, and so on. The poem, by contrast, considers the event more symbolically than tropically. It sets up and then explores the relationship between nature and machinery and between human effort and natural forces. It does this through realistic descriptions of actual events and scenes – the pillars, the mud, the "boys" working, Allan's new diesel, and so on.

The poem is clearly oriented towards mediation. Textually, it presents the new bridge as a praiseworthy object, specifically because of its mediatory functions, which include its literal bridging between riverbanks and its symbolic rapprochement between fertility and production. Unlike the contentious letters, the poem is celebratory and affirmative. It is associated with the commencement of work on the new bridge, while the letters concern a perceived need for that structure. The poem rhetorically suggests that the adversary has always been nature, not the community's apathy or the Highway Department's neglect. Thus the poem's potentially critical last two lines refer to the opinion of the writer himself rather than, as in his letters to the editor, to those responsible for the problem.

Bob Raymes's poem retroactively redefines the issue to minimize its contentious, potentially community-splitting qualities by raising it to a level above that described in the letters to the editor, transcending the letters' word for word, township for township, and other oppositions by analogy and mediation. Raymes chose to write a poem because its generic meaning – an orientation towards harmony – is appropriate to a resolved problem and because the kinds of comments he wished to make are best expressed in verse. The poem functions finally to mark the resolution of an issue that was previously problematic and contentious.

RESITUATING ACCOUNTABILITY:
"MANSE PERSPECTIVE"

In addition to its special symbolic language, by which it attempts to transform its audience's perception of reality, usually through analogy and mediation, folk poetry is marked by its function to resituate and alter personal accountability for a statement. Poets can thus express, in public, opinions that their community might find inappropriate in another expressive form – say, as a joke, or as a letter to the editor. Two poems, the second written in direct response to the first, are examples of these processes and of how written poetic performances imply and concern individual as well as community views.

The first, published in December 1982 in his weekly column "Meanwhile, back at the ranch," by long-time Tara resident and newspaper editor Jim Merriam, describes his personal response to the Christmas season. United Church minister Roy Cowieson, a recent immigrant from Scotland, published his poetic counter-response the following week in his occasional column "Manse Perspective."

Tara, a small town in western Ontario where both Merriam and Cowieson lived when the poems were written, seems a harmonious place. It was settled in the mid nineteenth century by Irish immigrants and is surrounded by Scottish and Mennonite communities, but the public expression of its ethnic diversity is muted. The area is uniformly quite prosperous, and there are no obvious discrepancies in wealth. Farms and outbuildings are in good repair, and the land is ideal for beef cattle. Tara's population consists primarily of retirees from nearby farms and people who work in Owen Sound or at the Douglas Point nuclear power station, each about twenty miles distant. Tara may be primarily a bedroom and retirement community, but its residents have historical and social ties in the area. Despite this generally benign aspect, rifts appear, as they do in any community. This is the concern of Merriam and Cowieson's poetic dialogue.

When he wrote the poem discussed here, Jim Merriam was in his late thirties. His family came from St Thomas to Tara when he was a few months old. At seventeen, a high school drop-out, he got a job as a cub reporter for the *Owen Sound Sun Times*, the daily paper in a nearby community. He has worked as a newspaper and television reporter and editor in Lethbridge, Alberta, and the Kitchener-Waterloo area of Ontario, and in Tara he managed his late father's hardware and antique businesses and bred horses. He lived with his second wife, her daughter, and his daughter and son on a farm just outside Tara.

Roy Cowieson, the Tara United Church minister, was in his early forties. He was born near Glasgow, Scotland, and grew up in that city. After completing the equivalent of grade ten at school and working for twelve years, he felt called to the ministry. He trained in Scotland but came to Tara, his first parish, in 1978. He began writing a column in the *Tara Leader* shortly after he arrived, "commenting on community things: people and local issues" (T84–48).

Cowieson and Merriam are in many respects peers. Similar in age and in occupational and professional standing, both stand somewhat apart from the rest of the community because of their professions – but in different ways – and both have relatively powerful positions. Though Cowieson is formally educated and Merriam mainly self-taught, they were high-school drop-outs and had a wide variety of jobs during their lives. Each also has, because of his work, done considerable writing in several genres, and both have written other poetry.

Yet there are also significant differences between the two. Though Cowieson is a newcomer to the region, he was invited to become minister and he won widespread community acceptance. Merriam's case seems almost the opposite. He says: "My wife and I live com-mon-law and there's a segment of the community doesn't accept us because of that. They tolerate us, but we don't get invited to their homes. And I've lived here all my life. But they don't approve; they make that quite clear" (T84–51). However, he is by no means a social pariah, especially among his circle of drinking buddies.

Merriam and Cowieson are both informal and friendly people. Each has an awareness of the implications of his role in the community and something of a sense of humour about it. Their different lifestyles and positions in the community, however, have set up a public per-ception of them as adversaries. Cowieson suggests: "People keep on thinking that Jim and I have got a vendetta going. And they've a big surprise if they ever see us out doing something together, or at an occasion talking. I like to take a pot at Jim and he sometimes takes a pot at me, and others in the community do it from time to time at different events, but everybody gets on famously" (T84–48).

"Taking pots" at Jim Merriam consists mainly of commenting on his fondness for alcohol. When discussing with me the naming of Tara, Cowieson said, "Of course it only came around because there was a drunken brawl in the local hostel one night and they started singing that song, and people came up with that as the name for the village. The village is only named after a drunken occasion, so Jim Merriam fits into the scenery now very nicely" (T84–49). Cowieson's respect for Merriam, however, is obvious, and it was in part the stimulus for his poetic response. He said, "Jim writes every week without fail and people don't agree with a whole lot of what he says, but they never fail to read it" (T84–48).

Jim Merriam's personal views on religion conflict with those of the United Church minister, just as Roy Cowieson's attitude towards sobriety and its opposite clash with those of a pubgoer. Merriam does not belong to any congregation. His family was United Church, but he began to question the sincerity of the church's Christian sentiments when, as an Indian Affairs reporter in Lethbridge, he spent time on native reserves and saw the great discrepancies in wealth. To his mind, it was contradictory for the church to ignore the poverty on its own doorstep while "raising money for carpets." He sees the church's function in Tara as "a support structure, largely for old people. I don't think faith has a lot to do with it in a small community" (T84–51). Thus, we have a rather ironic situation in which a newcomer's poetry represents the community view whereas a more traditional resident's work contends with it.

When I asked Roy Cowieson why he wrote a poem in response, he said: "Well only because he wrote a poem and I thought 'Anything Jim Merriam can do, I can do the same.' He has a background in the United Church and he's quite one of the colourful characters of the community, anti-establishment in many senses. And I have his mother in the congregation, and the people in the congregation have a great respect for him. And that was partly to get back at him. It was just a fun thing, not to be taken seriously" (T84–48). The last – humorous but not serious accountability – is equally true of Jim Merriam's poetry, which is "something that just sort of comes to me. You usually try to make it light, maybe humorous if possible. I'm not real good at it, but I have a lot of fun doing it. And it's sort of spur of the moment, saying 'I'm just sitting here. Well, I should be saying something about Christmas. How am I going to do that?' And if I'm in the right humour, it might be in the form of poetry" (T84–50).

The festive season – a time when Merriam says "the creative juices flow" – his associations of Christmas with poetry, and a copy deadline all resulted in this original poem, which unintentionally opened the poetic dialogue:

Christmas is just days away,
And so it's time for me to say,
If all the hubbub makes you gloomy,
It doesn't mean that you've gone loony.

They start the thing so bloody early,
Sane men have often been driven squirrely,

With all the cheer and all the splash
Designed to get your hard-earned cash.

The music that is so very good
Is played and played, until I could
Wring the neck of every singer
Who wants to be a Yule bell ringer.

And then there is that shopping chore
That really can become a bore,
Imagine spending all that money
For a toy to break a week from Monday.

Or, if you're buying clothes and tools,
For those too old to play like fools,
You get to see them stashed away
About supper time on Boxing Day.

The clothes are never worn or seen,
Unless there's a party next Hallowe'en,
And the tools we needed, as all could see,
Are last used taking down the Christmas tree.

Now you all might think I'm a Christmas grinch,
That's not the case, in fact, it's a cinch
I'll get the spirit with a resounding crash
The day before the Yuletide bash.

Then I'll rush and hurry from store to store
On Christmas Eve, not a minute before,
And spend myself right into debt,
Using six month's pay I haven't earned yet.

But on Christmas Day we'll all be happy,
We'll eat and drink, then take a nappy,
Then wake up tired and grumpy and sore,
And wonder whatever it all was for.

The only good thing about the whole season,
Is the spirit that shows for no good reasons,
We fight and chew and bitch all year,
Then call each other the best friends dear.

That's the nicest thing we can say,
About the season and Christmas Day,
It's worth all the fussin' and all that goes in it,
To have all those friends, if just for a minute.

Now I really should end this dumb little poem,
But I haven't mentioned writing home,
And all old friends both timid and bold,
Whose importance is something dear to hold.

I'll never get around to sending cards,
And writing letters I find is real hard,
So I'll send them copies of this little rhyme,
So they'll know I miss past Christmas times.

Enough being serious, with sentiment sloshin'.
We'll end with just one word of caution,
If you rant and rave and sound like me,
You can't peek for your name under the tree. (*Tara Leader*,
   8 December 1982)

Most of these comments about Christmas could be quite acceptable
to the community. It is common to lament, as Merriam does, the
commercialization of Christmas. But Merriam describes his own Christmas behaviour not as mediation between the extremes outlined in
the first six stanzas, on the one hand, and the culturally understood
ideal, on the other, but as an uneasy compromise between the two.
He opposes this in the next four stanzas with one kind of excess
that is positively viewed and valued – surplus friendliness. The poem
suggests that the Christmas season is set apart from the rest of the
year: "We fight and chew and bitch all year / Then call each other
the best friends dear." According to the poet, then, it is "Worth all
the fussin' and all that goes with it / To have all those friends, if
just for a minute."

In viewing excess positively, the poet sets up a mediation. Although
the profusion of commercialization and "fussin'" are not idealized,
they are seen as enabling factors. The general spirit of plenty allows
the undoubtedly valued excesses to take place, so the poet concludes:

We'll end with just one word of caution
If you rant and rave and sound like me
You can't peek for your name under the tree.

In other words, the Christmas celebrant must finally transcend the event and season's negative aspects in order to participate in its positive qualities.

Cowieson's poetic reply ignores to some extent the above moral. It does not counter Merriam's attitude. Instead, it adds material and makes explicit the positive cultural expectations and associations that are only alluded to in Merriam's poem. Most obviously, this includes the religious aspect:

It's not a carol, a psalm or a hymn,
Just a few lines in rhyme to my friend "Jim."
Last week in The Leader, his poem I did read,
A reply I reckoned is just what he needs.
AT THIS CHRISTMASTIME.

Poor Jim, running hard to find Christmas cheer,
As most people do at this time of the year,
Battling crowds and stores, and your own folks too,
Whose plans are made and you've just got to do
− WHATEVER THEY DO − AT CHRISTMASTIME.

Some folks had reached the end of their tether,
"No Christmas cheer, in this mild weather."
As though the season depends on a good fall of snow,
And the light of Christmas − to make goodwill grow
TOWARDS CHRISTMASTIME.

At least friend Jim before his poem ends,
Had mentioned the season is good for being friends
With those we don't like and seldom ever love,
Due to that spark that comes from above
ONLY AT CHRISTMASTIME.

That spark I believe is the real Christmas story,
Of a human E.T. come from a home up in glory,
And stayed for a while to make us see reason
That love depends not on snow or the season
OR EVEN CHRISTMASTIME.

So the real Christmas spirit is not held in a glass,
Nor found in the store, or in wallets, alas!
But was found in a stable, dirty and mean,
By the smell of your ranch, Jim, you'll know what I mean,

He came not as a king, but lowly and humble,
That hard hearts of women and men might just crumble
And melt into dust that He turns into gold,
New life which has purpose, a life He now holds
STARTING THIS CHRISTMASTIME.

For you Jim and yours, a Scots word, "AWRABEST,"
In this season of cheer may you all be blest
With good friends and some fun, and a barrel of coke,
Each drink passed your lips, you'll see as my joke;
But I do trust these lines leave you not in the lurch,
But uniting with us "Round the Manger" at church;
We might be "United" – but are really a branch
Leaning over to touch all who live in that ranch
AND BEYOND, THIS CHRISTMASTIME. (*Tara Leader*, 15 December 1982)

Cowieson immediately counters Merriam's suggestion that deplorable excesses are essential to the season. To him, the snow and lights are not enabling factors but extraneous details; they detract from rather than enhance the true spirit of the season. He shows that the commercialism that Merriam sees as necessary is instead antithetical to Christmas. The significance of the season is not in the mediation between the approved and the disapproved, the former neutralizing the negativity of the latter, but in direct inversion, where the "dirty and mean" or "lowly and humble" are more valued than a king; and in oppositional reversal, where hard hearts and dust become golden. He suggests that though Merriam lives and works on a ranch (which Cowieson makes a local signifier of the Christmas stable), he cuts himself off from a similar reversal. The cause would be understood by the community; it is Merriam's lack of interest in the church.

In Cowieson's eyes this is very strong criticism. He suggests that on a spiritual as well as a sociocultural level, Merriam prevents his own redemption by avoiding the church, the only means for a necessary reversal or inversion of human life to the transcendent plane. The poet mitigates this judgment somewhat in the final verse and the opening of the third by suggesting that on a secular level, if not on a spiritual one, Merriam is as good as the next person. If he cannot be approached spiritually, at least he can join in the cheer and fun of the season, as Merriam maintained in his own poem. However, Cowieson makes his preferred solution explicit: "But uniting with us 'Round the Manger' at church; / We might be 'United.'" Clearly, the poet feels that if Merriam were to attend church, the valid mediation point, even he could achieve the spiritual reversal.

Rather than directly countering Merriam point by point, Cowieson extends and even ridicules some of his adversary's arguments. This additive process might appear anomalous in prose, but poetry implicitly calls attention to its own symbolic content. Likewise, read as prose, Cowieson's direct references to Merriam, such as "By the smell of your ranch, Jim, you'll know what I mean," are humorous insults: recall that Cowieson stated that humour was one of his reasons for replying in verse. Yet read as poetry they must be interpreted as references to familiar local signifiers of the humanity and accessibility of religion. As this is an essential aspect of the poem's meaning, the local signifiers are elevated and altered and their sense becomes specific, particular, and special.

The "politeness" quality of poetry[9] means that its presenter can say things that would otherwise be inappropriate. Direct personal criticism of insiders in small towns is inappropriate. By voicing his comments – which include criticisms of Merriam – in poetic form, Cowieson does not risk damaging his own or his subject's personal "face," partly because the genre itself, in the community's perception, is considered benign rather than malignant in intent. It is general cultural knowledge that poetry is safe and inoffensive, and these qualities are manifest in its use. If someone wished to be contentious, he or she would do it in a letter to the editor, at certain local meetings, or in a session with cronies at the firehall, perhaps. One newspaper editor comments: "I have run poetry that I haven't read. I should have asked you to shut that [the tape recorder] off, but I have. I've never run a letter to the editor I haven't read, but it would be rare that a poem would be a vindictive sort of knife twisting kind of thing. In my experience they're going to be nice and lighter and softer."

In this particular example, Cowieson sees the major criticism of Merriam to be the drinking references: "Well, I sort of go over the Christmas cheer bit, kind of heavily. Poor Jim, he enjoys drinking and he doesn't hide it. He has a farm, and he's got horses on it. And he even talks sometimes about giving his horse a drink just to give it some extra spark, that sort of thing. So basically that's why I mentioned the barrel of coke. He drinks a bit and now he's trying to get across that Christmas cheer is something different than what's canned, in a bottle, or whatever" (T84–48). To make such comments baldly without redressive action[10] in the local paper would certainly be considered insulting at the very least. But the use of the poetry frame makes the statement amusing instead. It refers to something that is well known in the community, so although this aspect of the poem's content is textually off the record, reference to drink and to

Merriam by the United Church minister is understood to signify over-indulgence in alcohol. The commentary is artistically redressed, however. It takes place as part of the wishes "For you Jim and yours, a Scots word, 'AWRABEST' / In this season of cheer may you all be blest," which explicitly indicate the tone: jocular and well-wishing rather than abusive and condemnatory. Also, the poem's symbolic language – specifically the reversal and inversion of oppositions – indicates that from Cowieson's point of view (representing the community), Jim Merriam, sinner, can be saved.

Roy Cowieson is very aware of this altered accountability aspect of poetry, and he exploits it: "Maybe for me it's a cop-out, that I'm not actually saying something direct, but in a poem it's like a throw-away comment, like you're saying something as you're walking away. Maybe that's the way I see poetry. I think that if I had to answer what Jim had said in a serious way, it would probably be much more personal, and I may well have to attack some things he's saying. Whereas in a poem, I'm not saying something too seriously, so I can be let off the hook" (ibid.). The poet, in using an artistic form, can make his comment without necessarily being made responsible for its superficial semantic content. While a poet is obviously accountable – clearly one of the reasons Cowieson wrote his own poem was to take Merriam to task for his statements – this is a marked and particular accountability, using a local form of "poetic licence," in which the content is generically redressed and made more benign. Poetry has in addition a kind of impersonality; it is understood that verse is about the community as a whole and that its commentary is general, though its underlying referent may, in fact, be individual and personal.

The use of poetry is, in addition, appropriate to Cowieson's social persona and role in the community. It allows him to make, through indirection, statements that are essential to his role as a minister and to his self-image: "I think if I started moralizing and being serious, [the community] would think I was taking ill or something, right? So it's just part of [my] personality, eh? That it comes through that way. You see, the Scottish personality, the Scottish humour, is always laughing at these very serious moments in life" (ibid.). The current cultural definition of the minister's role allows Cowieson to be a model rather than a direct chastiser. Through his humorous poetry he can express personal opinions and the community's ethos alike without over-reaching local expectations of neighbourly behaviour.

The special semiotic of folk poetry – its tacit generic meaning – was not a conscious reason for this poet's choice of genre, but its implications for accountability certainly were. Cowieson, as he says, chose to reply in verse to match Merriam's poem. Yet it was more than simple parallelism; poetry was a particularly appropriate form for Cowieson to use to make the public commentary he wanted to make. A prose rebuttal of Merriam's poem would undoubtedly have had a very different textual content because Ontarians understand that verse has distinctive and special meanings and readers are likely to have heightened awareness of the genre's metaphorical and symbolic qualities. Answering in poetry and using its marked poetic language allowed Cowieson to be critical of Merriam, yet to do so in an appropriate way.

SPECIAL ACCOUNTABILITY, GENERIC MEANING

Throughout this chapter we have considered these two functional aspects of folk poetry more or less in isolation from one another and from their common relationship with Ontario communities. Yet these functions do relate to one another: the poet's special accountability for his or her verse-making is partly the result of folk poetry's special language, and aspects of that language mitigate the poet's responsibility for his or her commentary. Both special accountability and generic meaning indicate and involve an appropriate response to community dynamics. Both help to make what may locally seem strange or alien more apposite, or to laud the particular aptness of some event or scene. Poetry can serve these functions as it concerns events and activities that have already taken place, and evaluates them retroactively.

In chapter 2, I indicated that folk poetry in Ontario is mainly demonstrative: it evaluates current activities and refers to the past. Most of its topics concern what is happening now or has already taken place, not what will occur in the future. Contrast this, for instance, with the more frequently forensic and deliberative aspect of the letter to the editor. That genre attempts to predicate future action, whereas poetry describes current activity and contextually refers to the past. The letter to the editor is a sensitizing and future-contentious genre, while the poem is a sensitizing and past-and-present–evaluative one. The letter to the editor assumes a stance on one side of a community rift; the poem mediates it.

Similarly, poetry's retroactivity affects its politeness quality. While its stance is evaluative, it explicitly urges action only in the rarest circumstances. Internal community criticism is almost invariably hypothetical and fictitious. Cowieson's criticism of Merriam, then, is stated in terms of what he *could* do rather than of what he *should* do. Similarly, the Brampton East Women's Institute members present popular verse that only alludes to the conflict at hand. Unlike the joke- and story-tellers, whose presentations openly acknowledge and artis- tically play upon the group's contentions, the presenters of poetry, advocates of mediation between the two points of view, textually approach the problem as indirectly as possible.

Likewise, though history and letters to the editor deal with fact, argument, and rational truth, poetry deals more with affect, symbolic relationship, and emotional truth. The methods of argument in non- poetic genres – as in Bob Raymes's use of exaggeration – may involve techniques other than mere statement of facts and indication of the speaker's qualifications to make such comments, but these must be present. So, Gerry Eagan speaks to those attending the community shower (through presenter Barb Partland) as the "Bard of Tecumseth." He explicitly represents the area. As such he is not advancing his individual opinion; he is reviewing and sharing common knowledge (and sometimes presenting new information as well) that is appropriate to the event. His text affirms that the community is one, but the fact that he can step out of his individual self into a persona as community poet reconfirms it.

Even folk poetry's subjects suggest this association. Jim Merriam's and Roy Cowieson's concern with Christmas, religion, and friendship, and Raymes's with modernization and agricultural fertility, are clearly emotional and sensitive topics about which local people feel strongly. Verse appeals to an understood community ethos and to the feeling – sometimes only minimally present – that an area's residents are communally one – ideally united rather than individually separate. It invokes, as in the Merriam and Cowieson poems, things that everyone in a community would understand and know about rather than par- ticular, individual, or special knowledge. Poetry comments on an issue in such a way as to assume a consensus about it, which is probably why Cowieson felt obliged to make his own opposing statement of another "consensus."

Here perhaps lies one more reason for the sophisticated condem- nation of folk poetry. It appears to be not only conservative and uncritical but also sentimental and moralizing. In the face of patent sociocultural complexity it simplifies issues and concepts. But appro- priateness can be a rare occurrence in modern Ontario society. Man- ifestations of propriety are seen as basic, emotional, even unremarkable. Folk poetry tries to see the best in everything and everyone precisely in order to create appropriateness; unlike letters to the editor, which point out deficiencies, poetry reinforces such appositeness. Even the exceptions to the sentimental tone of folk poetry – critical and con- tentious verse about nuclear war, the metric system, and other outsiders' activities and characteristics – moralize with a directness not often seen in academic verse.

The clearest example of the appropriation of contemporary culture in folk poetry occurs when a presenter uses a popular poem rather than an indigenous one. When the Women's Institute members used popular verse in their roll-call, it was very much in keeping with the presenters' necessarily indirect approach to the problem of intragroup conflict between the generations. More direct, specific, topical verse would have threatened the politeness ethos of both the genre and the group. However, the other aspect of appropriation – the explicit securing of a textually new, local meaning – is also evident in Ontario presentations of popular verse. Comparing the original poem and the altered versions, we can examine how a presenter changes and ultimately appropriates that original to his or her own contexts and uses.

CHAPTER FOUR

Appropriating
Popular Poetry

ACCOUNTABILITY
AND ATTRIBUTION

Folk poetry in Ontario is a vehicle for asserting community concerns in particular contexts. But it is also the product and property of individuals. People become involved with folk poetry in three culturally recognized types of roles: as author, presenter, and audience. We can tentatively use Roman Jakobson's schema of "factors inalienably involved in verbal communication" to sort out some elements in the communicative system of Ontario folk poetry: "The ADDRESSER sends a MESSAGE to the ADDRESSEE. To be operative the message requires a CONTEXT referred to ... seizable by the addressee and either verbal or capable of being verbalized; a CODE fully, or at least partially, common to the addresser and addressee; ... and finally, a CONTACT, a physical channel and psychological connection between the addresser and the addressee, enabling both of them to enter and stay in communication" (1960, 353).

The last chapter dealt extensively with the code of Ontario folk poetry. However, the notions developed there of author, presenter, and audience do not fit so easily into Jakobson's system. A local author, as originator of a poetic message, is obviously an addresser. But in the case of popular verse – not local in origin – the poem's original author is not the addresser, since a meaningful message must come from someone in the community. A local presenter can take an authorial-style role vis-à-vis popular verse. As we will see in this chapter, that individual, a sender making a poetic message available to the community, takes the role of addresser quite seriously and can alter and appropriate such verse. Here Jakobson's schema is particularly useful, showing the continuity and similarity between the author of local verse and the presenter of popular poetry. Further, a presenter may be a contact, when he or she reads or recites verse in public. Alternatively, the contact may be the local newspaper. And both have, in Jakobson's terms, contextual qualities. The community as audience is the receiver of the message – Jakobson's addressee.

Michel Foucault's "What is an Author?" (1975) asks the question begged by Jakobson's system: What difference does it make, in a given text, who is speaking? Foucault suggests that attribution of authorship turns a work into a commodity, a piece of property active in a relationship of power. Asserting "one can well imagine a culture where discourse can exist without authorship" (614), he suggests that we turn our attention to where discourse comes from, how it circulates, who can appropriate it, in what modes it is found, and so on, rather than to the idea of author as originator. This seems to be the only rational approach to Ontario folk poetry. In its system of communication, authorship is by no means a simple concept, and it is closely related to that of performance.

In Ontario the performer, who in Richard Bauman's (1977) terms is "accountable" for the poem's text, can be someone other than its composer-author. With respect to spoken communication, Bauman defines performance as "the assumption of responsibility to an audience for a display of communicative competence. This competence rests in the knowledge and ability to speak in socially appropriate ways. Performance involves on the part of the performer an assumption of accountability to an audience for the way in which communication is carried out, above and beyond its referential content" (11). His definition applies to Ontario folk poetry, whether it is performed in spoken or written form. Most commonly it is through their roles as presenters (addressers), not as authors (originators), that folk poets are accountable for their works. They are primarily responsible to their local audiences for content, for Jakobson's "message," which is shared with the significant others to whom their poetry is directed. Their works are not normally evaluated on poetic form and structure, that aspect of verse that results from the poet's activity in his or her role as versemaker. Though poems are evaluated for their apposite expression, local authorship multiplies local accountability. Usually, presenters do not take the same level of responsibility for the symbolic content of the popular poems they present as do local poets for their own works. Similarly, the makers of "home crafts" – quilts, knitted or crocheted goods, and so on – in discussing the value of their products, say that it cannot be reckoned in monetary terms – by hours of labour spent or the value of the materials used. Rather, they indicate that this value accrues from personal effort towards a social goal – making a present for a relative's wedding, or quilting for a raffle to support the church. The gift so created is valued qualitatively. This concept of gift-value, differing from use-value and exchange-value,[1] implicates some ways that poetry is evaluated in Ontario communities. Poetry is seen as "good" or "bad" not on its technical or artistic merits but rather in a hierarchy based on its specific situational appropriateness. In almost all cases, because of its current topical and local relevance, indigenously authored poetry is more highly valued than its popular counterpart. We can see this in the different uses of the two and the different ways in which accountability is acknowledged. Ideally, verse should have a local author who takes responsibility for its content and expression and thus for making it as topical, specific, and relevant as possible. Popular poetry, which is used when no local poem specific to the context is available, needs a community advocate who demonstrates its relevance to the rest of the group through his or her presentation. Such an advocate is not accountable for the poetry itself – line, verse, rhyme, and so on – but rather for its appropriate symbolic content. Because only other community members' comments are worthy of attention, the authors of popular verse – who are not "significant social others" – are quite irrelevant to the intended audience of local residents.

Presenter (addresser) and author (composer) can be theoretically separated, but in practice they can blend. Authorship is not an absolute; it is part of a continuum with presentation. This is obvious in situations where the two become merged or confused: when authorship is claimed when it conventionally would not be; when it could conventionally have been claimed but was not, and when it was not admitted but was anonymous or pseudonymous. We will consider several such cases.

Historically in Ontario, authors of non-indigenous poetry have often gone unrecognized. For instance, in the public-school readers where "Somebody's Mother" appears, its author is given as "unknown," though the first reader was published only four years after the poem's original American publication in 1881 (Burke and Howe 1972). In Ontario newspapers and other written media, authors of popular verse are rarely identified. In fact, along with differences in style and specificity of subject this is one way of distinguishing popular poetry from indigenous verse. Outsider poets whose names are published in weekly newspapers are almost invariably familiar: John Keats, Richard Armour, or Edgar A. Guest, for example. Authors of verses like "A Visit from St Nicholas" or "In Flanders Fields" may be well known but they are rarely identified, nor are authors of greeting-card verses given credit. If an attribution is made in the newspaper, it is something like "an old poem: Author Unknown" (*Carleton Place Canadian*, July 1982).

In community newspapers the name of the contributor (addresser) rather than that of the author is usually published, in the context of a formula such as "submitted by" or "contributed by." Addressers may suggest a poem's general relevance, as in "I'd like to pass on to you a very True & Touching poem I recently ran across" (*Symington Place Tenants' Newsletter*, June 1982), or they may emphasize a more specific meaning. For instance, in her *Grimsby Independent* "Looking Good" column (27 April 1983) Bette Potter discusses the changes an individual undergoes on the death of a spouse, and she closes with a poem, introduced thus: "To my mother's courage through the last months and in loving memory of my dad who died this week, I believe this poem has helped." Such verse achieves significance not from its original author but from its use. The extent of its relevance to important sociocultural issues is determined partly by the identity and importance of the individual community member who makes it available to the rest and partly by that presenter's ability to demonstrate the poem's relevance. The author has no role in this.

Indeed, popular poetry is rarely seen as a commodity to which an author is appropriate. Anonymity or lack of attribution does not mean that people believe in communal composition but instead that the writer's claim on a popular poem is not considered particularly strong, especially in comparison with that of a local addresser. The latter may on occasion even claim to have "written" a particular poem, but such accountability is often contextually very weak. For instance, Bill Crewson of Scarborough claimed authorship for "If God Should Go on Strike" not in social interaction with his community but in the fantasy-like radio programs he tapes for his own pleasure, using the pseudonyms "Country Bumpkin Bill" or "the Singing Ranger Jimmy West." The same poem has apparently been published in a popular international syndicated column, and an almost word-for-word version was submitted to the *Muskoka Free Press* by George Cottril of Huntsville, but Crewson calls it "some poetry I made up ... I just thought you might find it a bit interesting as it is very appropriate in these times which I have called 'If God Should Go on Strike'" (T83–24). Crewson is, of course, not the poem's author in a conventional sense, yet he is not a plagiarist. He is taking accountability for the poem's presence, as he says, for its "interest" and "appropriateness."

The opposite case, where an individual with every conventional right to do so is reluctant to claim authorship, can also occur. Exactly where a poem obviously based on another ceases to be identified with it and becomes another poem is difficult to establish. For instance,

Mary Dow Brine's "Somebody's Mother" and "An Act of Kindness" by William Dyer of Newmarket (which will be discussed below) are substantially similar, containing a number of almost identical lines and similar protagonists, yet the two have significantly different themes. Their similarities can be quantified, but their distinctiveness cannot. In his letter submitting "An Act of Kindness" to the local newspaper, Dyer does not say that he authored the work. In another instance, Mrs Astrida Reader of Paris shared credit with her mother-in-law for "It Is about Us" in the *Paris Star* (also discussed below), yet in an interview she explicitly denied her own authorship. Reader used several verses from a poem on an entirely different topic written by her mother-in-law, but more than half of "It Is about Us" was totally original.

Dyer and Reader do not consider themselves poets. Reader says: "My mother-in-law had a feeling for doggerel. She could do it in two minutes. I can't ... So I took my mother-in-law's poetry or it was doggerel and extended it ... I revised it altogether" (T83–39). Dyer says in his letter submitting "An Act of Kindness" to the Bradford-based weekly *Topic*: "I am accepting your invitation to submit a poem. I like poetry, but can't always find the words to express myself, probably due to limited education. I leave it to you to put in the correct punctuation, as I am very limited in that area."[2] Dyer's comment indicates a reluctance to be accountable for his work. He refuses to be responsible for a final version, leaving punctuation to the editor. Note also that he says he "submits" the poem, not that he "wrote" it. He shares this rhetorical insecurity with language with Reader, a polyglot who learned English only after she did Latvian, German, and French. She says: "My English is good but quite often the brain doesn't work to find the right expression or the right vocabulary for what I'm trying to say. One is smaller than the other or whatever, but at some times I feel my brain is faster than I can keep up with what I say" (T83–39). The fact that the prototype poem was written by her mother-in-law decreases the chance that she would be allowed by her family and community to "own" or author the poem.[3]

It is also possible for a poem to be attributed to more than one person. For instance, in the *Toronto Star* of 9 December 1983 a column by internationally syndicated American columnist Ann Landers was entitled "Will the real author of poem please stand up." Landers refers to "The Man in the Glass," which she had printed previously, submitted by a reader who said that her brother had written it. The columnist excerpts responses from eight individuals who dispute that claim: five attribute it to someone else – father, aunt, patient, friend, and rock group – and three say they wrote it themselves. It is difficult to draw any conclusions without knowing whether Landers's readers base their claims on actual texts in hand or on remembered performances. Possibly we have a situation like the Crewson one, where authorship follows accountability; or, as in the Dyer and Reader cases, a text may be similar in some ways – theme or content, for instance – though not identical to the one printed.

I suggest the last on the basis of personal experience. When I heard Mrs C.C.'s poem about the modern grandmother at the Brampton East W.I. meeting, I felt sure that it was a more or less identical version of another poem I had collected. My error was obvious when I examined the two texts side by side. This is a text of the earlier poem, from the *Blenheim News-Tribune* (26 January 1983):

> The old rocking chair is vacant today
> For Grandma is no longer in it;
> She's off in the car to the office or shop,
> Just buzzing around every minute.
>
> No one shoves Grandma back on the shelf
> She's versatile, forceful, dynamic;
> That isn't pie in the oven, my dear,
> Her baking today is ceramic.
>
> You won't see her trudle [sic] off early to bed,
> Or seek out a warm comfy nook,
> Her typewriter clackety-clacks through the night,
> For Grandma is writing a book.
>
> Without ever taking a look at her yarn
> To slow down her steady advancing,
> She won't tend the babies for you anymore,
> For Grandma has taken up dancing.
>
> She isn't content with the crumbs as of old,
> With meager or second-hand knowledge,
> Don't bring out the mending for Grandma to do,
> For Grandma has gone back to college.

Clearly, though they are thematically identical – or very nearly so – the two texts vary so substantially as to preclude even a relationship like the one between the Reader/Reader and Dyer/Brine poems. It is, of course, quite possible that if the two verses were not independently invented, one may have inspired the other, but this modelling does not in any sense reflect on their originality of composition.

Authorship, as seen here, is from an ethnographic point of view a variable and relative entity; presenters change poetry in ways very similar to those that Eleanor Long (1973) attributes to ballad performers and makers. Presenters of popular poetry may be conservative "perseverators," striving to maintain the text as it comes to them; "confabulators," who revise and add material; "rationalizers," who manipulate the text according to the message they wish to convey; or "integrators," who apply cultural models to texts of their own devising (231–3). The last are more properly authors than presenters of folk poetry, but these distinctions are not always clear.

The presenter and the author of indigenous poetry, of course, need not be the same person. On various occasions, like the wedding-shower example in the previous chapter, a local poet may be asked to provide verse that he or she is neither expected nor wanted to perform. In this situation, unlike the previous ones where the author is an outsider, it is the author, not the presenter, who has ultimate accountability for the poem and who is speaking for the community. Whether local poets are asked to write a work or write it on their own initiative, they are always credited in any verbal or written performance. The person who physically presents the poem to the community is only the medium of presentation – Jakobson's "contact" – rather than the sender of the message. Authorship is central because it is the writer who specifically addresses the relevant issues in the work.

Much of the evidence for the significance and meaning of accountability and authorship is negative. A contemporary poem, anonymously presented or submitted, has a very specific social meaning. Those who write poems are expected to be proud of their ability; whether considered a gift or a special interest, that talent is not something to be kept hidden. If a poem's authorship is suppressed and the identity of its composer unknown, the potential value of its commentary resulting from the author's social position and community role is attenuated. A local poet who is not willing to be accountable for a work is denying his or her social relations and is creating rifts in the community rather than bridging them.

Since most verse on local subjects is sent to the weekly newspaper, its editor receives a share of anonymous material, most of which remains unprinted. For instance, though the *Manitoulin Expositor* actively encourages contributions and prints pseudonymous material when the author's identity is known, "We have a policy of printing only things which are identified" (Mac Swackhammer, T84–40).

Most anonymous material sent to the local newspaper is "bitchy critical" (ibid.), like "Lamentation for a Golden Dream (or 'Flogging a Dead Horse')," in which a local mayor is castigated for attempting to renovate the town hall, thus forcing out the local theatre company.

The poem was submitted by "KB" and has not been printed in the newspaper to which it was sent. As folklorist Edward D. Ives suggests, the newspaper is not an appropriate place for such materials: "Being funny at some local townsman's expense was definitely out. There were outlets for such effusions, but the newspaper was definitely not one of them" (Ives 1971, 241). By sending the poem in effective anonymity, KB relinquishes the right to make a valuable critical comment by avoiding indication of the author's place in the community. That it was submitted to the newspaper but not published in it – though the work is probably not libellous – of course completely negates its value. Even the statement itself is lost.

Poet Gerry Eagan stresses the "fair-play" community ethos against anonymous works, and comments: "I sign my name usually to everything I write because I kind of believe in that. I don't believe in putting write-ups in the paper, especially if you're tearing somebody apart, and then just sign it 'an interested observer,' or something like that. So I usually sign everything like that" (T84–39). Critical discussion of community insiders – the mayor, the local police, etc. – is allowed and even expected. But in the newspaper it is unlikely to be in poetic form and ideally should be neither anonymous nor pseudonymous. Criticism of outsiders, and satirical discussions of national politicians, are considered quite appropriate for poetry and are always accountable and public.

If it was difficult to convince poets who had composed only one work that they had something to contribute to my study, it was even harder to convince collecters and presenters. They saw their involvement with verse as being passive rather than active and therefore found my interest somewhat strange. Collecting poetry is regarded in Ontario as a very everyday thing and not a practice of potential interest, as writing poetry is. Many collectors, however, are as ambiguous in their relationship to the communicative system as are presenters and authors. An individual who superficially appears to be a presenter may be simply a passive contact, or people may find themselves obliged to take on accountable presenter roles contrary to their initial intentions.

Many Ontarians collect poetry on a somewhat ad hoc basis, cutting out inspirational material and posting it on the refrigerator door, as Betty Burton does, or putting it in a box, a book, or an album. Some become active presenters of these works. They may accept accountability for a poem when they send it in a letter to a friend or relative and commend it as relevant to a particular situation, or when they submit it to the local newspaper, for example. Most poems that are thus performed publicly by someone other than their authors are popular imported works.

We should remember that appropriate *presentational* accountability within a community is weaker than local *authorial* accountability. Popular poetry is regarded as something to be used only when a more ideal, authentic, topical poem by a local author dealing with the specific situation cannot be found or created. For example, Mrs Shirley Laycock, my W.I. contact, apologized because none of the members of her branch "had the time" to write their own poems. She implied that reading popular verse for the roll-call was very much a second-best activity, to which she and her fellow W.I. members resorted only in the absence of the real thing, indigenous poems.

The poems presented at the Brampton East Women's Institute meeting provide a good sample of such works. They were selected from some common source for poetry – a bookmark, a calendar, a greeting card, and so on – and delivered in circumstances where there was some semantic correspondence between the poem's text and the current context. Thus, several poems about old age were read at the Grandmother's Meeting. Mrs C.C., who according to Mrs Laycock was well known for locating and reading appropriate poetry at meetings and who, except for the chairwoman, was the only person to read a poem directly echoing the topic of the meeting, said she did not collect poems. Rather, she suggested that she was always able to find them when necessary. The poem she read at the meeting I attended, for instance, came from her senior citizens' club magazine, which she had received on the day of the meeting.

Some collectors, like Lyda Johnson of Kincardine, send poems to the newspaper but never perform poetry orally, because of shyness and/or lack of opportunity. Much of the poetry that Johnson collects and presents is on the subject of old age: "Modern Grandmother," "Why Can Gram Be So Gay," "Somebody's Mother," or "A Thought":

She sits there waiting patiently
And wipes away a tear
Wishing that a visitor
Would suddenly appear ...

It's hard for her to understand
Just what's [sic] she's doing there
What happened to her family
And friends who used to care ...

So take her by the hand and say
How are you with a smile
And then sit close beside her
And just love her for a while.

The source of this poem was "the Ann Kelly column in the *Owen Sound Times*. A lady copied it from a Hanging in a Hospital room. Unknown writer" (Lyda Johnson, L 1985). To Johnson, the currency and popularity of the poem validates its importance. Its author is clearly a matter of disinterest to her, and its main significance is that it is a medium for her own communicative needs. Its topic concerns her in part because she is herself an older person whose family has moved away, and she uses the poem to make others aware of this by including it in letters, sending it to the local newspaper, and showing it in her scrapbook poetry collection to visitors.

Some people may find themselves more or less forced into public oral performance of poetry as part of a ritual function. It is a tradition at W.I. meetings that the chairwoman reads a "thought for the day" at the beginning of the meeting, and it is considered particularly appropriate – for reasons already suggested about poetry's separating and unifying function – for the "thought" to be in verse form. Any woman who becomes branch chair must constantly search for potential material and is thus a vigilant and attentive audience and collector of popular poetry, as well as a performer.

Even collectors who are usually passive non-performers by intention can be accountable presenters in their interactions with the people who examine their collections. When a group of friends or relatives gets together to look through such a collection, participants in the session can be alternately, or even simultaneously, presenter and audience. In one such instance, Evelyn Roberts of Paris borrowed a late friend's poetry collection so that she and her other friends could look through it together. Here Roberts was undoubtedly accountable for the entire event, since it was her idea and the session was held at her home. However, she and her friends traded the presenter's role about during the session when they read a poem from the collection or told an anecdote about the collector.

Roberts has her own collection of poetry in which the poetic material, whether it is kept in boxes or albums, is not separated from the photographs, newspaper clippings, and other memorabilia. Roberts was a schoolteacher in Paris, Ontario, and much of her collection is composed of poems by a local school superintendent celebrating the retirements of her fellow teachers. Most of these verses are on the original handwritten sheets; Roberts has taken on the role of verse archivist for her group as well as those of audience and occasional presenter. She attributes this to coming from "a family of keepers" (N 6 January 1984). Even an informal archivist like Roberts is in a certain sense accountable for poetry; she is responsible for its preservation and for making it available to others.

When someone other than the local author of a poem is given the task of reading it at a community event, as was the case at the shower in Colgan, great care is taken both to acknowledge the author and to indicate his or her accountability. The shower MC's comments identified the poet, Gerry Eagan, and described his valued qualities of talent and generosity. This mention of the author preceded the reader's very brief introduction. She acknowledged Eagan's authorship before beginning her performance of his poem. The groom reinforced it when he thanked "Gerry Eagan for that beautiful poem" (T84–46) and Barbara Partland for reading it, making the distinction between accountability and performance, and the order of their importance, quite obvious.

In all the commentaries from the stage, speakers described the positive qualities of the poem itself, not those of its rendition. Backstage afterwards, however, the poet and the reader discussed the performance and congratulated one another on their respective talents. Eagan explained to me that Partland's skill showed that she was accustomed to performing poems. He commented that her performance was much better than any he could have done. Evidently, readers can acquire a reputation for proficient presentation of poems. Yet the distinction between addresser and contact remains vital; the message originates with the poet, who is the addresser; the reader is only a medium for the presentation of the words.

I know of no one who has publicly presented materials by known others as a sender rather than as a contact for presentation. Privately, however, such action is possible, as when a resident of a community sends an absent relative the latest work by a local poet. In this case the immediate sender – the relative – is accountable for a different kind of content in the poem. That is, he or she is responsible for the poem as a general example of activities at home, as a valid kind of memory, rather than for the poem's situational meaning in its original circumstances of presentation.

In some unusual cases a local poet, though author of a work, may not be accountable for its symbolic content. When Lynn Allison's wife asked him to write a poem for her family's reunion, she was responsible for the poem's symbolic and topical content, and thus she is the accountable addresser. Her husband, as writer, is author and in part also contact, but he cannot be said to be accountable in the usual sense.

APPROPRIATION AND VARIATION

The foregoing considerations are significant because they help us to understand how and why popular poetry is textually appropriated by local Ontario addressers. A close examination of variation between texts shows the extent to which these people make a work their own, and their culture's. Folksong scholars, for their part, have devoted extensive study to this kind of continuity mixed with variation. For instance, Tristram Potter Coffin (1977) observes that traditional balladry is affected by the stabilizing influence of print, general trends in folk art, and singers' personalities.[4] He tries thus to explain the reasons for continuity and variation, as well as the forms of their textual manifestations. Folklorists usually assume that texts that are transmitted primarily in written form, as contemporary Ontario folk verse is, do not vary at all. Yet this is not the case.

This assumption fails to recognize the presence of a vital living tradition. Little research has focused on the traditional qualities of modern Anglo folk poetry; as we saw in chapter 1 most analysts of this material have dealt in a rather different way with its forms. Here, however, we can demonstrate that continuity and variation (Sharp 1907) alike are as present in folk poetry as in other genres of folklore. Since even a superficial examination of the texts reveals clearly the continuity aspect, my analysis is directed more to demonstrating the presence and purpose of variation.

Poem variants must exhibit enough textual similarity that the inference of conscious modelling is plausible. In other words, variants are genetically related one to another. Variation can be seen first on the level of the text, in the use of alternative and/or unique words. Second, variation occurs on the deeper levels of structure, both in sequence (syntactic structure) and in composition (paradigmatic structure). Third, there is variation on the level of semantics, most frequently in the poems' topics and/or in their protagonists. The distinctions among these kinds of variation can be seen in the analyses that follow.

Clearly, the three levels are not always completely separable, and as some striking examples show, variation in the words of the text, even in its structure, does not necessarily mean there is a change in its meaning. Nor does textual or structural continuity correlate with semantic continuity. Context – poetic as well as social – is all important in determining what a poem means to a community, and in no example here is the notion of a literal, a-contextual meaning reasonable.

Types of variants seem to fall into two categories. The first group comprises poems that retain some degree of identity with their prototype. They are "versions" of one another, in the conventional sense. But others depart strikingly from the meanings and intentions of their models, nevertheless retaining structural similarities; these are sometimes called parodies. The models for this type come from various sources. The song prototypes can be "Clementine," "The Yellow Rose of Texas," "My Bonnie Lies over the Ocean," the theme song from the television situation comedy *The Brady Bunch*, "Auld Lang Syne,"

"The Battle Hymn of the Republic / Solidarity Forever" (a common subject for parody and parodic verse; see, for instance, Jorgensen 1983), and the hymn "God Sees the Little Sparrow Fall." It is difficult to see any common thread joining these originals other than a certain currency and availability. The poem models found in my collection are Edgar Allan Poe's "The Raven," Joyce Kilmer's "Trees," the nursery rhyme "Ten Little Indians," William Wordsworth's "She Dwelt among the Untrodden Ways," Clement Moore's "A Visit from St Nicholas," the Twenty-third Psalm (King James version), and the works of Robert Service. Again, I find no striking semantic, structural, or textual similarities among these verse prototypes.

Rarely, a poet will use a more proximate source, as Astrida Reader did in employing her mother-in-law's poem, but I have seen no examples of a new poem being based on another local song or poem. As Ed Miller of Haliburton suggests, however, this can occur:

E.M.: Now a lad got up at Kinmount. Now he sang "The Haliburton Highlands." But he changed the words and –
P.G.: To "The Yellow Rose of Texas?" [Mr Miller's "Haliburton Highlands" is sung to that tune.].
E.M.: Well, he had a tune to it all of his own, you know, but he had the same swing to it and "Haliburton Highlands," but he had different towns and stuff like that, see? But I knew the minute he started that it was my song. (T84–24)

If this case is exceptional, I have no way of knowing, since I could not identify local poetic prototypes without the assistance of local people and since my source for most of this material was the community newspapers.

Throughout, the lack of direct correlation between textual and semantic as well as between structural and semantic change is obvious, and it is contrary to what I expected. Even the grossest textual variations can have minimal semantic effect, and the merest textual and structural changes can have great semantic consequence. Variation can be properly understood only within the context of the poem as a whole, and in some aspects only within its sociocultural and performance context as well. Let us consider several different versions of Ontario folk poems.

"A Little Mixed Up"

This first example is of two versions of the same poem that are almost identical, similar in all but textual matters. The versions of "A Little Mixed Up" come from the *Stittsville News*, 27 April 1983, and the *Paisley Advocate*, 2 March 1983. Material from both variants is presented alone; material from the Paisley example only is in parentheses; and material from the Stittsville example only is bracketed:

Just a line to say I'm living
That I'm not among the dead
Though I'm getting more forgetful
And more mixed up in (the) head.
            [my]

For sometimes I can't remember
When I stand (on) the stair
            [at the foot of]
If I must go up for something
Or (I've) just come down from there(.)
   [have I]   [?]

(And) before the fridge (I) often (stand)
[ ]   [so]
My poor mind (is) filled with doubt
            [ ]
Have I (just) put the food away, (or)
      [come to]   [ ]
(Have) I (come to) take (it) out.
[Or do] [ ]   [some]

And (there's sometimes) when (it's) dark (out)
      [there are times]   [it is]   [ ]
(With my nightcap on my head)
[And I am dressed for bed]
I (don't know) if I'm retiring
   [can't tell]
Or (just getting out of bed).
      [have just got up, instead]

So if (it's) my turn to write you
      [it is]
There's no need (of getting) sore
                  [to get]
I may think that I have written
And don't want to be a bore.

(So) remember – I ( ) love you
[Please]   [do]

And I (do) wish ( ) you were here
   [ ]   [that]
But now it's nearly mail time
(So) I must say "Goodbye, ( ) dear."
[ ]   [my]

I stand before the post box,
[With the letter in my hand,
Good gracious! What has happened?]
(With) my face (so) very red
[ ]   [is]
( ) Instead of mailing (you my) letter
[For]   [your]
I (had) opened it instead.
  [have]

Textual differences between these two versions occur in words that carry a minimal semantic load, or are synonymous: extended or contracted verb forms, such as (it's) for [it is]; verb number (there's) for [there are]; and interrogative rather than declarative form (I've) for [Have I]. Or words with little semantic value like (and) are omitted, or others put in their places: (I) for [so] or (it) for [some] in the third verse.

Variation also exists where synonymous or nearly synonymous words are used, as in (don't know) for [can't tell] in the fourth verse. Where entirely different lines are used, as in verse four (With my nightcap on my head) for [And I am dressed for bed], again the sense is similar; the night-cap in the Paisley poem is a synecdoche for the content of its corresponding line in the Stittsville poem. At least one pattern is evident here; where the Paisley poem has contractions, the Stittsville version uses the extended form.

There is no substantial difference in the structures of the two works. Even where two additional lines are found in the Stittsville version, they make no change to the work's structure; they are elaborating and essentially redundant expressions. Note that their presence may be related to the special performance context of this version. The Stittsville version was printed as "recited" by Mrs Bertha Desjardin at a dinner given for seventy-five guests on her ninety-eighth birthday. The additional lines (they make a six line verse in a poem otherwise containing only four line verses, so it is safe to assume that they were added to a prototype) in Desjardin's version set up, yet postpone, the punch line, and are thus very appropriate in an oral performance. There is no evidence that the Paisley poem is otherwise more similar than the other to a common prototype, but the types of differences between the two seem analogous to those that result when a text is memorized for recitation. In sum, no major textual, structural, or, of course, semantic differences are evident between these two examples.

"Wonderful Grandma"

In two versions of "Wonderful Grandma," however, aspects of the main protagonist's character vary subtly as a result of alterations in the text. The textual variations themselves are similar to those outlined in the example above, yet there they produced no semantic differences. A version from the collection of Lyda Johnson of Kincardine is probably from the *Free Press Weekly*, a farm paper from Winnipeg, now defunct, that was popular in Ontario through the first half of this century. The other was published in the *Almonte Gazette* with the attribution "by Cora Yuill." Mrs Yuill has also read the poem, with considerable success, at her senior citizens' association meeting. The Johnson version is in parentheses, Yuill's in brackets, and shared material unmarked:

(Who'll) take Grandma, who will it be
[Who will]
All of us want her, I'm sure you'll agree
Let's call a meeting, let's gather the clan
In such a big family (there's certainly) one
                          [there must surely be]
Willing to give her a place in the sun.

Strange how we thought (that) she'd never wear out
[But] See how she walks, it's arthritis no doubt
(Her eyesight is faded, her memory is dim
She's apt to insist on the silliest whim)
When people get older they become such a care
She must have a home but the question is where.

Remember the days when she used to be spry
Baked her own cookies and made her own pie
Helped us with lessons and mended (our) seams
                          [the]
Kissed away troubles and mended our dreams.

Wonderful Grandma we all loved her so

Isn't it dreadful (she's) no place to go
[she has]
One little corner is all she would need
A shoulder to cry on, (her) Bible to read
[and a]
(A chair in the window, the sun coming through
Pretty spring flowers all covered with dew.)

(Who'll) warm her with love so she won't mind the cold
[Who will]
Oh who will take Grandma now that she's old
What nobody wants here, (oh) yes there is one
[ah]
Willing to give her a place in the sun.

[Where] She won't have to worry or wonder or doubt
And she won't be our problem to bother about
Pretty soon now god will give her a bed
But (who will) dry our tears when dear Grandma is dead.
[who'll]

Superficially, textual variations in the two versions of "Wonderful Grandma" are fewer and less pervasive than those in "A Little Mixed Up," which might suggest that they should be semantically closer. But this is not the case. An important difference of meaning occurs where there is unique material – in the two couplets of Johnson's version that are absent from Yuill's. In the total context of the Johnson poem these lines are simply additive. They do not alter the sequential structure and have similar semantic content to that of the preceding lines, which concern the deterioration associated with old age. The first couplet adds the weakening of sight, memory, and mental ability to the suggestion that arthritis is affecting the grandmother's ability to function. The second adds a few niceties – a chair and flowers – to the grandmother's meagre and easily satisfiable needs – shelter, comfort, and a Bible. The couplets' absence from Yuill's version, however, places another valence on their meaning in the total context of the Johnson poem.

The Yuill grandmother is clearly less pathetic than her Johnson poem counterpart. Her problem is physical, not mental, and her needs are correspondingly more instrumental and less expressive. Though Yuill would not confirm this, I suspect that deliberately or unconsciously she excised the couplets from a prototype in order to present a more univocally positive picture of the grandmother. She takes authorial credit for the poem; this is appropriate, especially because she has in fact changed its meaning. Note again that the same kind of variation had no semantic weight in "A Little Mixed Up."

"The World Is Mine"

In a third example, "The World Is Mine," there is minimal textual change (as in "A Little Mixed Up") yet also some semantic variation (as in "Wonderful Grandma"). This poem is obviously very popular in Ontario; I located four versions of it. One is from the *Lambeth News Star* of 3 February 1983, with the author given as unknown. Another was sent to me in manuscript form by Mrs Evelyn Sample of Almonte, who found it "in a magazine" and had submitted it, under the title "Don't Whine," to the editor of the *Almonte Gazette*, but it was not printed there. Sample commented, "Now can you believe why the Editor of the Almonte Gazette would not print such an inspiring poem, about things we take so much for granted?" (L 5 April 1985). A third version was published in Hazel Levere's column, "Star Dust," in the *Smiths Falls Record News* of 26 October 1983. She had asked a friend to locate "a certain piece of verse that had been read at a W.I. convention some years back. It made quite an impression on me." A fourth text appeared in the *Rainy River Record* of 12 January 1983. The addresser was Dr Tennyson Guyer.

The line numbers of the poem are here in brackets, and the versions are designated as follows: 1: Smiths Falls; 2: Rainy River; 3: Lambeth; and 4: Almonte. Parentheses indicate synonymous words used in parallel positions:

```
[1]
1–3  Today upon a bus I saw
4    Today           I saw
[2]
1    A lovely (maid) with golden hair
2–3  A        (girl)  with golden hair
4    A lovely (girl)  with golden hair
[3]
1    She seemed so gay and oh
2–3  She seemed so gay       I envied her
4                            Envied her
[4]
1    I     wished    I were     so fair
2–3  And wish   that I were half so fair
4    And wished    I were     so fair
```

[5]
1   When suddenly   she rose to (leave)
2–3   I watched her as she rose to (leave)
4   When   she rose to (go)
[6]
1   I   saw her hobble   down the aisle
2–3   And   saw her hobble   down the aisle
4   She   hobbled down the aisle
[7]
1   She had one foot   but
2–3 She had one   leg and wore a crutch
4   She had one   leg   wore a crutch
[8]
1   As she passed – a lovely smile
2–3   But as she passed – a   smile
4   And   a   smile
[9]
1–4 Oh God forgive me when I whine
[10]
1   I have two feet   the world is mine.
2–4 I have two   legs the world is mine.

[11]
1   And when   I stopped to buy   some sweets
2–3   Later on   I   bought some sweets
4   Then I stopped to buy   some sweets
[12]
1   The (lad) who served me   had such charm
2–3 The (boy) who   sold them had such charm
4   The (lad) who   sold them had such charm
[13]
1   He seemed to radiate good cheer
2–3   I thought I'd stop and talk awhile
4   I   talked   with him
[14]
1   His manner was so warm and kind
2   (If I were) late t'would do   no harm
3   (If I were) late would do   no harm
4   (My being) late   was no harm
[15]
1   I said "It's nice to deal with you
2–3   And as we talked   he said
4   And as   I left he said to me

[16]
1   Such courtesy I seldom find."
2–3   "Thank you sir you've really been so kind
4   "You've   been so kind
[17]
1   He turned and said "Oh thank you ma'am"
2–3   It's nice to talk to folks like you
4   ( )
[18]
1   And then I saw that he was   blind
2–3   Because you see   I'm   blind
4   "You see" he said "I am blind."
[19]
1–4 Oh God forgive me when I whine
[20]
1–4 I have two eyes – the world is mine.

[21]
1   Then   walking down the street I saw
2–3   Later walking down the street I   met
4   Later   I saw
[22]
1   A child   with eyes so   blue
2–3 A   boy with eyes so   blue
4   A child   with eyes of blue
[23]
1   He stood and watched the others play
2–3 But he stood and watched the others play
4   Watching   others play
[24]
1   He   seemed to   know not what to do
2–3   It seemed   he   knew not what to do
4   Not knowing   what to do
[25]
1   I stopped a moment   then I said
2–3 I   paused and then I said
4   ( )
[26]
1–4 "Why don't you join the others dear?"
[27]
1   He (looked)   ahead without a word
2–3 He (looked) straight ahead without a word
4   He (stared)   ahead without a word

[28]
1   And then I knew he could not hear
2–3 And then I knew he couldn't   hear
4   He could not hear
[29]
1–4 Oh God forgive me when I whine
[30]
1–4 I have two ears the world is mine.

[31]
1   With feet   to take me where I'd go
2–3   Two legs to take me where I   go
4   With   legs to take me where I   go
[32]
1&4   With eyes to see the sunset's glow
2–3   Two eyes to see the sunset's glow
[33]
1&4 With   ears to hear what I would   know
2–3   Two ears to hear what I   should know
[34]
1   ( )
2–4 Oh God forgive me when I whine
[35]
1–4 I'm blessed indeed! The world is mine.

The Lambeth and Rainy River examples are so similar (their single difference is an alternation of "would" for "t'would") that we may conclude they are very close to the prototype. Their extreme geographical separation (Lambeth is just outside London, in central Ontario: Rainy River is on the Minnesota border, over four hundred kilometres west of Thunder Bay) yet almost contemporary publication date is inferential confirmation of this; no direct connection between the two is likely, so they may each have come from an independent source.

The Almonte and Smiths Falls versions are remembrances or rewritings of a prototype. Both are metrically somewhat different than Lambeth–Rainy River. I know of no direct connection between them. It is interesting that they are semantically so similar. Perhaps a correspondence in cultural view has produced parallel alterations.

Almonte and Smiths Falls describe the girl as "lovely." In line 1 the watcher is drawn to observe the girl as she is leaving (the other two imply that she has been observed continuously). The past tense is maintained in line 4. The sequence of incidents in the Lambeth–Rainy

River verses, "Today ... Later ... Later," is instead "Today ... And when ... Then" (Smiths Falls) and "Today ... Then ... Later" (Almonte). In Almonte and Smiths Falls the speaker "stopped to buy" rather than "bought," and the seller is a "lad," not a "boy."

In both, too, the poem's central lines vary significantly from the prototype: lines 13, 14, 15, 16, and 17 are completely different in Smiths Falls, and Almonte has line 17. This is because the poems' protagonists are different. In Lambeth–Rainy River the emphasis is upon the male speaker's kindness as he leaves; this takes up only one line rather than two, as in the others. The female speaker of Smiths Falls elaborates on the lad's, rather than the speaker's own, positively valued qualities of warmth, kindness, and courtesy.

In both lines 12 and 22 the "boy" in Lambeth–Rainy River versions is instead a "child." He is "seen" rather than "met" by the speaker. This is more semantically consistent with the later events of the poem, which indicate that the child/boy does not address the speaker. Finally, lines 31, 32, and 33 change the redundant "two" to "with."

Some changes in Smiths Falls and Kincardine appear to be those of the confabulator type of redactor (Long 1973). These two are more internally consistent and less textually repetitive than Lambeth–Rainy River. They are structured with the eight-line stanzas emphasizing the positive characteristics of the handicapped individuals, and the two-line choruses and five-line conclusion concentrating on the speaker. The Lambeth–Rainy River prototype lacks this organized structure, instead alternating its protagonists within the verses. The speaker, whose sex is male in Lambeth–Rainy River, female in Smiths Falls, and not stated in Almonte, is portrayed somewhat differently in each, as are some of the individuals he/she meets.

"The Modern Grandmother"

In the next set of examples of this poem, which we discussed earlier, minor semantic and textual changes, by now familiar from previous examples, predominate. The first, from a column by Alvin Armstrong in the *Blenheim News-Tribune* of 26 January 1983, is introduced thus: "One of our versemakers has his version of the modern Grandma." The second, from the collection of Lyda Johnson of Kincardine, is probably from the *Free Press Weekly*. Common material is unmarked, Blenheim material in parentheses, and Kincardine material in brackets:

The old rocking chair is vacant today
(For) Grandma is no longer in it
[Cause]

She's off in the car to (the office or) shop
                    [golf or to]
Just buzzing around every minute.

No one shoves Grandma back on the shelf
She's versatile, forceful, dynamic
That isn't [a] pie in the oven, my dear
Her baking today is ceramic.

[Down go the pins as she takes steady aim
"It's a strike!" she yells at the bowling game
She pulls on her wig and is ready to go
Out for the evening to play at bingo.]

(You won't see her trudle [sic] off early to bed
Or seek out a warm comfy nook
Her typewriter clackety clacks through the night
For Grandma is writing a book.)

In the Kincardine version, the stanza above follows rather than precedes the next.

(Without ever taking a look at her)   yarn
[She no longer sits around knitting up boxes of]
To slow down her years steady advancing
She won't tend the babies for you any more
(For) Grandma has taken up dancing
[Cause]

She isn't content with the crumbs as of old
With meager or second hand knowledge
Don't bring out the mending for Grandma to do
(For) Grandma has gone back to college.
[Cause]

[So the dust gathers thick on Granny's old chair
While she is away gallivanting
Tomorrow she leaves for Hawaii you know
To rest neath the palm trees enchanting.]

In these texts, unlike the previous examples, we can observe fairly
extensive structural variation; the arrangement of stanzas in different

sequences is clear. Semantic variation, too, is striking. As in the versions of "Wonderful Grandma" discussed earlier, original material appears in one poem to be simply additive, but its absence in the other causes semantic variation. Where stanzas are common, they share nearly identical lines.

However, the two stanzas found only in the Kincardine version emphasize the leisure activities of the modern grandmother's life: she plays bingo and bowls, and goes on a vacation to Hawaii. In contrast, the Blenheim-only stanza has the grandmother using her time productively rather than for relaxation and self-indulgence; instead of going to bed early, she writes a book. This divergence is also reflected in the work-play dichotomy in the last line of the first stanza: the Blenheim grandmother goes to the office, whereas the Kincardine grandmother golfs. And rather than taking a traditional child-care role, the Blenheim grandmother contests her expected lot by becoming productive economically. Instead of contributing to the family unit in the only way possible – and thus fulfilling traditional cultural expectations and earning a respected if non-productive place in the family – the Kincardine grandmother devotes her time to selfish leisure activities. Rather than taking care of people and providing food for them by baking pies, the Kincardine grandmother makes useless ceramic objects, and she goes out dancing instead of baby-sitting. She is (passively) wasting her time rather than (actively) using it badly. The Kincardine grandmother is perhaps more laughable than her Blenheim counterpart, who more effectively threatens the status quo. The Kincardine poem is equally ambivalent and/or implicitly critical of the grandmother's behaviour, but she is faulted for spending her time in a frivolous and valueless way, not for doing so in a way that is in traditional Ontario culture explicitly disapproved of. The poem is, of course, intended to be funny, but humour very frequently concerns culturally ambivalent issues.[5] The issue, appropriate for humour because it is problematic, is poetically apposite for the same reason.

A third grandmother poem, read by Mrs C.C. at the Brampton East W.I. meeting described in the previous chapter, differs completely in all but semantic aspects. Note, for example, the identical references to chairs in the final verses of this and the Kincardine poem, though their texts are quite different. In the context of the meeting, this poem can be seen as a positive force for the integration of younger and older members. Beside the other poems, however, its critical stance towards the grandmother who shirks her traditional responsibilities is evident. The first two stanzas suggest the grandmother's expected role in producing utilitarian objects by knitting, tatting, and crocheting, and serving the family by baby-sitting. In the last two stanzas, she combines the Kincardine grandmother's frivolity – touring, exercising, skiing, and curling – with the Blenheim grandmother's productivity – taking clients out to lunch. The final comment, "Grandma's off her rocker," suggests not only that she literally spends no time in her chair but also, colloquially, that her abrogation of culturally defined responsibilities is truly deviant. The poem, in focusing less specifically on the grandmother's current faults and in giving a final punning comment, has a less overtly critical attitude than the other two, but it is also more open to alternative interpretations.

It seems ironic that the semantic differences between the two textually near-identical poems, Blenheim and Kincardine, are greater than those between either one and the Brampton poem. Yet because they are so alike, it is easier to see Blenheim and Kincardine as variants of the same poem. Only by considering all three poems together – and only chance made all three versions available – can one see that they all form part of a semantic continuum.

"Somebody's Mother"

A really noteworthy example of the range of variation in Ontario folk poetry occurs in versions of "Somebody's Mother," by American children's author Mary Dow Brine. First published in Brine's *Madge the Violet Girl and Other Poems* in 1881 (Burke and Howe 1972), it was reprinted in the *Royal Reader, Second Book*, of 1883, in the *Second Reader* of the Ontario Readers throughout its series of editions (1884, 1909, and 1923), and in the *Canadian Catholic Reader, Second Book*, of 1899. In each of these volumes the poem's author is "unknown." The poem's diffusion was unusually wide and deep, for Ontario schoolchildren educated between the 1880s and the 1940s – and possibly later – used at least one of these readers. Moreover, to many of those who saw it there, "Somebody's Mother" did not remain a poem only to be read in a textbook or learned as a "recitation."[6] It enjoyed great popularity outside the school and childhood milieux. It was printed four times in the "Old Favorites" column of the *Family Herald and Weekly Star*.[7] It was frequently anthologized, with credit to its author, in collections of popular poetry such as *The Family Album of Favorite Poems* (Ernest 1959). And it has retained this popularity, as the presence of two versions of "Somebody's Mother" in my survey collection shows.

The popular origins of "Somebody's Mother" in the late Victorian vogue for sentimental verse are as certain as its current popularity in Ontario. Indeed, there appears to have been something of a fad in "Somebody's [Relative]" poems around the last quarter of the nineteenth century. For instance, a humorous monologue/song, "Somebody's Child," considers a parentless child's search for his relatives (Spaeth 1927, 67–8). An even clearer relationship between the highly serious if mawkish "Somebody's Mother" and the poem "Somebody's Grandpa," published in 1880 (Spaeth 1926, 139–40), is obvious; common to both poems is an elderly person who, unaided by passing crowds of adults and schoolboys, is assisted and defended by a single child.

Similarities are also evident in poetic form. The initial rhyme in "Somebody's Grandpa," lay / way, echoes the opening grey / day in "Somebody's Mother." This suggests that the second author may have been aware of the earlier poem and to some extent modelled his or hers on it. Both old people are described as "grey," and note the topical, semantic, and textual similarities between the following sets of lines:

Of the hurrying throng that pass'd that way
Not a word of his sad life no one could tell. ("Somebody's
   Grandpa")

And:

She stood at the crossing and waited long
Alone, uncared for, amid the throng. ("Somebody's Mother")

In both poems the descriptive material above is immediately followed by the arrival of a crowd of boys. Though in the Grandpa poem they are actively there to "scoff, jeer, and tease," in the Mother poem they are like the rest of the throng and merely ignore her. In both poems a child of the opposite sex to the title character offers himself or herself as helper, at the same time invoking familial relationships. The little girl in the Grandpa poem says, "He's somebody's grandpa! Don't hurt him please," and the boy in the Mother poem comments, "She's somebody's mother, boys, you know." Though there is a lengthy intervening section in the Grandpa poem, both conclude with similar morals:

Oh dear little children! never forget,
Though the life of a man may be sinful and wild
There may still be hearts to whom he is dear;

He may yet own the love of an innocent child.
He's somebody's grandpa, brother, or friend
You may bruise some child's heart when you laugh at or tease.

And:

She's somebody's mother, boys, you know,
For all she's aged, and poor, and slow;

And I hope some fellow will lend a hand
To help my mother, you understand,

If ever she's poor, and old, and gray
When her own dear boy is far away.

"Somebody's Mother" shares with other popular late Victorian poems an attention to youth, age, and the meaning of family relationships. The moral that one should be kind to others is not the poem's only message. It also stresses that the essential ties that bind people – family, friendship, and so on – are common to all individuals. It is very much a small-town Ontario community value that interpersonal relationships rather than individuals' particular characteristics should be emphasized, and the poem's expression of this ethos earns it current acceptance in the province.

Like many other school-reader poems, "Somebody's Mother" was often recited in class and at school concerts,[8] and the superficial changes that result when a piece is recalled and written down from memory are evident in the following version. Lyda Johnson of Kincardine submitted it to the *Kincardine News*, 4 May 1983, as "Poem for Mother's Day." (Common material is unmarked; material from the Brine poem is in parentheses, and material from the Johnson version is in brackets.)

The woman was old, and ragged and gray
And bent with the chill of the winter's day;

The (street was) wet with (a) recent snow,
  [streets were]   [ ]
And the woman's feet were aged and slow.

She stood at the crossing and (waited) long,
[waiting]
Alone, uncared for, amid the throng

Of human beings who passed her by,
(Nor) heeded (the) glance (of) her anxious eye
[Non (sic)]   [a]   [to]

Down the (street) with laughter and shout
          [road]
Glad in the freedom of "school let out,"

Came the boys like a (flock) of sheep
                    [block]
Hailing the snow, piled white and deep.

(Past) the woman so old and gray
[Passed]
Hastened the children on their way.

(Nor) offered a helping hand to her
[None]
So (meek) so timid, afraid to stir
    [week (sic)]

Lest the carriage wheels or the (horses) feet
                              [houses (sic)]
(Should) knock her down in the slippery street
[Would]

At last came one of the merry troop
The gayest laddie of all the group

He paused beside her and whispered low
"I'll help you across if you wish to go."

Her aged hand on his strong young arm
She placed, and so, without hurt or harm

He guided (the) trembling feet along
          [those]
Proud that his own were firm and strong

Then back to his friends (again) he went
                    [ ]
His young heart happy and well content.

She's somebody's mother, boys, you know
(For all she's aged, and poor, and slow;)
I hope some fellow will lend a hand
To help my mother, you understand,

If ever she's poor, and old, and gray,
(When) her own dear boy is far away.
[And]

(And) "somebody's mother" bowed low her head
[Then]
In her (home) that night and (the prayer) she said
　　　[prayers]　　　　　　　[these words]

( ) God be kind to (the) noble boy
[Was]　　　　　　　[that]
Who is somebody's son, and pride, and joy.

In most circumstances this poem has been unusually resistant to change. The texts in the "Old Favorites" column of the *Family Herald* are identical to the published prototype, and even the alterations in the Johnson version, above, are minimal. A few are clearly typographical errors, such as [block] for (flock); some replace words with synonyms, such as [road] for (street); others alter verb form, such as [waiting] for (waited); and in several cases words are excised completely, added, or replaced with syntactically equivalent ones, as in [would] for (should). Also, there are alterations of word order in the penultimate couplet. However, these have little effect on the poem's overall meaning.

The only major semantic change in the Johnson version is the excision of the second line in the original fifteenth couplet. This line deals with the pitiful state of the grandmother, describing her as "aged, and poor, and slow." Since identical information has been introduced earlier, Johnson evidently saw or unconsciously perceived it as unnecessarily repetitious.

"An Act of Kindness"

However, there is a second version of "Somebody's Mother" that manifests considerably more unusual and pervasive changes. The Brine poem is obviously the prototype and inspiration for "An Act of Kindness" by William Dyer of Newmarket, a work he submitted to the Bradford-based weekly *Topic* in July 1983. Recall his letter accompanying the poem, quoted earlier: "I am accepting your invitation to submit a poem. I like poetry, but can't always find the words to express myself, probably due to limited education. I leave it to you to put in the correct punctuation, as I am very limited in that area." Lest his recomposition be seen as a simple act of plagiarism, we should understand that Dyer never actually says that he was the author of the poem. Since his punctuation was faultless, his letter's closing sentence appears to function as a disclaimer of performance, which Richard Bauman identifies as a typical marker or key: "The conventional means used to announce performance may amount to a surface denial of any real competence at all ... Such disclaimers are not, of course, incompatible with taking responsibility for a display of competence, but are, rather, concessions to standards of etiquette and decorum, where self-assertiveness is disvalued" (Bauman 1977, 21–2). Evidently, the markers of written performance and accountability are similar to those of verbal art.

Folklorists have found traditional songs that were considered to be an individual's property (Pocius 1976, 109–22). We have already encountered Michel Foucault's (1975) suggestion that the concept of authorship itself is based primarily on notions of the ownership of a text. Authorship and plagiarism are problematic notions and become even more so in traditional communities, where the originality of a poem's content is not what makes it valuable. Johnson and Dyer evidently know "Somebody's Mother" from its unattributed publication in the school readers. Its author is not only unimportant; she is also unknown.

In the following transcription of "An Act of Kindness," parallel lines from the prototype appear in parentheses below the appropriate lines in the Dyer version.

The woman was old and slightly lame
(The woman was old and ragged and gray)
And walked with the aid of an old brown cane
Her feet were wet from the slush and snow
(The street was wet with a recent snow)
She was ragged and cold and moved so slow
(And the woman's feet were aged and slow).

She stood at the corner of Water and Main
(She stood at the crossing and waited long)
Trying to cross but all in vain
A crowd of shoppers went hurrying by
(Of human beings who passed her by)

But none paid heed to her anxious eye
(Nor heeded a glance to her anxious eye).

She started to cross when the light turned green
When a car roared by that she hadn't seen
The careless driver ignored her plight
And drove right through against the light.

She stumbled back to the curb once more
And then amid the traffic's roar
A voice beside her strong but low
(He paused beside her and whispered low)
Said, "I'll help you cross if you care to go"
("I'll help you across if you wish to go").

Standing beside her was a lad in jeans
The shabbiest kid I had ever seen
He had patches on seat as well as the knees
So poorly dressed I thought he would freeze.

"Thank you" she said and took his strong young arm
(Her aged hand on his strong young arm)
And they crossed the street without any harm
(She placed and so without hurt or harm)
"You are kind," she said "for one so young
"Your parents are blessed to have such a son."

Now he didn't leave her there on her own
But carefully took her to her home.
Then down the street he whistling went
(Then back again to his friends he went)
He was happy and his heart was content
(His young heart happy and well content).

And the little old lady now safely inside
Had tears in her eyes that she couldn't hide
She bowed her head and through tears of joy
Thanked God above for that kind young boy
(God be kind to that noble boy
Who is somebody's son, and pride and joy).

To see both the form and the meaning of Dyer's intensive appropriation of the Brine poem, we need to examine closely the relationship
between the two works. Here a semiotic framework for this analysis

is helpful because it reveals a greater variation between the two works than might first appear, at the same time suggesting the semantics behind their divergences.

The Brine poem is in rhyming couplets; Dyer's was printed in *aabb* quatrains. The Brine poem is slightly longer, totalling thirty-eight lines to the Dyer work's thirty-two. They have similar metrical structures and syllabic counts per line. Moreover, fourteen lines in "An Act of Kindness" – nearly half – have textual parallels with lines in "Somebody's Mother." Yet, though Dyer's work is on one level an updated version of "Somebody's Mother," in which cars replace horses and carriages and the boy wears jeans, both the poem's paradigmatic structure and the meaning emerging from it vary significantly from that of the prototype.

In the Dyer poem the signifying images in symbolic opposition have three possible relationships to one another. They may *correspond*, as do the old woman's cane and the boy's jeans in the first and fifth stanzas. Corresponding signifiers are structural equivalents; both of the above, for instance, indicate the outcast status of their owners. Signifiers may also *contrast*, as the old woman's silence in stanza two does with her speech in stanza six. These oppositions are enabled by other actions in the poem. That is, the boy's kindness allows the old woman to speak and signal the social tie between them. Or, signifiers may *differ*, as the heedlessness of the shoppers in stanza two does from the boy's kindness in stanza six. Whereas contrasts focus on symbolic oppositions tied to the poem's context, differences carry value – one is seen as positive and the other as negative – and there is no reconciliation between them. Kinds of movement and sound, as well as persons, can be value differences if they are used to represent positive and negative qualities, and if they are never reconciled.

We also need to examine some variations in the manifest content of the two works. Protagonists in the Brine poem are the old woman, the throng, the boys, and the "gayest laddie." In the Dyer poem they are the old woman, the shoppers, the driver, and the "lad in jeans." The Brine poem is not specifically located; it could take place in a town or in a city. The Dyer poem, however, bears a close particular resemblance to small town Ontario, where "Water" and "Main" are common major street names. The predilection among small town drivers – and pedestrians – to ignore traffic signals is also a recognizably though not uniquely Ontarian characteristic.

It might seem surprising, since "An Act" takes place in a small town, that its main characters – the old woman and the boy – evidently meet for the first time. But in this 1980s community life has become increasingly impersonal, and the oldest and youngest generations are the most likely to be unacquainted since they have no set of patterns for everyday contact. Older residents of Ontario towns have usually retired there from farms in outlying areas and may thus see themselves as part of another group than do the town's families, many of whom are newcomers.

Under these circumstances the boy might be an object of fear for the old woman, but the Dyer poem makes them structurally analogous; they correspond to one another in that one is over-old and the other is over-young. Both wear signs of their common outcast status: the woman is "ragged" and walks with a cane; the boy is "shabby" and wears patched jeans. Both suffer in the cold weather because of their poor clothing.

Their relationship is one of mutual assistance: he helps her home, and she gives him a reason to be cheerful. The boy's advantages of physical strength and kindness do not set him apart from the old woman as an individual; they are the catalysts or enablers of the symbiotic relationship between the two. Note also that the street crossing is accomplished by the two together: "they crossed the street." The central difference in values of the Dyer poem separates the lone, slow moving old woman in the first stanza and the heedless, hurrying crowd of shoppers in the second.

Relationships in the Dyer poem vary from those in the Brine prototype. In the street crossing in "Somebody's Mother," for instance:

He *guided* the trembling feet along, [my emphasis]
Proud that his own were firm and strong.

The street crossing emphasizes striking variations between the two, and throughout the poem the relationship between the old woman and the boy is less corresponding than contrasting. She is alone; he is part of a group. She is meek, timid, afraid to stir, trembling, old, ragged, and gray; he is strong, young, gay, firm, and hastening. He assists her from his position of physical strength, which contrasts with her weakness. She is analogous not to the boy but to his mother and all mothers, as he explicitly states.

The two poems further diverge in thematic/paradigmatic structure (see Figure A). The Dyer poem is composed of two blocks of verses, in which quatrains one through four parallel quatrains five through eight. One and five introduce and compare the two main characters. The old woman's immobility and silence in two contrast with her eventual speech and movement in six; the unsuccessful attempt to cross the street in the former differs from a successful crossing in the latter. In addition, the crowd of heedless shoppers in two has a value difference from the single kind boy in six, and in two no close relationships are mentioned, while in six the boy is identified as a

Figure A
Thematic paradigmatic structure of William Dyer's "An Act of Kindness"

Stanza one		*Stanza five*
PERSON (woman) over-old	=	(boy) over-young
cane, ragged	=	jeans, shabby
MOVEMENT standing	=	standing

Stanza two		*Stanza six*
MOVEMENT no crossing	/	successful crossing
SOUND (woman) silent	~	speaks
PERSON (woman) alone	~	with boy
(shoppers) heedless, relationless	/	(boy) kind, son

Stanza three		*Stanza seven*
PERSON (driver) careless	/	(boy) careful
(woman) alone	~	with boy
SOUND (traffic) roar	~	(boy) whistling
MOVEMENT (driver) careless, fast	/	(boy) careful, slow

Stanza four		*Stanza eight*
PLACE curb	~	home
SOUND (traffic) roar	/	(woman) crying
(boy) strong low voice	~	(woman) praying

Key
= relationship of correspondence
~ relationship of contrast
/ relationship of opposition

son. In three the careless speeding onrush of the car, different from the careful slow progress to the woman's home in seven, and the traffic's roar, contrasting with the boy's whistling, signify the general value-differences of danger and safety in the two verses. Finally, in four and eight, stumbling to the curb's temporary safety contrasts with the more secure, permanent safety of home, while the sounds of the traffic's roar and the boy's voice in four have difference and contrast, respectively, with the weeping and prayer of the woman in the conclusion of eight.

Semantic domains – that is, topical categories – in which the Dyer poem's action takes place are those of person, movement, place, and sound. Particular kinds of people, movements, places, and sounds represent the poem's major symbolic and cultural concerns, which are cruelty and kindness, danger and safety. These pairs of differences, which can be aligned with some symbolic oppositions above, are unlike those that either correspond to or contrast with one another. What might otherwise seem a mere contrast may be a value difference in a particular context; for instance, the apparent "contrast" in the domain of sound between the traffic's roar and the boy's whistling in quatrains three and seven in fact aligns in the domain of person with the careless driver and the careful boy, who are different. This produces an analogical message that driver is to boy as careless is to careful as roar is to whistle as cruelty is to kindness as danger is to safety. However, the woman's silence and aloneness in two contrast with, rather than differ from, her later speech in six because that speech signals the beginning of the mutually beneficial relationship between her and the boy. Similarly, the curb contrasts with home because the former is the milieu for the meeting between the woman and boy. Thematic/paradigmatic relations between the two blocks of verses are oriented towards dialectic or synthesis, as a series of problems raised in one through four is resolved in five through eight.

We should also note that each successive pair of stanzas shows some kind of relationship of value difference. In one and two it is between the old woman and the crowd; in three and four between her move away from the curb and her return to it, as well as that between the careless driver, effectively disembodied in his car, and the helpful boy, at this point a disembodied voice. Five and six express difference between standing and crossing; they perhaps contrast description and speech as well. The final two stanzas differentiate between weeping and prayer and being outside the home and inside it. One and two consider individuals and groups who deny or ignore each other, while three and four deal with the quality of relationships that are initiated and affirmed. Five and six emphasize movement. Seven and eight concern particular signifiers, one dealing with qualities of sound, the other with the old woman's position inside or outside her house.

These symbolic oppositions are elaborated as the poem's meaning unfolds. We see contrast and correspondence in the relationship between signifying images of the old woman and the boy, though the two differ from the rest of the world. Because of these contrasts and correspondences, they can develop solutions to their problems. Thus, in the second set of paradigms the unsuccessful crossing in two becomes successful in six because the protagonists' contrasts are complementary. This synthesis comes about when the old woman and the boy create a relationship of friendship by speaking and crossing the road together. These contrasts and correspondences persevere

Figure B
Thematic paradigmatic structure of Mary Dow Brine's "Somebody's Mother"

Couplets	Individual	Group	Inactivity	Movement
1–2	old woman		still	
3–4	old woman		still	
		throng		hurrying
5–6		boys		hurrying
7–9		boys		hurrying
	old woman		still	
10–12	(boy separates)		(he pauses and whispers)	
13	(boy and old woman)		(he guides her slowly across street)	
14–17	boy			lectures
		boys	listen	
18–19	old woman			prays

Key

( ) intermediary between individual and group, inactivity and movement

throughout the poem, implicitly fostering the concluding, more permanent syntheses in the last two paradigmatic sets, wherein the woman affirms her religious faith and her renewed trust in mankind, and the boy achieves the contentment resulting from friendship and good deeds.

In contrast to the Dyer poem, the Brine poem reveals a more straightforward structure (see Figure B). The major oppositions throughout are between individual and group and between action and inaction. There are no complex relationships of difference, contrast, or correspondence. The initial analogy, as stated in couplets one through nine, is of individual is to group as inaction is to action. The old woman, by herself, is immobile, while both the throng and the boys are hurrying. In couplets ten through twelve, one boy separates himself from the group; he is then neither strictly alone nor truly part of the group. He pauses, neither movement nor stasis, but intermediary between them. And he whispers, neither loud speech nor silence. Then in couplet thirteen the boy and the woman (again neither strictly a group nor exactly individual) move. She does so tremblingly; her movement is partly involuntary. He guides her (directing the movement of another, not self-directed) across the street. These

three couplets, concerning mediating states between oppositions previously made explicit, enable a reversal to occur in the final couplets,
where the boy, an individual set apart from the group, lectures his
friends on the subject of mothers and kindness to elderly women.
The boys are placed in the inactive role of listeners. Similarly, the
old woman takes an active speaking role in the final couplet; she
prays. The analogy is thus reversed from its initial state and becomes
individual is to group as action is to inaction.

The two poems are superficially quite similar. Both deal with "acts
of kindness" and with their opposites as well as with situations of
danger and safety. The Brine poem's approach appears more shallow
and is reflected less clearly in its thematic/paradigmatic structure. But
these shared concerns are probably what interested Dyer in "Somebody's Mother" and form the base of his elaboration of the poem.

However, the textual similarities (word for word and line for line)
between "An Act of Kindness" and "Somebody's Mother" are not
echoed in their paradigmatic structures. As Figures A and B show,
the two works are very divergent. The structural changes in Dyer's
version correlate with its social and contextual variation from
"Somebody's Mother." The relationships between characters and the
concepts of age, of youth, and of their cultural significance differ. In
the Dyer poem the main protagonists are analogous, and their relationship becomes symbiotic; in the Brine poem they are in opposition,
and their relationship becomes one of dependence on youth by age.

It is obvious that the cultural contexts of the two works are separated
widely in time and space, and the changes in poetic signifiers and
in their relationships correlate in part to the changes in social relations
in small Ontario communities. "Somebody's Mother," like its nineteenth
century verse cognates described above, is about the need for young
people to respect their elders and treat them kindly. "An Act of
Kindness" is about something rather different. It points out, for
instance, that the natural authority of age and experience has deteriorated to the point that the older members of the community are as
marginal as the young. Moreover, it explains these changes to its
readers; more than simple artful discourse, it seeks to help them to
see their community and lives in a different way.

On the surface the divergences between "An Act of Kindness" and
"Somebody's Mother" might suggest that Dyer's appropriation of
Brine's work was relatively simple, that he merely took lines from
her poem that seemed useful and composed new ones when necessary.
But if my analysis is correct, we can conclude that Dyer's work
reveals not only a rewriting but fully a reconceptualizing of Brine's

poem. What he has made is an intensive appropriation. Lyda Johnson, on the other hand, writes primarily to maintain the text. The authority – in the sense of responsibility rather than of authorship – of addressers like William Dyer for their texts bears little relationship to any standard literary measure of originality. The poems these individuals use as prototypes remain recognizable because at least some aspects of the worldview and ethos expressed in them remain fitting. Consequently, Lyda Johnson could present "Somebody's Mother" with only the most minimal alterations; she assumes that its appropriateness can be perceived by her audience. William Dyer, on the other hand, wants to make the poem's message, as he sees it, as explicit as possible. He changes some parts of it but still includes much that is also found in the Brine and Johnson versions.

VARIANTS AND PROTOTYPES

The verse considered above, from "A Little Mixed Up" to "An Act of Kindness," retains semantic connection with its models and thus suggests a considered use of a prototype because of, rather than in spite of, its meaning. In contrast, the following poems have a much less clear and obvious relation with the works on which they are based. In some cases poems with very different topics and themes share a common prototype: these are modelled on the Christmas carol "We Three Kings," "Clementine," the Twenty-third Psalm, and Clement Moore's "A Visit from St Nicholas." Variants like these have been termed "parodies" by some folksong scholars. Peter Narvaez, for example, defines folk parody in mainly structural terms: "The essence of folk parody is that, as an artistic form of communication, it is built upon a pre-existing aesthetic structure and that in this building process the content or meaning of the initial structure is substantively but not substantially altered" (1977, 32). I choose, however, to avoid "parody" as a general characterization for this material because standard usage of this term includes an intention to ridicule not present in most folk versions,[9] and I identify verse as parody only when it makes clear oppositional or contrastive use of elements in the paradigmatic structure of its prototype.

The poems that we will now consider make little or no semantic reference to their prototypes. What, then, suggests the model's use? In many cases, its mere presence and currency are sufficient, but usually it is the model's paradigmatic and poetic structure – metre and rhyme especially – that local poets find valuable. Even where local poets have considerably altered syntagmatic structure and text, paradigms can be common with the prototype. For example, a friend reported hearing the bluegrass tune "Fox on the Run" used as the basis for a song about the late Terry Fox, performed for a cancer fund-raising campaign on local television. "Fox on the Run" seems an obvious choice for a prototype because of Fox's name and running activity. Yet any closer semantic similarity to the prototype's topic or characters would clearly be inappropriate.

Many poems and songs used as models for Ontario folk poetry are learned in childhood: at school, at camp, and in the playground. As such, they are very familiar to almost anyone brought up in the province. People rarely learn so thoroughly the verse they encounter as adults as they do the poems they memorize for a class recitation or the songs they sing repeatedly at camp-fires in childhood. Evidently, adult poems are simply not well enough known, or sufficiently ingrained, for use as structural models. The prototypes associated with Christmas, though, are somewhat anomalous. They are learned in childhood but retained in the active repertoires (see Goldstein 1971) of most adults. Local newspapers usually publish carol texts at Christmastime, so they are also part of Ontario folk poetry as the genre is described here.

Robert Service Variants

The poems below use Service-like characters and language, and play with his symbolic oppositions such as wild / tame, dangerous / safe, and strong / weak (Hirsch 1976, 132–3). For example, in his jazz, blues, and ragtime shows, Mose Scarlett has been known to recite "The Fortune of Billy McCree." This is the one item in his extensive poetic (not sung) oeuvre that he performs in this context. His poems, written under the nom de plume of J[ustin] P[lainfield] Moseley, are usually sent in greeting cards or very occasionally published in news-letters. In one such performance, at the Free Times Cafe in Toronto, Scarlett explained how he had started the poem for amusement one Christmas Eve and was halfway through it when he realized that he was writing it on his wife's Christmas card. It was too late to get her another, so he decided to alter the poem to refer to his gift – a conventional use for Ontario folk poetry – a sheepskin coat:

'Twas in the dim light of a shivery night
That I stumbled on Billy McCree;
I could see in the snow, as I bent over low,
He lay crushed 'neath a wind blown tree.

Though his presence I'd stirred, there did come not a word

From his lips that were swollen and parched;
And his hideous grin spoke of liquor and sin,
As he lay there so still, as if starched.

He had one punctured eye that stared up at the sky,
Whilst the other'd been ripped from his head –
And it didn't take much, with some poking and such,
To determine that Billy was dead.

His nose, like a screw, had been twisted askew
And his teeth rattled loose in his jaw;
Little more could I see, for the rest of the tree
Covered all but his cold iron claw.

But though he looked sore as he lay in his gore,
Some great comfort still glowed in this beast,
For though battered and torn, the fine sheepskin he'd worn
Had saved him from freezing, at least!

The character of Billy McCree – his gruesome aura and the "liquor and sin" – as well as aspects of the poetic structure are shared with Service's popular works. Yet the topic of this poem, and its particular expression, are Scarlett's own.

Another Service-like work is by Jim Merriam of Tara, whom we have met before. It is less consistently cast in the Service idiom than is Scarlett's. Other than its parallel use of part of the opening line of "The Shooting of Dan McGrew" – "A bunch of the boys were whooping it up" (Service 1940, 29) – its main connection to the Service works is its interest in the drunkenness of the protagonists and their activities in primarily male contexts. It tells about a bus trip taken to Montreal by a group of men from Chesley and Tara to see a baseball game. The poem suggests that other activities prevented the viewing of baseball, and Merriam concludes:

Now this little poem is not very good
The rhymes are poor and few,
But it saves explaining a baseball trip
Without seeing a pitch or two

All things will be quiet in old Tara town
And parts of Chesley too,
'Til all these poor fellows recover a bit
And find out just what they did do!

And there is only one tiny wee moral
To this silly little poem,
If you want to see a good baseball game
Turn on the TV and stay home. (*Tara Leader*, 1 September 1982)

Considering the specificity of the events discussed in this work, it might have been difficult to find a poem – by Service or anyone else – that could have been textually paralleled more closely, but this was not in any case the poet's intention. He confirms that character similarity and poetic structure were his main reasons for using the prototype: "The rhyme and the flow of it seemed to fit the occasion. And the beginning line, 'A bunch of the boys were whooping it up,' just suited the whole thing perfectly. It was just that it suited to what we had been doing. So that's – really just fit, it fit perfectly" (T84–40).

"Ten Little Indians"

Elements of structure are quite clearly the reason why Gary Ziegler, an Ontario Provincial Police Community Service officer, chose "Ten Little Indians" as the model for his "A parable (in rhyme) for careless drivers":

10 little drivers, cruising down the line, one had a heavy foot and then there were nine;
9 little drivers, the hour was late, one dozed a moment and then there were eight;
8 little drivers, the evening felt like heaven, one showed off his driving skill and then there were seven;
7 little drivers, their lives were full of kicks, one bought a bottle and then there were six;
6 little drivers, impatient to arrive, one ran a stop sign and then there were five;
5 little drivers, wheeling near the shore, one viewed the scenery and then there were four;
4 little drivers, happy as could be, one passed upon a hill and then there were three;
3 little drivers were busy it was true, one neglected car repairs and then there were two;
2 little drivers, and the day was nearly done, one did not dim his lights and then there was one;
1 little driver who is still alive today, by following the safety rules, he hopes to stay that way!

The moral of the story:
Speed limits are set for your safety. A tired driver is a dangerous driver. A car is no place for a clown. Gasoline and alcohol are a deadly mix. Don't gamble years of your life to save a few seconds. Always keep your car in safe condition. Adjust your driving to existing conditions. (*Manitoulin Expositor*, 26 January 1983)

Folklorists Iona and Peter Opie give complete texts for nursery-rhyme prototypes of Ziegler's poem. In one, implicitly or explicitly violent deaths overtake six of the ten "little nigger boys," who are choked, chopped in half, stung by a bumblebee, got in chancery (a boxing hold), swallowed by a red herring, hugged by a bear, and frizzled up. (Some of these – swallowed by a "red herring," for instance – can be interpreted other than as violent deaths; they are ambiguous, metaphorical, or proverbial expressions.) Five of the events that reduce the group's membership are self-imposed or reflexive: "One choked his little self," "One overslept himself," "One said he'd stay there," "One chopped himself in half," and "He got married" (Opie and Opie 1951, 327–8). In another version there are, similarly, both violent deaths for the "ten little Injuns" – tumbling off a gate, breaking one's neck, tumbling down a cellar, tumbling overboard in a canoe, or being shot – and self-imposed or reflexive fates: "One toddled home," "One broke his neck," and "He got married" (ibid., 32).

The fates of the drivers in the Ziegler poem are all self-imposed and reflexive, and their deaths are implicitly violent. The final driver's destiny – unlike those of the rest of his driving cohort – is not death but survival, as is true of the final and other "Injuns" and "nigger boys." The paradigmatic structural elements and their relationships in the Ziegler poem and its prototype are very similar. Syntagmatically, all the variants exhibit a serial restatement of similar structural material, though not an incremental but a "detrimental" repetition. The apparent textual connection between the poem and its prototypes results from the fact that their structures are remarkably superficial; text and structure are almost identical.

There are obvious semantic differences between the prototypes and the Ziegler poem, and the characters involved (if they could be so called) are the key. Though the protagonists of the nursery rhymes are both racially described and stereotyped groups of "others," Constable Ziegler's drivers are clearly intended to be viewed as "selves." The moral of his poem relates to the behaviour of the poem's readers and is explicit about the connection between the poem's events and its semantic and moral point. Certainly the nursery rhymes are not warnings to children about how to avoid chopping themselves in half or shooting one another, but the Ziegler poem explicitly advises against the activities it records.

"We Three Kings"

One of two variants of the Christmas carol "We Three Kings" in this sample is lexically quite close to its prototype, even including the description that the protagonists are "from Orient," which is nonsensical here but serves to identify the model more clearly. While they were at a church summer camp, Betty Bohlender and her fellow cooks presented this variant at a skit night. Instead of bearing gifts, they brought food:

> We four cooks from Orient are
> We have travelled from afar
> Food we bring you, songs we sing you
> Everything's up to par.

The first two lines above are clearly parallel, and the following cooks' list of the food they bring is parallel to the kings' inventory of gifts:

> We hope you liked our remon [sic] pie
> Extra flavor came from the flies
> Shreddies, rice flakes, squares and cupcakes
> And many more surprises.

A second variant has a slightly different relationship to its prototype. As with the first, commonalities between the two are paradigmatic, but in the second, textual parallels are less evident. The similarities concern travel (the Grand Valley minor hockey team travels to another town to play its team) and the word "star," referring in the new context to a particularly valued player:

> We the Atoms of Grand Valley are,
> To Hockey games we travel afar.
> Erin and Hilly [Hillsburgh],
> Don't be silly –
> Hail to Atom stars.
>
> Oh, – Star of shinny,
> Shine on us!

Star with many an exciting rush,
Northward leading –
Shelburne conceding,
Losing two games with little fuss. (*Grand Valley Star and Vidette*,
    22 December 1982)

This poem was published at Christmas, a time when carols like its
prototype are almost impossible to avoid, and this may have influenced
the writer's choice. But textual elements of "We Three Kings" may
have suggested some of the content – for example, "Northward leading" – which might not have been included in a poem based on
another prototype.

"The Yellow Rose of Texas"

In some Ontario folk poetry, there is no common sequential structure.
For instance, Edward Miller's "Haliburton Highlands," sung to the
tune of "The Yellow Rose of Texas," has only a few tenuous connections
with its prototype:

I've lived in the city of Toronto, and I've roamed through Montreal
And went to the island of Expo and there we had a ball
With its aerial rides and go go trains and so many sights to see
But those Haliburton Highlands is where I long to be.

Some folks go to Florida and roam through Disneyland
Others like the Everglades where nature sure is grand
Some like New York city with the Statue of Liberty
But these Haliburton Highlands is where I long to be.

Some boys joined the army and to Europe they did roam
Some came up through Italy and seen the sights of Rome
And some are now on Cyprus in the Mediterranean sea
But these Haliburton Highlands is where I long to be.

I've seen the Vermont Mountains, and New York's Lake Champlain
And spent the day on the sand bars along the coast of Maine
We went for a swim in the ocean it was cold as ice to me
But these Haliburton Highlands is where I long to be.

We travelled north through Ontario where we were western bound
To the foothills of Alberta and Coronation town

We saw the wheatfields in Saskatchewan as far as I could see
But these Haliburton Highlands is where I long to be. (Broadside
published in Haliburton, undated)

The rhyming structures of the variant and prototype are similar ("be"
for "me," etc.), but some metrical stretching is necessary to fit Miller's
song into the prototype tune. Common to both, also, is first-person-
singular commentary, which emphasizes personal experience.

"Bygone Days"

Earlier, I referred to Astrida Reader's "It Is about Us," which recruits
members for the Home and School Association, and its prototype
"Bygone Days" (Reader 1958, 35–6), by the writer's mother-in-law.
This poem is something of an anomaly because it comprises both
completely original and clearly modelled sections that have different
poetic structures. After the first three stanzas of "It Is about Us,"
which are totally original, come five stanzas altered from "Bygone
Days" in tense and person only. Three more original stanzas follow,
but the final stanza of both poems is identical:

Nigh sixty years ago
In Beddec [sic], Nova Scotia
The year is 1895
Our Home and School was born then.

Mrs. Alexander Graham Bell
Was the nobelest of Founders,
But she had no telephone –
To bring the parents out.

She quickly asked her husband
To get a telephone invented
So Home and Schoolers – even then
Could come to Meetings from far and near.

No indoor skating rinks had they,
No hockey boots or skates,
And when in school no scribblers
But had to write on slates.

How well do they remember the
Slate cloth makes them sick

For when they had no water,
Saliva did the trick.

However did they manage
To exist without TV?
Without chips and Coca Cola?
This thing amazes us.

No motor cars adorned their streets,
But one thing known for sure,
Their legs were made to walk with
We don't use them any more.

No "baby bonus" graces their mails
No cheques of unemployment
But people worked for honest pay
Which gave them much enjoyment.

We have come quite some way now
Still passing Resolutions comes April – every year;
And w're [sic] still looking for quality in education here
For all the children everywhere.

But if you parents don't come out to talk,
To every meeting that is called,
How will you know what ails the system?
How will you ever help the child?

Come join your Home and School Association
Elementary or Senior High
The educators need your quality of knowledge
The child will thank you many fold.

For what we get, is what we give
In service to mankind:
This purpose was ordained for us,
That happiness we'll find. (*Paris Star*, 13 October 1982)

Reader's interest in giving some history of the Home and School Association suggested the use of the other poem's initial five stanzas. The final stanza was probably most instrumental in her choice of a prototype, however; it is obviously rhetorically applicable to her purpose. Its meaning in the prototype is fairly general, relating to the value of hard honest work; stanza eight of the new variant immediately precedes the final stanza in the prototype. Its new poetic context makes this verse an explicit suggestion of the value of joining Home and School. As with other examples we have seen, meaning is dependent upon the poetic context.

"Trees"

Basil Scully's "Sophistrees: A Treebute" (*Manitoulin Expositor*, 2 March 1983), as its initial, fourth, and sixth stanzas show, is based upon Joyce Kilmer's "Trees" (see Ernest 1959, 247). Model stanzas from the prototype appear in parentheses below the Scully verses:

I pray that I may someday see
An MP [member of Parliament] with integrity

(I think that I shall never see
A poem lovely as a tree.)

An MP who is not obsessed
My tax deductions to divest.

An MP who won't scream at thee
"The media did this thing to me."

An MP who will always wear
Her halo with a touch of flair

(A tree that may in summer wear
A nest of robins in her hair;)

Within whose heart no rancor dwells
To label critics "infidels."

MPS are made with votes from me
And 'tis our votes will set them free.

(Poems are made by fools like me
But only God can make a tree.)

In addition to other poetic structural similarities, the second stanza takes its rhyme from the prototype's pressed / breast.

Though the Scully poem shares text and poetic structure with its prototype, it twists paradigmatic structure so that it is in ironic opposition to the prototype. Kilmer gives the tree qualities of beauty and perfection, while Scully gives the MP a number of serious imperfections: lack of integrity, vanity, and so on. The Scully poem also warns the MP of the god-like position of the voters who are the source of her power. Part of the humour in "Sophistrees" is the ironic contrast between Kilmer's sublime point of view and Scully's down-to-earth one. Because of its ironic use of paradigmatic structural elements from the prototype, this example closely resembles parody as it is traditionally defined.

Psalm Twenty-three

Two similarly parodic poems based on the Twenty-third Psalm criticize national politics:

> The Government is my Shepherd
> Therefore I need not work.
> It alloweth me to lie down on a good job.
> It leadeth me in the path of the parasite for Politics' sake.
> Yeah, though I walk through the valley of laziness and deficit spending,
> I will fear no evil,
> For the government is with me
> It prepareth an economic utopia for me
> By appropriating the earnings of my grandchildren.
> It fillith my head with false security,
> My inefficiency runneth over.
> Surely the Government shall care for me
> All the days of my life
> And I shall dwell in a fool's paradise forever. (*Arthur Enterprise News*, 13 October 1982)

Called "A Psalm for Today," this poem – which of course shares a common sequential structure with its prototype – contrasts the contentment of a true paradise evident in the original with the "fool's paradise" in the new version.

"The Gospel According to St Pierre [Trudeau]," from the collection of Katherine Smith of Agincourt, blames the former prime minister of Canada, Pierre Trudeau, and the Liberal party for Canadian poverty:

> Pierre Trudeau is my Shepard
> I shall not want

He leadeth me beside still factories
And abandoned farms
He restoreth my doubt about
The Liberal Party.
He annointed my wages with taxes
And inflation so my expenses ...
Runneth over my income,
Surely poverty and hard living follow
The Liberal Party.
And I shall work on a rented farm and live in a rented
    House forever.

"A Visit from St Nicholas"

The most popular model for Ontario folk poems is Clement Moore's
"A Visit from St Nicholas," known as "Twas the Night before Christmas." There are four variants in this sample. Moore's prototype is
certainly the best-known poem relating to a season or holiday, with
the possible exception of Colonel John McCrae's "In Flanders Fields,"
which is associated with Remembrance Day.[10]
    Mose Scarlett and his friend Tina Cohen's Christmas greeting variant
comes close to literary parody. Its tone and theme oppose that of the
Moore poem. Beyond the opening line, resemblances between their
sequential structures are limited, but Cohen and Scarlett (who is
unusually conscious of metre and rhyming technique) maintain strong
commonalities of poetic structure with the prototype poem:

'Twas a week before Christmas, and all over town
The first snowflakes landed and quickly turned brown.
An army of dumptrucks assaulted the road
Their cargo of crystals to pit and corrode.

Our government toasted their raises "Hear! Hear!"
And chose resolutions to break the next year.
The post office workers stood ready to strike
Delaying all parcels to pick what they'd like.

Some shops were bemoaning their minuscule trade
Left over from long ago's Santa's parade;
While elsewhere, consumers, like mechanized elves
Were pushing to grab all the stock from the shelves.

A bland Muzak carol of Christmas did sing
One's only relief, the cash register's ring.

Yet, somehow or other, despite all this dread,
Old Santa still plotted his journey by sled.

And in his great wisdom he'd park on each roof
For here in our city, we've all seen the proof
That if he, like us, drove by road from afar
A swarm of "Green Hornets" would ticket his car

But still we count blessings in families and friends,
And as you're among them, this greeting extends
The warmest of wishes for joy and good cheer,
With strength to survive all the hubbub next year!

"Twas the Even of Christmas," composed and read by James Brady
for a Delhi church Christmas concert, displays greater textual and
structural similarity to its prototype and is not a parody. It uses the
most familiar parts of the Moore poem – its opening and closing –
as poetic structuring models and employs some common content. In
both poems the appearance of Santa Claus is heralded by a strange
sound. In Moore's he is "a right jolly old elf" who is "dressed all
in fur"; in Brady's he is a "cuddly old elf" who is "dressed all in
red." Brady's poem names individuals: the pastor who played Santa
Claus, his wife, and the widow of a former pastor. Brady told me
that these people were mentioned because "they had been so much
a part of the Delhi congregation for so many years" (T84–16).

Michael Giffen's variant of "A Visit from St Nicholas" follows the
prototype most closely of all the examples here and, like the Brady
poem, names many community members. The italicized sections are
shared between prototype and variant:

Twas the night before Christmas
And *all through the* Glen,
Not a creature was stirring,
Not even Frank's old hens.
Elwood put candy canes in his bus *with care,*
In hopes that Shirley wouldn't find them *there;*
Errol was *nestled all snug in* his *bed,*
While visions of a new pick-up *danced in his head;*
Sally *in her kerchief*
And Fred *in* his *cap,*
Had just settled down for a quiet *nap,*
When out on the lawn
There arose such a clatter,

They *sprang from* their *bed*
To see what was the matter;
And *to the window* they *flew like a flash*
Johnnie, Jamie, Joseph in their toboggan did crash.
What to Betty's *wondering eyes should appear,*
Bonnie working overtime.
Sorting Giffen's gas bills for the New Year;
A little grey car zoomed around in the night
Who else would it be but Debbie Nightingale in flight;
Then there were the Shields boys on top of the hill,
Jim asked if his horse would win;
Harold said, "It probably will
After the medicine I fed it last week,
That old gray mare should run like a streak."
Our two neighborly ladies were stopped by John Brown's truck
Their names happened to be Mrs. Hartley and Mrs. Tymchuk;
They were headed for Elwood's with bags at their side
But everyone knows, they accept no rides.
So this is the story of our quaint little town,
Pretty and small, and so nice to come down
And visit the people full of great cheer,
Who wish you a Merry Christmas
And a Happy New Year. (*Creemore Star*, 22 December 1982)

Identity with the prototype breaks down as Giffen brings in particular
characteristics and anecdotes about individuals. The familiarity of "A
Visit"'s text lessens further into the poem, making the prototype's
sequential and paradigmatic structure less evident as Giffen's poem
progresses.

The fourth variant on "A Visit" is Doreen Young's Block Parents
poem, considered in chapter 2, dealing with a fictitious incident in
which a Block Parent assists Santa Claus. It shares with its prototype
a first line and a common metre, but little else.

"She Dwelt among the Untrodden Ways"

Though the following example is textually the most similar to its
prototype – and might have served to initiate this discussion – it is
placed here because it is perhaps the most striking demonstration of
semantic variation imaginable. It shows clearly the lack of correlation
between textual and semantic change. Only one lexical item is replaced
– one proper name takes the place of another – but in context its
semantic alteration is drastic:

She dwelt among the untrodden ways
Beside the springs of Dove:
A maid whom there were none to praise
And very few to love.
A violet by a mossy stone
Half hidden from the eye!
Fair as a star, when only one
Is shining in the sky.
She lived unknown, and few could know
When Karen ceased to be;
But she is in her grave, and oh,
The difference to me!

Except for the substitution of "Karen" for "Lucy," this poem is identical to William Wordsworth's "She Dwelt among the Untrodden Ways." It was submitted as a memorial to Karen Hunter of Alliston, a young woman murdered during a convenience store robbery in June 1983. The letter that accompanied the poem in the newspaper explains the circumstances:

To the people of Alliston I wish to express my heartfelt thanks for all your gracious help during this difficult time. The ways in which you have shown your support for me and your care and concern for Karen and those who loved her have been deeply touching.

Because of the memories associated with the store, I have decided to leave the business, but could not do so without saying how much I have appreciated your patronage over the years. It would, of course, be impossible to thank each of you personally, so please accept this as a poor substitute for the gratitude I feel. (Cheryl Overland, *Alliston Herald*, 15 June 1983)

One could hardly over-emphasize the amount of community disruption caused by the robbery and murder and by the others like it that occurred in other communities that same summer (see Bob Raymes's poem on a similar topic, discussed in chapter 2). In a small town like Alliston violent deaths from anything other than automobile accidents are almost unknown, and homicide is truly shocking. All but one of the letters to the local newspaper two weeks after the event were on the topic of the murder. In addition to the poem and letter above, the chief of police, "a police officer's wife," and another citizen responded to criticisms in the previous week's newspaper of the quality of police protection in the town; the murdered girl's family thanked the town for donations and kindness; and one merchant criticized others for staying open during Karen Hunter's funeral. The crime was clearly interpreted very personally by many town residents. Cheryl Overland's poem is her response to the event. Wordsworth's poem, of course, similarly mourns the death of someone close to the poet, but to the people of Alliston who read it, Cheryl Overland's variant refers specifically to Karen Hunter's early death and to its effects on what seemed hitherto an innocent, untouched community. An understanding of the context is necessary for the outsider to grasp this, but obviously the poem is substantially different semantically from its prototype; the character it discusses and the specific topic of Karen Hunter's death are not shared with Wordsworth's poem.

We might assume that the intention of a poet in (re)writing a version of another poem is more reproductive than creative and that of a poet composing new stanzas structured on a prototype is more creative than reproductive. Yet, like other common-sense generalizations, this one has some obvious problems. The Karen Hunter poem, for instance, seems difficult to range on a creative-to-reproductive continuum, as does the William Dyer version of "Somebody's Mother." They are paradoxically neither, or perhaps both.

As we have already seen, a presenter's authority for his or her text may have little relationship to any standard measure of its originality. Instead, poets who compose or present versions of other poems are happy with their semantic contents – or at least with some aspect of them – and so feel no need to make alterations. Those who write parodic style variants may be struck, consciously or unconsciously, by paradigmatic similarities between the situation in the prototype and the one they wish to present, or by the usefulness of some other structural aspect, syntagmatic or poetic, in organizing their thoughts. We can fairly say, though, that Ontario addressers do change semantic aspects to fit their culture's notions of appropriateness – Cora Yuill's "Who'll Take Grandma" is perhaps the best example. It is also true that apparent semantic inappropriateness – between a "trivial" nursery rhyme and Gary Ziegler's highly serious poem about safe driving, for instance – is no deterrent for poets wishing to model their work on another.

Meaning in Ontario folk poetry, as in all culture, is always contextually based. Thus it is difficult to conclude that the poetic works highlighted in our discussion as having a close identity with their prototypes will always possess it. There is always a chance that some refiguration or new context, like the one occurring with the Wordsworth/Overland work, will make a particular poem semantically different from a prototype or cognate. But there are some obvious checks on this process. First, the Wordsworth poem is not indigenous and in an Ontario context seems difficult to relate to the usual configurations of folk poetry. Second, its textual ambiguity assisted its refiguration into Overland's intended context.

But it is hard to imagine the same process working on a poem like "The World Is Mine." Its meaning is explicitly outlined in the text itself, and the only plausible changes to that meaning – a sarcastic or ironic tone – would be contextually inappropriate in the Ontario communities under consideration and odious to most poets and presenters. A poem like "The Modern Grandmother," locally interpreted as humorous, has an indeterminacy of meaning related to the social ambiguity of its topic in Ontario, not to a textual vagueness.

Evidently, cultural appropriateness and the appropriating of poetry – the passive and active uses of "appropriate" – are not as separate from one another as they might at first appear. As poets make their poetry their own, whether or not they model it on a pre-existing prototype, they do so by making it culturally apposite. Ontario folk poetry must fit the authors' and/or presenters' notions of what is right and proper – poetically, syntagmatically, paradigmatically, and semantically. Clearly modelled and more original poetry alike must fit canons of appropriateness in form as well as in content. This brings us to a group of poems on the same topic for which there are no common prototypes but which nevertheless retain common expression and a shared worldview and ethos. The appropriation of popular poetry, discussed above, leads in the final chapter to a discussion of the appropriation in poetry of an individual who was made to represent a cultural ideal. We return once again to the community and to versemakers as its representatives creating expressive forms that address local concerns.

CHAPTER FIVE

Appropriating a Hero

During my initial search for Ontario folk poetry, conducted in the summer of 1982, I discovered two poems in the *Agincourt News* about Terry Fox, the young man from British Columbia who ran his "Marathon of Hope" from St John's, Newfoundland, to just outside Thunder Bay, Ontario, in 1980. I soon recognized that this was a special phenomenon; genetically unrelated texts on the same topic (as opposed to genetically related ones such as those discussed in chapter 4) are extremely rare. I encountered more Terry Fox verse in the regular course of my research, but most of the works discussed here came into my hands as a result of specific inquiries.[1] And I could have found many more, in Ontario and elsewhere – Betty Fox, the runner's mother, reported, "We have received hundreds of poems" (L January 1983) – had I continued my search.

Though the poems discussed here are marked because they share topic but not text, they obviously partake of the other qualities of Ontario folk poetry. They are communicative; they address problematic and conflictual situations; they are presented in the usual contexts of community newspaper and meeting; and (with one exception, presented for the sake of information) they are composed by individuals whose primary identities are not as versemakers. These poets represent the full range from one-timers to self- and community-defined local versemakers. The sheer number of Terry Fox poems makes this a striking group; however, it also indicates their distinctive significance. The fact that so many people chose Fox as their topic confirms his particular appositeness. We will discover that this group is, paradoxically, both unique and representative.

My discussion in this final chapter centres on twenty-one of the thirty poems in my sample. These works are by pseudonymous versemakers or by ones I was able to contact personally. Some of the poems possess intrinsic interest, and some display the symbolic system of heroism associated with Terry Fox more clearly than the rest. Nevertheless, each example adds evidence of the *shared* quality of the meanings that Ontario people assigned to Fox and of how poets interpreted those meanings. Of course, there are a few unconventional poems. As we might suspect, the pseudonymous verse differs in meaning and intent from most of the pieces by named authors. Two wealthy poets who do not see themselves as participants in Ontario community culture interpret Terry Fox differently from others. Even the professional songwriter's piece shares more symbolic qualities with Ontario folk poetry, and its appositeness is indicated by the fact that his well-publicized song subtly influenced some of the early local verse. Finally, one poem not specifically written for Fox but previously used as a memorial to another young cancer victim was distinctive.

Local poets do not usually make outsiders the object of repeated, lavish praise, as they did Fox. Outsiders are most often portrayed as sources of disjunction, not as examples of appropriate behaviour and morality. Fox was unusual, however, precisely because his actions typified traditional values. And in a sense he hardly seemed an outsider. The subject of considerable publicity, Fox entered Ontario communities on a day-to-day basis and became a familiar figure through television and newspaper reports. Two facts – media coverage of Fox's Marathon of Hope and his actual running through small Ontario towns along his Trans-Canada Highway route – made him a community member in an atypical, idealized way. The poems reflect this familiarity; most address him as "Terry."

Fox's special, marked, and different qualities are clearly understood by local poets. They saw him as a hero, not as an average person. Further, because he created a (temporary) gestalt of national unity, Fox became a distinctively *Canadian* hero. His archetypification in verse as a pattern for Canadian heroism is noteworthy; there was no clearly understood, expressed tradition of Canadian heroes into which he could fit. In order to create such a paradigm, poets describe Fox as everyman[2] or mythical hero, or some combination of the two. But the view of Fox in the poetry – the predominant aspect of his heroism – changed as the events of his life in the public eye unfolded. We can see this as a process of forming a "legendary"[3] national hero from the combined qualities of the mythic and everyman hero.

A sketch of the basic facts of Fox's story is helpful before we proceed further.[4] He was born 28 July 1958, in Winnipeg, Manitoba. His father was a Canadian National Railroad switchman. In 1968 the family moved to Port Coquitlam, British Columbia. In high school Fox was a good student and very active in athletics. He attended

Simon Fraser University, hoping eventually to teach high-school physical education. On 3 March 1977 he was diagnosed as having osteogenic sarcoma, a tumour of the connective and supportive tissues, in his right leg. Five days later the leg was amputated above the knee. It was highly probable that the cancer had already spread to his lungs, so Fox began fourteen months of chemotherapy. He continued athletic activities none the less, and joined a Vancouver wheelchair basketball team.

Terry Fox's Marathon of Hope was inspired by an article he read on Dick Traum, an above-the-knee amputee who completed the New York City marathon. Fox began training in March 1979 for a projected run across Canada, with the aim of raising one dollar from every Canadian for cancer research. With support from the Canadian Cancer Society and financial assistance from several corporations, he began his marathon on 12 April 1980 in St John's, Newfoundland, first symbolically dipping his artificial leg in the Atlantic Ocean. (He intended on completion of his run in British Columbia to dip his leg in the Pacific.) For the duration of the run his younger brother accompanied him in a van driven by his childhood friend, Doug Alward.

Leslie Scrivener of the *Toronto Star* began weekly reports early in the run, but the Marathon of Hope received its greatest national attention and support when Fox reached Ontario. By 12 August breathing difficulties and chest pains forced him to terminate his run after 144 days and 3,339 miles, just outside Thunder Bay, Ontario. He had completed almost two-thirds of the distance across Canada, but the cancer had spread to his lungs.

On 7 September 1980 a CTV national television network telethon raised $10,179,768 for the Marathon of Hope. A number of awards and honours were given to Fox, including the Companion of the Order of Canada. By January 1981 the cancer had spread to the abdomen and the lymph glands surrounding the aorta, and Fox received interferon treatment from then until shortly before he died, on 28 June 1981.

Poetry was only one possible response to Terry Fox's inspiration, as the versemakers themselves indicate. Two became Cancer Society volunteers. Most donated money, but others involved themselves in the actual fund-raising. Some ran in the annual marathons held for cancer research; as Crystal Davies commented, "I was very happy to participate in the 1982 Terry Fox run and will be happy to do so in 83 84 85 86 etc" (*Newmarket Era*, 23 March 1983). Others assisted in fund-raising by producing records or tapes of their songs and donating the proceeds from sales to the Canadian Cancer Society.

Other Canadians made artistic and hortatory efforts. There were letters to the editors of local newspapers and letters to the Canadian Cancer Society accompanying donations. A feature film, *The Terry Fox Story*, was made of his life. A 1,661 line epic, "The Song of Alopeix," was written by James Lord, a sixty-nine-year-old graduate student of English literature at McMaster University in Hamilton. A wealthy Terry Fox enthusiast, Leon Mayzel of Toronto, opened the Terry Fox Bookstore and donated material on Fox to school libraries across Ontario.

The response of poets, however, was to create the figure of Terry Fox as a Canadian hero. Canadian folklorist Carole Carpenter suggested to me that Fox possessed qualities that could make him a hero only in this country. She considers Fox's journey across the land, overcoming the physical environment, particularly characteristic of Canadian heroism, a theme that such works as Margaret Atwood's *Survival* (1972) maintain is of major significance in Canadian literature and culture. However, the verse below shows that the physical environment, though important to several poets who wrote about Fox, is by no means their major concern.

Some who would argue with Carpenter's analysis might suggest that what was typically Canadian about Terry Fox was his failure to achieve his goals – in this case, running across Canada and finding a cure for cancer. Writer Pierre Berton, for instance, has commented that "the feeling has been with us for a long time – that we are a nation of losers" (1975, 1), though he qualifies this by saying "it is only the professional writers, the literary artists, who have seen us as losers; not the ordinary people" (4). Berton discovers patterns in the kinds of characters Canadians view as heroic. The unifying theme is "a sense of *aloneness*"; the "greatest adulation [is] for single sportsmen in single contests" (11). Examples are Marilyn Bell's first solo crossing of Lake Ontario and Ned Hanlan's rowing feats. The human symbols of the country are "lonely men with lonely jobs" (13): the bush pilot, the trapper, the explorer, and the Mountie.

Berton's patterns clearly appear in the poetic archetypification of Terry Fox. An archetype is an ideal pattern, not a real person, so the portrayal of Fox as a Canadian hero has proceeded along predictably selective lines. This recalls to mind the active meaning of appropriation; Fox is taken over by Ontario folk poets who use him as a figure for expressing community ideals. Critic Kent Steckmesser notes that "as symbolization proceeds ... the actual individual who lies at the bottom of the legend tends to become irrelevant" (1965, 251). Fox was not in fact alone on the road, but only one poetic work mentions "a brother and a friend" who accompanied him. Indeed, several poems comment upon his aloneness and the solitary nature of his run, though it was generally reported that he had a support group in the van that followed him and that for various durations other runners ran alongside him.[5] Certain of Fox's characteristics, such as perseverance, are emphasized, while others, such as intelligence, are ignored. Ontario folk poetry responds to Fox's dignity in the face of a crippling and disfiguring disease and to his choice to raise funds through the *public* act of running the marathon. Poet Helen Parkin commented that she wished her own daughter, who had also had a leg amputated because of cancer, could have lived to see Terry Fox. The girl had been embarrassed and ashamed of her disfigurement, and she might have felt differently, said Mrs Parkin, had she attended the Marathon of Hope rally in Toronto's Nathan Phillips Square and seen that "people were looking at him, not at his artificial leg" (Q 29 February 1984).

As a mythic hero, Fox is presented in these poems as a greater-than-natural force, mastering cosmic disjunctions. As an everyman hero he overcomes more mundane difficulties – environmental, physical, spiritual, and social. And as a national hero, he is described as conquering barriers to Canadian unity.

Let us focus first on the mythic hero. Critic Joseph Campbell sees a pattern common among mythic heroes in all cultures. The "separation from the world, a penetration to some source of power, and a life-enhancing return" (Campbell 1968, 35) that he describes in literature are also evident in ritual (van Gennep 1960, Turner 1969). The mythic hero is "a personage of exceptional gifts ... He and/or the world in which he finds himself suffers from a 'symbolical deficiency'" (Campbell 1968, 37). Campbell's insights are echoed in poetry about Terry Fox. He is seen as dying to the world and being reborn (ibid., 35–6); undergoing trials and victories of initiation (36); tests and ordeals (97); (symbolically) confronting society "with his ego-shattering, life-redeeming elixir" (216), taking "the return blow of reasonable queries, hard resentment, and good people at a loss to comprehend" (216), and "effecting a reconciliation of the individual consciousness with the universal will ... through a realisation of the passing phenomena of time to the imperishable life that lives and dies in all" (238). And the mythic vision of Terry Fox finally returns to his human-ness as Campbell suggests: "not human failure or superhuman success but human success is what we ... have to be shown" (207).

Everyman heroes, in contrast, are human throughout. One analyst of popular culture feels that Lenny Skutnik, who rescued one of the passengers on an airplane that crashed into the Potomac River in Washington, DC, exemplifies everyman heroes, who are "ordinary mortals thrust by chance or circumstances into extraordinary situations.

Unlike most mortals, however, they do not back off; they accept the challenge, rise to the occasion, and thereby raise themselves above the legions of the Average" (Rollin 1983, 29). The everyman hero is like the Rabelaisian "great man," as described by M.M. Bakhtin: "The great man ... is profoundly democratic. In no sense is he opposed to the mass, as something out of the ordinary, as a man of another species. On the contrary, he is made of the same generally human stuff as are all other men ... Nothing in him is incomprehensible or alien to general human nature, to the mass of men ... The great man ... is ordinary man raised to a higher power. Such greatness diminishes no one, for everyone sees in such a man a glorification of his own human nature" (Bakhtin 1981, 241). As an everyman hero, however, Terry Fox manifests particular qualities, operating in a number of different spheres of activity. In the environmental sphere he triumphs over weather, or the road; in the spiritual he is never discouraged; in the physical he is presented as untiring; and in the social he typifies valued qualities of community.

As is generally true of contemporary Ontario folk poetry, most Terry Fox verse avoids tropic language. Though poets sometimes describe him metaphorically – as a giant, for instance – they more commonly use broader symbolic concepts – the run or the battle are examples – to characterize their perspectives. They use elaborating symbols more frequently than summarizing ones and, as discussed in chapter 1, root metaphors more than key scenarios. Their poetry attempts to sort out and understand the complex nature of Terry Fox's meaning. Thus, what we need to consider now is not how Fox's illness and Marathon of Hope fit mythic or everyman archetypes but how those archetypes are communicated in poetry.

One striking thing about this twenty-one item collection is that it divides readily into two clusters of fairly unified works. Ten poems were written at the Marathon of Hope's conclusion or shortly thereafter, and clearly refer to it. Ten were composed immediately following Terry Fox's death and were written, most poets told me, on the day his death was announced. Two other groups are less symbolically coherent, yet obviously different from the others. Two poems were written before the marathon's end and eight written considerably after Fox's death, either to evaluate the runner's significance or to remind others of his link to the annual marathons held in the early fall to raise further cancer research funds. Fox is initially used as an instrument for reflection on the nature of Canadian culture, heroism, and so on, rather than as a simple metaphor, though he later becomes a sacred, emotional, and non-reflective national symbol.

The first group of works, written during the marathon, is concerned

with the separation of the runner from the community, mainly sym-
bolized by the run. In the second group "run" and "battle" symbolize
initiation; that is, the end of Fox's marathon is seen as a test or
ordeal he must undergo. In the third group, written at Fox's death,
the emphasis is on some aspect of return, either in "battling" or in
"dreaming." The final group re-evaluates Fox and his significance. No
single poem in any group completely indexes its category, and some
texts are more representative than others, but each example includes
some characteristics of the group as a whole.

SEPARATION:
THE MARATHON OF HOPE

The two song texts representing this period differ from those associated
with the later events. This is by far the smallest group, and the only
one represented entirely by songs, or even in which songs are in a
majority. One, released during Fox's run, was a professional production, though the motives of its producers parallel those of community
poets and presenters. The other, never published or released, was
written by an amateur musician.

These two texts share an uncomplicated notion of Fox as an everyman hero. Unsurprisingly, mythic elements are not at this point part
of his poetic meaning. While his run continued, he was seen as
nothing more than a special individual, and the two lyrics reflect this.
They represent his special qualities mainly in the human domain,
rather than in the environmental or social ones. Though both
songmakers see Fox's heroism in the human sphere, one presents the
obstacle against which he strives as physical, chorusing "Run, Terry,
Run," while the other choruses "Courage," referring to Fox's evident
triumph in the spiritual realm.

Vern Kennedy, "Run, Terry, Run"

Though this first example is a professional production, it fits quite
readily into its group. Like the previous examples of apposite popular
verse we have seen, it has influenced local poets, and its echoes can
be heard in a few later works. The production of Vern Kennedy's
"Run, Terry, Run" involved much co-operation, as an undated press
release (preceding 1 July 1980) suggests:

Vern Kennedy of Take One Singers has written and arranged a song,
"Run, Terry, Run," to support Terry Fox, the young Canadian cancer
amputee who is running across Canada in support of the cancer cause

... The singers, studio musicians, studio and even transportation is being supplied gratis.

Copies of the song on tape will be sent to radio stations between Mr. Fox's current location in rural Quebec and Ottawa where he hopes to arrive for Canada Day, July 1. A single will then be released in both languages also gratis by Waterloo Records of Waterloo, Ontario. All royalties through PRO will be assigned to the Terry Fox cancer run by Mr. Kennedy and the Take One singers.

The singers are trying to find a sponsor to cover the cost of travel to Ottawa so they can be there to sing Terry's song for him in person when he reaches that city. (Scrivener collection)

As in the case of later fund-raising songs, personnel worked free of charge, equipment was donated, and proceeds were given to cancer research. Most poets and songmakers who composed works during Fox's lifetime shared with Kennedy a wish to perform for the man himself, but they also wanted to communicate with the general public.

As its chorus suggests, this song concentrates on encouraging Terry Fox to continue overcoming the physical challenges facing him:

Run, Terry, Run,
Leave your troubles behind you;
Run, Terry, Run,
To where the rest of the world will find you ...
Through the rain and the sun,
Run, Terry, Run.

Run, Terry, run,
Though you have every right to be bitter;
Run, Terry, Run,
Show the people you're no quitter ...
Show them you're number one,
Run, Terry, Run.

Life's a long, hard road, and you've just begun.
But you do your best 'til the job is done.
'Cause you've got a lot of pride,
And there's something deep inside,
Tells you life's no easy ride,
When you decide to run.

Run, Terry, Run,
Let every step you take remind you;

Run, Terry, Run,
You've got a lot of good folks behind you ...
And a lot more to come,
Run, Terry, Run.

Run, Terry, Run,
We'll be running right there beside you;
Run, Terry, Run,
With your faith in a dream to guide you;
There's a race to be won ...
Run, Terry, Run.

Just one step at a time, that's the only way,
Keep your goal in mind each and every day,
When the road is getting rough,
You may think you've had enough,
But we know you're made of the stuff,
That'll make you stay.

Run, Terry, Run,
Run, Terry, Run,
Run, Terry, Run,
Run, Terry, Run!

The song gives a strong impression of collective attention; there are references to "the rest of the world," "the people," "a lot of good folks behind you ... / And a lot more to come," and even an assertion that "We'll be running right there beside you." It is an exhortation from the community to Fox himself. No disjunction exists on the social level; "we" are united in support of Terry Fox. The central root metaphor of the road creates and maintains this pattern. M.M. Bakhtin suggests:

The road is a particularly good place for random encounters. On the road ... the spatial and temporal paths of the most varied people – representatives of all social classes, estates, religions, nationalities, ages – intersect at one spatial and temporal point. People who are normally kept separate by social and spatial distance can accidentally meet; any contrast may crop up, the most various fates may collide and interweave with one another. On the road the spatial and temporal series defining human fates and lives combine with one another in distinctive ways, even as they become more complex and more concrete by the collapse of *social distances*. (1981, 243)

An appropriate metaphor for Terry Fox's activity as a national hero in uniting the country, the road appears repeatedly in the poetry about him. Here the run is expressed in the human physical domain – as a marathon – rather than in the environmental one. The run symbolizes life ("Life's a long, hard road"). It is a "job" – work – rather than a "ride" – play; it is a material metaphor of Fox's physical perseverance.

Ross Knechtel, "Running Man"

Poet Ross Knechtel wanted to record his composition "Running Man" to raise money for the marathon but was unable to find a backer. A teacher in his early forties,[6] Knechtel told me that on the day Fox passed through Toronto, he went to watch the run "instead of painting the hallway" (Q 16 March 1984). The teacher was profoundly moved by the experience and had no difficulty composing a song about it, saying: "If it matters, you can write about it." He suggested that Terry Fox's uniqueness and superiority made him both admirable as a person and a suitable subject for poetry.

Knechtel's song concentrates on Fox's spiritual qualities:

The beholder sees what he will see
What you saw was a plan to set you free
The runner has a way to go
What drives him? It's courage we all know.
The fallen knows where he will land
The doubter never can take a stand
But you, you lay your cards all down
What drives you through each and every town?

Courage
To make good a promise.
A plan.
Run across Canada, gutsy running man.

The scoffers know where they can go
The doubters send them all below
The runner has a will to live
Just watch him and know that he can give.

Courage
To make good a promise.

A plan.
Run across Canada, gutsy running man.

"I'm no different than I was before
"Each day my living means much more
"He did it, I'm going to do it too."[7]
His own words, he means them, and they're true.
Cause he has

Courage
To make good a promise.
A plan.
Run across Canada, gutsy running man.   (Scrivener collection)

Knechtel's perspective on the community obviously differs from Kennedy's. Where Kennedy asserts that "we" support Fox, Knechtel dwells on the detractors: "the fallen," "the doubters," and "the scoffers." He contrasts the scepticism of these generalized others with Fox's spiritual everyman qualities of courage and vision. But Fox is named only through his defining characteristics, as "the runner" and "gutsy running man." This pits figure against figure and representative against representative, *not* individual against community.

The quotations from Terry Fox manifest the spiritual qualities needed by an everyman hero – humility, purpose, and determination. In this, he is not very different from Kennedy's hero. Persevering and continuing the run are central to both poets and are expressed in direct exhortations to Fox.

INITIATION: TERRY FOX'S
MARATHON ENDS

The second group comprises nine poems and one song lyric associated with the end of Terry Fox's cross-Canada marathon. One poem was published in a community newspaper; one was printed in a Canadian Cancer Society newsletter; and one was posted on the bulletin board in a Canadian Cancer Society unit office. The song was recorded by its composer. The other five poems are apparently unpublished but were sent to Leslie Scrivener for publication in the *Toronto Star* and/or to be passed on to Fox himself. I discuss six of the ten examples here.

Not surprisingly, these poems represent more diverse views of Terry Fox than do the previous examples. Several poets consider Fox's everyman heroic qualities in terms of the physical environment and social domain rather than the purely physical or spiritual. Others perceive Fox as a mythical hero, as reflected in the associated symbols of mountain, giant, and battle.

Grampa G, "The Incredible Fox"

The pseudonymous Grampa G's "The Incredible Fox" dwells on its subject's transcendent characteristics, presenting a thesis that places Fox's special mythic qualities in the foreground, primarily – as in the Knechtel song – through his contrast with others:

No man is a mountain,
So I have been told.
No matter how rich,
With his oil or his gold.

No man is a mountain,
Though he be a king,
A prime minister's son,
Or most anything.

No man is a mountain,
Not even a rock,
No man is a mountain,
Except TERRY FOX.

This poem was sent to Leslie Scrivener, perhaps after the author saw his pseudonym in her column of 22 September 1980: "A sweaty maintenance man, who would identify himself only as 'Grandpa G' wheeled his 13 month old grand-daughter Bonnie Jean from King City to City Hall yesterday, filling a large pail with donations [to cancer research]." Scrivener could give me no more information about the writer.

The poem offers an analogy between Terry Fox and a mountain. Grampa G employs this obviously appropriate elevating analogy to set up negative comparisons in the social sphere. Qualities of elevated social position and status – wealth, birth, and political power – are explicitly rejected as indicators of "mountain"-like characteristics. Implicitly, it is not through his social attributes that a man becomes a mythic hero. While the poet is not explicit about the actual source of the man's mythic-heroic essence, he maintains that only Terry Fox has this special quality. The poem's title confirms this; Fox is, exceptionally and superlatively, "incredible." Though democratic in intent, this view of Terry Fox contrasts sharply with that of the road-metaphor poems.

Costas Cokkinos, "One-Legged Giant"

Costas Cokkinos sent his poem, "One-Legged Giant," to the *Toronto Star* editor hoping that Fox would read it there, but it was not published. Cokkinos, like Grampa G, sees Fox as a mythic hero, but in addition he explicitly views the marathon as a symbolic gesture actively unifying the Canadian nation:

His fiery torch
Casts a gigantic
Luminous golden ray
Of unity and hope
From coast to coast,
Terry Fox,
One-legged giant
With a fiery torch
Another glorious
Runner of Marathon.

A boy, a man,
One-legged giant;
A Colony, a Dominion,
Now, a great free land,
Terry Fox and Canada;
A new Promethean
With a noble face,
Running,
From coast to coast
With his fiery torch
Heralding unity and hope.

Terry Fox
Son of all Canada
Of the east and the west
The present and the past;
A boy, a man,
One-legged giant

With a fiery torch,
Eternal symbol
Of unity and hope.

Born in Athens, Greece, in 1915, Cokkinos came to Canada in the early 1950s but returned to continue political activity in his native country in 1967. He retired to Canada in 1979. He has written several polemical and poetic works, mainly in his native language. At the time of this poem's composition, Cokkinos said, he felt very emotional. He indicated that Fox's "human significance" (Q 24 February 1984) was great and suggested that the man looked like a classical Greek athlete. Poetry was the only way to express his feelings about the "unbelievable" phenomenon of Terry Fox, which he saw as indicating the "beauty of gesture" and the "perfection of humanity."

Cokkinos's poem, like Grampa G's above but unlike others in this group, makes no reference to Fox's cancer or to his fund-raising activities. The work, in fact, makes only one mention ("one-legged") of his individual human or everyman qualities, and this allusion to physical disability is contextually presented as an inherent part of the man's heroism. Cokkinos concentrates triumphantly on Fox's mythic and nationalistic qualities. His characteristics heroically transcend the human sphere – he is a giant and a new Promethean – or nationalistically typify its best qualities – he is noble and glorious. Like the previous work, Cokkinos's considers Fox in terms of elevating analogies.

Notice that Cokkinos's first stanza presents the poem's initial organizing symbols: the torch, illuminating Fox's mythic (hope) and national (unity) importance, and the metaphorical-symbolic view of Fox as a "one-legged giant." As Fox the colossus encompasses Canada "from coast to coast," this stanza summons up further mythic-heroic aspects of its subject, relating Fox to a traditional Greek figure, the torch-bearing Marathon runner. The second stanza shifts the focus to the run's nationalistic aspect. Cokkinos sets up the association boy is to man is to one-legged giant as colony is to Dominion is to great free land, then relates them to Fox and Canada. The transcendence of the nation from infancy to maturity is enabled by Fox. Cokkinos told me that he saw Terry Fox as the first true Canadian hero; in the poem he relates having such a hero to the special qualities that make a country more than just an aggregation of people occupying a given space. Symbolic and actual existence, with respect to nationhood, are, to this poet, totally congruent.

Cokkinos's view gains depth when he calls Fox "a new Promethean." Prometheus stole from the gods an essential element, fire, conventionally understood as making possible mankind's elevation from the animal to the fully human. Terry Fox's "fiery torch" has the same effect on Canada. Here mythical and national elements cannot be separated except analytically; they refer to, and reinforce, one another. At the end the poet relates the symbolic domain of nationhood to that of the family and emphasizes his previous assertions. To Cokkinos, such a hero is not an ephemeral phenomenon. As Canada's son, Terry Fox encompasses time and space to become eternal, just as nations and families continue beyond the lifetimes of their constituent members.

Helen Parkin, "He Alerted a Nation"

Helen Parkin sent "He Alerted a Nation" to Leslie Scrivener on 10 December 1980 with a note suggesting "What I would dearly love is for Terry himself to see it via publication in a Vancouver newspaper":

O Canada, vast and wide
To Terry Fox we look with pride
He jogged across your highways long
Repeating oft, his plaintive song

He stirred the hearts of millions
As he gallantly endured
The muscle spasms, aches and pains –
That others might be cured

To re-inforce his message
To make us "feel" the pain
Once more he was afflicted
Cancer – struck – again!

What a challenge! What a dream!
He reached across the land
And gently plucked us one by one
Out of the blinding sand

Now we've got to face it
Cancer's got to go
We've all been robbed of loved ones
Some – not long ago …

So let's keep going "kinda wild"

From oldest old to little child
The Fund is swelling by the hour
For Cancer Research, that spells POWER ...

Yes – Canada, vast and wide
To Terry Fox we look with pride
Our Heritage – our Seeing Eye
God Bless you Terry, you're *Some Guy*!

Mrs Parkin is in her fifties. She was born in Dublin, Ireland, and came to Canada in 1964. Her interest in Terry Fox arose from personal experience; her younger daughter had died of cancer, and her knowledge of the illness is evident in the poem. Like Cokkinos, Parkin sees Fox as a national hero, but her poem operates mainly on the everyman social level, though it includes some mythic symbolic images. The notions of Fox as a national figure and as one who indexes valued community qualities become self-reinforcing and interrelated, as mythic and national ones did for Cokkinos.

Parkin's first three verses introduce Fox and his cause, viewed in terms of national pride, social awareness of the cancer problem, and Fox's self- sacrificing nature. The human, physical aspect of Terry Fox – Parkin characterizes this entirely in terms of cancer – is included, but as an example of the adversity he faced rather than as the level on which he transcended the everyday. Atypically, Parkin views cancer not solely as a scourge but also as the factor enabling Fox to become an everyman and national hero. She commented to me that she knew, when the cancer recurred at the run's premature end, that death would soon follow. For her, the physical sphere could not be a signifier of heroic status, since it is precisely where the man's only-too-human, mortal qualities would be evident.

The fourth verse is a central and linking one. Fox is portrayed implicitly as a giant – this root metaphor is used somewhat differently in the previous two poems – who has a visionary, prophetic effect. Because of his run the community and nation can now "see" the problem of cancer, and his heroism enables us collectively to face a serious social problem hitherto ignored because we have been hiding in the "blinding sand." The last verse re-emphasizes the vision metaphor: Canada looks with pride to Fox, "our Seeing Eye." The poem goes on to address the problem to be faced collectively – cancer – and the solution – we should be like Terry Fox and go "kinda wild" (a quotation from the man himself). The poet's exhortation echoes those in the first group, asking not for support for Fox himself – she knows there is little hope – but for cancer research.

Joe St. Denis, "The Courage of Terry Fox"

The next poem in this group is by Joe St. Denis, a part-time professional musician and salesperson in his forties, who wrote "The Courage of Terry Fox" with his cousin Roger Morin, partly inspired by a relative's death from cancer (*Sudbury Northern Life*, 19 November 1980). His recording of the song was authorized by Fox himself, and St. Denis pledged royalties from his record album – which also included other songs – to the marathon. However, he comments: "I presented $2500.00 to the cancer society in Sudbury Ontario – one month after Terry died. Although my pledge was based on the recording being a profit, I had to dig in my own money because 1st – the record did not make a profit and 2nd – I felt I was obliged to give something" (Q March 1984).

His song makes explicit its connection with fund-raising:

The story's bout a man who has cancer
He said he'd fight right until the end
That's why Terry ran through our country
To try to save the lives of fellow man.
But to do what he had done showed great courage
Cause Terry Fox has only got one leg.
This man has been struck by this monster
And his goal is to bring him to an end.

Chorus:
So people ask put all our hands together
And pull a little harder for our friend.
We must show him that we're all behind him
To save the lives of people in this world.

The love for life is a greater satisfaction
Than all the gold and riches in this world
But to put your life on the line for the world
Is a courage that very few have got.
But Terry Fox has taught us all the lessons
That everyone important in this life
So to raise the gold that Terry always wanted
We'll help him to achieve it with this song.

Chorus

St. Denis's poem works on the everyman spiritual and social planes.

Fox's main characteristics are sacrifice and courage. But though the writer apparently sees him as an everyman hero, he expresses Fox's experience in terms of the tests and ordeals of mythology; he is "struck" by a "monster." Fox's perseverance, which is praised in the first group of poems, can no longer be contained within the road metaphor; it is restated as a "fight." As Joseph Campbell suggests, "The battlefield is symbolic of the field of life, where every creature lives on the death of another … effecting a reconciliation of the individual consciousness with the universal will. And this is effected through a realisation of the passing phenomena of time to the imperishable life that lives and dies in all" (1968, 238). Thus, in Christ-like sacrifice, Fox "puts his life on the line for the world" and "tries to save the lives of fellow man." But St. Denis affirms that the proper response is collective action on behalf of Fox and his cause. The battle's reconciliation comes because Fox's attempt to raise "gold" to save lives will be successful. The ultimate stress is upon spiritual qualities enabling a transformation of the social sphere.

Grant Filson, "Go Terry Go"

Grant Filson's "Go Terry Go" was published in the Cancer Society's *Education Insight*, June 1981.[8] Now retired, Filson was a zoning-plan examiner for the city of Toronto for thirty years. Terry Fox's run had a profound effect on him. After witnessing the "triumphant journey into Metro [Toronto]" (Q 24 February 1984), Filson began working as a volunteer for the Canadian Cancer Society. He speaks of Fox's effect on his life in religious terms, calling it "a conversion." In conversation Filson commented on Fox's creation of national unity and on his own emotions, but his poem concentrates upon Fox as an everyman hero who triumphed over the physical adversity of the environment and his disease.

Go, Terry, go.
You can do it. We all know that you can.
The miles were long and the pavement hard,
But you won many hearts as you ran.

Run Terry, run.
From the hilltop high you could see
The long narrow road ahead. A lonely road,
An uncertain road, Oh! would it ever end?

Run Terry, run.
The hills were high and they wearied you so.

If you could only quit right now
With your spirits very low.

Run Terry, run.
You cannot quit. Remember the boy who also lost a limb.
The joy you shared and a bond was made
At the lake where you went to swim.

Run Terry, run.
You finally made the hill. You felt so good
And you smiled with joy. You did it, you know,
With courage, pride and will.

Run Terry, run.
Gale force wind blew snow and rain.
The icy air made your body shake,
And you worried as you felt the pain.

Run Terry, run.
There were cities and towns and people too,
To cheer you on your way. It helped a lot
To hear them shout. It really made your day.

Run Terry, run.
Fortune and fame were not your game,
Achievement not your goal. You did it all
To help the sick. That was the only aim.

Run Terry, run.
You mastered your fears. You endured the wind
And the rain. As the miles went by,
You conquered your aches and pain.

Go Terry, go.
There's one more mile to conquer,
One more hill to climb. A million hearts are praying,
And they'll run for you, this time.

Filson's poem echoes the Kennedy song's "Run, Terry, Run," and like it employs the road as a metaphor. Here, the road is a meeting place for Fox and his community. The first stanza suggests his collective effect of "winning hearts," extended in a real-life key scenario in the fourth. The incident alluded to, in which Fox went swimming with a young fellow cancer amputee he met along the road, was heavily covered by the media. It indexes Fox's social goal of helping other cancer patients, as well as highlighting a major force that impelled him in the first place: the apparent hopelessness of the disease's young victims. By implication, this encouragement and reminder makes poetically possible the physical and environmental achievement (stanza five) and reinforces Fox's "courage, pride and will."

Thus, the road also expresses the human, physical aspect of the everyman hero who overcomes the environment. This is the only work in the entire sample where the latter is so important. Fox's tests and ordeals are the environmental ones of miles, hard pavement, hills, icy wind, snow, and rain, but they are also the human physical – exhaustion – and spiritual ordeals – uncertainty, loneliness, low spirits, and the urge to quit. The ninth stanza restates Fox's goals in terms of environmental and physical human adversity. It also affirms Filson's sense that as an everyman hero, Fox did in fact overcome the adversities that faced him. Stanza ten brings the road, the battle, environmental adversity, and spiritual qualities together, calling cancer "one more mile to conquer / hill to climb."

Zorro, "Marathon of Hope"

"Marathon of Hope," by Zorro, was sent to Leslie Scrivener on 8 September 1980 for publication in the *Toronto Star*, with a letter suggesting that any payment for the poem should go to the Cancer Society. As one might by now expect of pseudonymous poems, it is somewhat problematic. It differs from other Fox poetry in its unusually contentious tone:

Run Terry, run ...
For you have shown us
That life is not an apple pie,
You sweat, you suffer, and you die.
However, if you can stop and think,
There is a bit of Terry in all our kind,
We failed ourselves and the world to bring
The happiness and peace of mind.
In search for cure it's not a shame
To settle for a smaller prize,
To help our Terry to the fame
May help you more than you realize.
Like his end is the beginning,
Terry made us understand
With his team in research winning,
Shall prevail and never end.

For this occasion it's quite rare
Having such a marathon dancer
And your DONATIONS ...
Be aware,
Will help and further the cause of CANCER
Don't ask for what? and/or for who?
To satisfy your selfish clue,
Could be well for your future son,
Run Terry, run ... run ... run ...

Though this poem's extremely contentious and negatively blame-laying tone is anomalous in this collection of works, its symbolic content fits well with others in this section. In the "Run Terry, Run" chorus Zorro invokes culturally understood signifiers of Fox's activities also common to several examples above. Zorro sees Terry Fox as an everyman hero in terms of his social effects and uses the poem to condemn those who lack his community spirit.

Zorro's aim is predominantly hortatory. He indicates that Fox is himself a signifier of proper community values, and he asks the community to avoid letting Fox's evident physical failures ("you sweat, you suffer and you die") overshadow his social achievements of raising money for cancer research. He invokes the proverbial knowl-edge that "life is not an apple pie" to indicate that even in not overcoming physical adversity, Fox exemplifies the traditional value of hard work. To Zorro, as to Kennedy in the previous section, Fox's run is work, not play.

But Zorro softens his denunciation of the community by admitting that Fox's positive characteristics are found in "all of our kind." Others can symbolically participate in Fox's heroism (though they cannot exemplify it as he does) by honouring him as he deserves ("helping our Terry to the fame") and contributing to his cause ("your DONATIONS"). He suggests that it is inappropriate to question the pur-pose or value of such activities; their inherent, understood, inchoate value will be demonstrated in terms of preservation of community within the family metaphor ("could be well for your future son"). By invoking the domain of family, Zorro emphasizes collective and indi-vidual unselfishness.

This group of verse has several common qualities. The "Run, Terry, Run" chorus of Vern Kennedy's song influenced a number of poets. However, the run itself – central signifier of Kennedy's "Run, Terry, Run" and of Ross Knechtel's "Running Man," both written before the run's end – and its major significance – evidence of Terry Fox's perseverance – give way to a more complex vision of the man and his activities. The poems of the second group, centring on the end of the marathon, begin to indicate the differences appropriate to expressing the characteristics of everyman and mythic heroes. The mythic hero is described in the third person, through elevating analogies between Fox and mountain or giant. No mention is made of cancer, fund-raising, or other mundane matters; and no exhortations are addressed to Fox or to his community. The everyman hero, on the other hand, is invoked in terms of "you" and "us," and his real-life activities are foregrounded and made symbolic.

Evidently, the fact that Fox's own run ended made its use as a signifier somewhat problematic. Poets who continue to use the run as a symbol expressly indicate how Fox overcame adversity despite having to halt his marathon. In the first group of songs his significance is as a quotidian exemplar, an idea extended in the second group. After the run's end Fox is encouraged to continue as an indicator of positive qualities to community and nation, but several poets exhort both to become actively involved in his run. The run can no longer signify simple perseverance on Fox's part; it comes instead to indicate his courage and determination. Perseverance becomes less important than Fox's effects on the community and the nation. And new metaphors – the giant, the mountain, the torch – show how Fox transcended the human sphere. Alternatively, analogies to Christ and references to Fox's visionary qualities indicate his still-human transcendence of the norm.

Terry Fox as a poetic figure becomes more human – a number of poems urge "Terry" personally to continue the run, not give up hope, and so on – yet, paradoxically, also increasingly remote. The poets' personal involvement is obvious in the way they direct expressions to Fox, but their perception of him indicates his more exalted status than in the two early songs. This applies to the works that view Fox's heroism as mythic, social, or environmental – symbolic stances not seen in the previous series – but also to those that like the first two songs, see him primarily in everyman physical or spiritual terms.

RETURN: MEMORIALS TO TERRY FOX

The previous group presented Terry Fox primarily as an everyman hero and secondarily as a mythic hero. The next series of poems cannot be concerned with Fox's mastery over physical obstacles; thus concentrate instead on his wider implications: the national hero as social everyman and mythical hero combined. Though some poets in this group maintain a view of Terry Fox as a spiritual everyman hero, or as an exemplary or inspirational figure, they include additional symbolic aspects.

This group includes one exceptional poem. It was written as a memorial to a cancer victim, but Fox was not its original subject. Naturally, then, this purely memorial poem does not present Terry Fox as a hero. Addressed to his family, it associates him with the spiritual plane.

Helen Parkin, Untitled

The anomalous example is Mrs Helen Parkin's second work concerning Terry Fox. It is a rewriting of verses she originally composed for a family whose child had died in the hospital where her own daughter was being treated for cancer. The principal change made to the original was the initial date:

> June 28 it came to pass
> His pilgrimage was o'er
> He bade farewell to loved ones
> And knocked on heaven's door.
>
> God greeted him with outstretched arms
> "You're here at last my boy."
> He clasped him to His Sacred Heart
> And heaven rang with joy.
>
> "You've had a long hard climb, my boy,
> "And not once did you balk."
> Then Jesus smiled, said "Rest a while,
> Then rise up, son, and walk."
>
> Tears of joy o'ercame the boy
> His voice sang through the font
> "Oh Lord, you are my shepherd
> And nothing do I want."

This poem shares with the St. Denis work in the previous group an explicitly Christian perspective. The resolution of Fox's problems resides in death and in the rewards awaiting him in heaven. But the most anomalous aspect of Parkin's poem is its treatment of the heavenly sphere alone, whereas other Fox poems involving Christian redemption explicitly indicate the rewards the man receives for his described activities in the everyday world. Here, Fox is not a hero but a pilgrim soul received into paradise. His earthly personality, achievements, and activities have no place; he occupies a plane of existence where such things can have no significance. The adversity he faced, though, is alluded to in the heavenly reward that makes it possible for him to walk; implicitly he reaches heaven physically as well as spiritually whole.

Since Parkin did not originally write this work to refer to Fox, its uniqueness is not surprising. It is one of the few not referring to the man by name, and the only one not employing the common symbolic root metaphors – the road, the dream, and so on – cited in other poems of this group. Technically, this memorial is not a Terry Fox poem, since with merely a date change it could be used with equal effect to refer to the death of almost any male individual. But it does share with the other works in this group, and with other memorial verse, an explicit attempt to find a solution for the problem at hand, death. Parkin's answer is Christian immortality and the opportunity Fox has in heaven to do what he could no longer do on earth, walk normally. The poem also shares with other Terry Fox verses some of the less central signifiers associated with the man, weeping and climbing, which increases its appropriateness.

Katherine Smith, "Terry Fox"

Understandably, Terry Fox had a great emotional effect on young people, many of whom identified strongly with him. Katherine Smith of Agincourt was fifteen when she began doing volunteer work for the Cancer Society, inspired by Fox's example. She wrote the following poem on the day she heard about his death. She sent a copy to the Fox family and showed it to another Cancer Society worker, who posted it on the bulletin board there, where it was seen by the editor of the *Agincourt News*. He asked for permission to publish it, and did so on 8 July 1981.

I get a feeling
Deep inside myself
When remembering the courage
Of a one legged running man.

The freckle-faced child of yesterday
Still shining deep inside,
But now a man of twenty-two
Fighting pain he tries to hide.

His gait is music to my ears
'Cause it means the spirit still burns,
Smiling faces drown his fears
The faces of those who've learned.

I can tell he's someone special
This young man with a dream
Nothing was able to stop him,
Nothing, or so it seemed.

Then outside Thunder Bay,
Terry's cancer had returned.
The country didn't know what to say,
So instead we gave all that we earned.

Life is full of struggles
Where hopes and dreams are few,
But the best dream is Terry Fox,
And he means a lot to me and you.

Although we lost our hero
We shouldn't be too sad,
I'm sure that Terry's happy,
'Cause he's gone to be with God.

He lost the final battle
But in his way he won
There is hope for all the others,
Another battle has begun.

The initially personal nature of the poet's reaction to Fox's death
is evident; she speaks in the first person singular for the opening
frame and throughout the first four stanzas. But she indicates a
time-limit for this personal reaction, altering expressive voice from
singular to collective when she refers to the end of the run. By this
time Fox becomes a figure whose significance applies to the entire
community. Of course, the end of the run was also the point at which
the folk poetic expression of Terry Fox's heroic qualities clearly began.
Concurrently, Smith's attention extends beyond Fox as an individual
– his gait, his physical appearance, his age, and so on – to wider
physical environments – "the country" – and spiritual spheres – "life."
This poem, like Parkin's second, sees Christian redemption for the
man as part of the resolution. "Our hero" – this work is one of the
few actually naming Fox as such – finds personal satisfaction in this
way, as the community does in participating in his cause, so that
both can be "happy." However, the poet also sees social effects as
resolutions; Fox's own hope enables hope for others with cancer
(stanza eight).

Smith emphasizes the spiritual aspects of Terry Fox's heroism – especially his courage. He is "someone special," and this is expressed in the symbol of the "dream." This signifier becomes increasingly important after Fox's death; only one earlier poem mentions it. The dream is the motive force inspiring Fox to raise money for cancer research through a cross-country marathon and allowing him to continue day after day. The illusory nature of the dream, on which the awful reality of the return of Fox's cancer and his ultimate death impinges, is implicit in its context, but the poets who use this symbol explicitly suggest that the community continues the dream. The dream is a symbol associated individually with Fox as an everyman hero, with his potential community effects, and with the notion of hope.

Smith also employs a battle metaphor. Like the dream this metaphor is both personal (Fox "fights" pain, for instance) and community/social (life is a struggle). The "battle" lost by Fox is taken up by the community, evidently so that the long-term war against cancer will be won. Here we have again Campbell's "reconciliation of the individual consciousness with the universal will" (1968, 238).

John Herron, "To a Boy with a Dream"

John Herron, in his early seventies, was born in Glasgow, Scotland, and first came to Canada in 1953. His poem was begun before Terry Fox's death but was not completed until after it:

Terry Fox you're here today
In our hearts you're here to stay
Your dauntless spirit must survive
To keep the Marathon of Hope alive.

We watched your progress day by day
And cheered you on along the way
Your courage and your obvious pain
No thought of self, no thought of fame.

Just a young lad with a dream
We thank you, Terry, for what you mean
To all the young folk who will follow through
To keep your dream alive for you.

We hope the doctors find the answer
And someday find a cure for cancer.

Herron's poem works almost entirely on the everyman social level. It opens by referring to Terry Fox's metaphorical presence "in our hearts"; his "dauntless spirit" survives, not through one individual, as in the previous poem, but in the collective mind and action. Rather than the end of Fox's run, or his death, Herron contemplates the man's active and lively symbolic presence in the community, even fictively addressing him throughout the poem. The "answer" or resolution of this memorial work, though collective, is on an everyday and physical plane; it is a cure for cancer, found by doctors. The continuation of the Marathon of Hope and its aim are of central importance. Herron sees that there is more than one individual in the collectivity ready to "follow through / To keep your dream alive for you." In the title and within the poem the writer refers to Fox's "dream" and its relation – as in the Smith poem – to both Fox's own activities and their collective continuation. But Fox is *"Just* a young lad with a dream" (my emphasis): he does not transcend the community; he exemplifies what is best in it.

Dorothy Herridge, "Marathon"

Dorothy Herridge is a retired secretary who was born in Somerset, England. She came to Canada with her husband Gordon in the 1950s. Her "Marathon" was published twice in the *Bolton Enterprise*, once when it was first written and again on the anniversary of Terry Fox's death. With the writing of this poem Herridge commenced a now extremely prolific poetic output:

He came to us and made us smile,
He came to us and made us weep.
We ran with him mile after mile,
And wept after his final sleep.

A victim of the dread disease,
He'd lost a limb, and what is more,
For him, there were no guarantees.
And who could tell what was in store?

Self pity was not in his soul.
He learned to walk, and then to run.
He trained because he had a goal
For Canada's own special son.

He called it Marathon of Hope.
His goal: to run across the land.
One wondered how on earth he'd cope.
To see such courage, Lord, 'twas grand.

The dollars came reluctantly at first,
Then they began to pour,
And Terry ran persistently,
And ran till he could run no more.

Three thousand miles he ran, and plus,
His running shoes and rolled down socks,
His guts, his gait, his pain, for us,
His Marathon, brave Terry Fox.

What more is there that we can say?
How long will cancer then endure?
Research now, we hope and pray,
To come up with a lasting cure.

Fox's ordeals are in the physical sphere: the adversities of cancer
and amputation, and the attendant uncertainty of the future. He is
also tested spiritually; his determination and physical achievements
are expressed in terms of a lack of "self-pity." Herridge's poem is
similar to Herron's in its collective voice and reference to the community, and in opening with an allusion to Terry Fox's effects on it.
As in the Herron work, Fox is a participant member of the collectivity,
not a lone runner: "He came to us" and "We ran with him." And
in both, resolution happens on the physical plane, consistent with the
central meaning of the marathon. Research, the end to which Fox
directed the money, enables the discovery of a cure for cancer and
thus the end of the physical adversity that Fox faced himself. However,
Herridge's is a more transcendent, nationalistic view of Fox's heroism,
one implying the same Christian notions as Joe St. Denis's song.

National and family semantic domains are again juxtaposed here:
Fox is "Canada's own special son." Family is a major level of community membership and to so designate the man is to underline and
reinforce connections suggested in the first stanza. Fox's "goal" is
partly nationalistic, seen in his land-crossing marathon. His significance
on this level, however, needs no resolution; he is fictively kin with
the rest of Canada, as our participation in supporting his run demonstrates.

Anne Boyes, "Terry Fox"

Anne Boyes, a former secretary and real-estate salesperson in her sixties saw Terry Fox on his run through Aurora, where she lives. She sent her poem "Terry Fox" to the Canadian Cancer Society with her annual contribution in September 1983, but she wrote the piece when Fox died.

History tells of many men,
  who rose to power and fame,
This, some won by violence,
  others on continents they sought to tame.

The year was 1980
  when Terry started his run,
His cause was not just for fame,
  or even have some fun.

He'd lost a leg to cancer,
  his days were full of pain,
But he did not let this stop him,
  he ran so we could gain.

His marathon he ran each day
  to help the cancer "Cause,"
He only asked our help to try
  to win the battle he'd lost.

At Thunder Bay his run was through,
  the cancerous growth had spread,
And Terry knew his fight was o'er,
  he knew he'd soon be dead.

A wave of love and emotion
  spread like none before,
And from every corner of the land
  the money began to pour.

I hope the gods will be kind
  to Terry now at rest.
To us he was a brave young man,
  who on earth did more than his best.

Let Canada honour Terry's name,
   his fight we'll not forget,
His "Marathon of Hope" goes on,
   for no cure is known as yet.

Boyes's initial reference to history implies that the national symbolic field will be central. The poet's sequential narrative of Fox's run is also an indicator of her association of the man with (Canadian) history. However, the allusions to "men / who rose to power and fame" are presented in opposition to Fox, whose "cause was not just for fame" (the same opposition that appears in Grampa G's poem). As an archetypical Canadian hero Fox makes his way into history not through violence but through self-sacrifice. The social and national spheres are congruent here; "our gain" is seen in terms both of cancer research in this verse and of national interest in the previous verses. As a Canadian hero Fox is perceived in contrastive terms, through what he is not rather than through what he is. This is again similar to the Grampa G work.

Boyes shares with some other poets in this group an almost positive view of cancer as a force impelling Fox's run and ultimately producing our "gain." Perhaps the Christian attitude towards the crucifixion as a preamble to redemption is an underlying analogy. Like Katherine Smith and others Boyes specifies a personal redemption for Fox, if in a more pantheistic than Christian sense. However, the importance of the cancer "Cause" is explicit, as is the essential nature of "our" participation, and this is expressed in the battle metaphor. Fox does not fight in isolation, but his personal battle is already lost; only the community can now win it. The spread of his cancer (stanza five) ends the run, but its juxtaposition with positive community effects (stanza six) indicates a transcendent view of the disease as an enabler. This is expressed in explicitly nationalistic terms – the money comes "from every corner of the land." The dual honouring of "Terry's name" and "his fight" is semantically linked, and contextually linked as well, in that Boyes submitted this poem with her contribution to the Cancer Society.

Andrea Koziol, Untitled

Andrea Koziol of London, Ontario, was eleven when she wrote her poem. She read it to close a speech on Terry Fox's inspiration for Canadians that she presented at a Canadian Cancer Society meeting in January 1984. Several workers at the Ontario division recalled the poem and mentioned it during my research visit there:

The sun rose,
He looked out over the sweeping landscape ahead of him,
And as the red tints of the sun turned to orange,
Then to yellow,
A new seed of hope was planted in his soul,
And as the sun rose further,
That seed bloomed,
For all to see,
Recognize,
And share.

He did not hide his dream,
It was as real to him, as it was to everyone.
But, one day he stopped.
The hope and the dream were still there,
But the strength wasn't.

The sun rose
But there was no one to look over the sweeping landscape
    ahead of them.
And as the red tints of the sun turned to orange,
Then to yellow,
A new seed of hope was planted in CANADA.

Koziol views Terry Fox as a national and mythic hero. She employs
two key scenarios that are unique in this sample: the sunrise and the
planted seed. She also uses the dream metaphor, and here as elsewhere
in this group it refers to the intersection of Fox's personal goals and
ideals with collective ones: his dream is what Fox shares with the
community and nation.

The sunrise scenario opens the poem, suggesting Fox's own experience of the day-to-day continuation of the marathon. But the sunrise
also represents the man himself, a visual manifestation of hope, presented as the growing seed. As it develops in Fox, the seed eventually
blooms and becomes visible to the community/nation, which can
thereby share in his hope. The second stanza turns to the dream as
a collective rather than a private vision. Like the sunrise and growing
seed it has a progressively public expression. Koziol, like her fellow
poets, sees the dream's extension beyond Fox's experience of it; explicitly "The hope and the dream were still there," though the marathon
ends. Night, associated with the dream and the run's end, intervenes
between the two sunrise stanzas, which are associated with the growing seed and the run's continuation.

Koziol's poem contains the clearest exposition in any of these Ontario folk poems of Campbell's vision of the mythic hero, wherein "the really creative acts are represented as those deriving from some sort of dying to the world; and what happens in the interval of the hero's nonentity, so that he comes back as one reborn, made great and filled with creative power" (1968, 35–6). Fox, as an (unnamed) individual, is only minimally present. His actions are almost purely symbolic – looking out over landscapes as the sun rises, for instance – and divorced from the everyman hero. Even the end of his run is viewed in terms of faded strength, not the repulsiveness of a diseased, deteriorating body. Koziol's Fox, unlike that of other poets, does not run or battle; he only dreams. He exists as a symbol more completely than as a human being.

Shadrock Porter, "Crown Him Hero"

Shadrock Porter is in his early forties. He was born in Guyana and came to Canada in 1979. He recorded his song "Crown Him Hero" in November and December of 1983 and donated recordings to the Cancer Society. Porter told me that he sees Terry Fox as a heroic and inspirational figure, and likens him to Marcus Garvey and Martin Luther King (N 24 March 1984). He commented that every part of his song, including the music that imitates the rhythm of his run, is about Terry Fox:

Hip hop so long, hip hop so long, goodbye.
Hip hop so long, hip hop so long, goodbye.

It was 1980, the twelfth of April,
He started on a journey with his brother and a friend.
Dipped his leg in the ocean and set on his way
For B.C. backed in motion, at twenty-six miles a day.

Chorus One
So long, goodbye,
So long, goodbye,
So long, goodbye,
So long, goodbye.

He was inflicted with cancer, but only one leg.
Born to save the world and he did it oh so well.
So much money raised, I can never understand,
He never wanted praise, oh such a simple man.

Chorus One

[spoken] You were born for a reason.
You were born for a cause.
And even though now you're gone,
Your name still lingers on.
You are like a silver lining behind a dark cloud.
You are what men should be: determined and proud.
And even though now you're gone,
And our tears spring all right,
It's real and all men, rich or poor, sick or well, will have to die.
So walk on, Terry, walk on by.

Chorus Two
Crown him hero, crown him man,
Crown him hero of this land.
Crown him hero, watch him toil,
Crown him hero, Lord, of the soil.
Yeah, goodbye.
Crown him hero, crown him man.
Crown him hero, lord of the soil.
Crown him, crown him.

[spoken] Great men has come, great men has gone.
If we ever do remember them, Terry Fox was one.
He were just twenty-two, but he was a man all right.
He had to do what he had to do. Man, he was out of sight.

Chorus One

[spoken] He had a courage, he had a guts.
Reaching across this land with a leg that wasn't much.
Every day another mile; one foot forward, no more to follow.
He was here yesterday for a while, but never, never tomorrow.

Chorus One

[spoken] The courage that touched so many souls,
The love that reached so many hearts,
I tell you what, we won't let you die, Terry.
We'll resurrect that flame that flamed inside of you.

Chorus Two

Here Fox is a national and mythic hero. Shadrock Porter's lyrics are explicit about Fox's activities and life, beginning with a narration of the key events of the run. This is the only work in which the runner is not metaphorically alone but is accompanied by his brother and friend. Significantly, Porter is also the only poet to refer to Fox's symbolic baptism of his leg in the Atlantic before setting out. Combined with the allusion to the journey to BC, these reflect Fox's nationalistic goal of uniting the country.

As in the previous examples, Fox is viewed in Christian terms as a specially selected individual "born to save the world." Yet he is also a selfless and "simple man" and one who betokens the best of humanity. Everyman spiritual and physical domains in the first two stanzas are soon transcended in later stanzas that offer a new perspective. The third stanza fictively addresses Fox, metaphorically and symbolically considering his national and mythic significance. In a purposeful universe, he was "born for a reason ... for a cause," and his death does not mean that his influence ends. He is an exemplar of "what men should be – determined and proud." As a man, Terry Fox dies; but on the plane of mythic and national heroism his "name still lingers on" and he can "walk on by." Thus, retroactively, the repeated "so long, goodbye" in the first chorus and opening two lines is a farewell to Fox's physical self and, by implication, a welcome to his national and mythic transcendence of that state. Death, to Porter, is what Fox shares with other men; like Christ, however, he is more significant for the special characteristics and heroic qualities that he does not share with others.

In nationalistic terms Fox is a hero "of the land" and "of the soil." Mythical and national qualities combine in stanza five, when Fox reaches "across the land with a leg," a reference congruent with Cokkinos's and other mythical visions of Fox as a giant. Mythically and nationally in the final stanza Fox reaches and touches souls and hearts, who are incorporated into his resurrection. In this sense Fox will not die if we resurrect his "flame." Fire metaphorically refers to the phoenix-like life-in-death concept expressed in this and other mythic heroic verse.

In this third group of works the family becomes even more prominent as a field of symbolic activity than in the previous one, implicating as it does here both community and nation. As we have seen, most poets present Fox as an individual transcending the human everyman sphere rather than as one circumscribed by it. Root metaphors for his activities are the battle and the dream rather than the run. The latter loses its aptness as metaphor because Fox was unsuccessful in his attempt to complete a cross-Canada marathon. Unlike the battle metaphor, the run carries no association of a temporary setback leading to an ultimate victory. Likewise, the "road of trials," which Campbell associates with the initiation phase of the hero's progress, is inappropriate now that Fox's tests and ordeals are over. Similarly, his physical run is no longer possible, but his social/national/mythic dream, collectively shared, continues.

The dream metaphor, as we have observed, finds extensive expression in this group. The association between dreaming and death – death is a permanent dream state, or dreaming a temporary death – is obviously understood by the poets but is nowhere made explicit. Used thus, the dream asserts that Fox's death is only a temporary setback. Perhaps paradoxically it also refers to Fox's goals. Thus, the concern in almost every example with the discovery of a cancer cure as a result of the marathon becomes associated with the social, national, and mythic aspects of his heroism. The dream root metaphor is complex, incorporating the long-term cancer cure and collective participation while emphasizing continuation and remembrance rather than ending and forgetting.

Unlike the first two groups of poems, which show little need for resolution – most were hortatory, suggesting to Fox that his run could continue, often addressing themselves directly to him – the third group evinces a need for some method to deal with the human tragedy of death, especially that of a youthful, inspiring, admirable public figure. Indeed, a resolution of personal salvation for Fox himself in his heavenly reward constitutes the entire body of the Parkin poem. Most others include this or some other resolution: the renewed hope for a cancer cure, for instance, or even, as in the final few examples, Fox's own "crowning" as a mythical or national hero.

RE-EVALUATION: COMMUNITY ACTION AND INDIVIDUAL VIEWS

Poems in the final group diverge more than the previous ones in intent and expression, though the poets are united in wanting to bring attention to Terry Fox. Some urge participation in annual community Marathon of Hope runs, held in early fall to raise funds for cancer research.[9] As a headline from the *Acton Free Press* of 14 September 1983 suggests, local residents see such runs as actions equally supporting cancer fund-raising and Terry Fox himself. I quote the entire story:

WHY I RUN FOR TERRY
All kinds of people run for Terry, but the common thread of their desire is admiration for Terry and his dream of finding a cure for cancer. Four of the more prolific Fox run fundraisers from previous years shared their

thoughts this week for the events committee and the *Free Press*. Here's what they had to say.

Mary Beth Dowell – Terry was a courageous young person. I would like to see his dream come true. I'd like to know that a cure for cancer can be found.

Rick Dodds – I run for Terry Fox because I admired what he tried to do and research against cancer is important. Terry showed a lot of courage.

Ed Leatherland – I admire Terry's courage and determination as he ran for his dream for a cure for cancer and I am running to help see his dream realized.

Peter Cassa – I want to raise more money than I have previously for Terry's dream. I will make more than I made last year. I made $300 last year. This year I want to raise $600. I run for Terry because after what someone did on one leg a person with two legs should do more. I hope the people of Acton will support the run even more than they have in the past so we can raise even more than last year.

Some of the versemakers in this group re-evaluate Fox's significance. Two of them do so from viewpoints that seem anomalous, and their apparent motive for writing is to assert and advocate their own views in dialogue with a community whose perspective on Fox is quite different. As in the previous group of works, the emphasis is not on Fox's everyman human qualities but on his social, national, and mythic significance.

Bonnie Hind, "Terry"

Bonnie Hind is a schoolbus driver and farmer in her forties, well known in her area as a poet and songmaker. She explained to me that the song "Terry" was the third she had written on the subject and the only one she found successful. She wrote it "with one word on my mind, 'HOPE'" (Q March 1984). The song was sent to the Fox family, printed in the *Glencoe Free Press* of 3 November 1983, and distributed to Canadian radio stations and local schools. Intended as a fund-raiser, it was recorded in both English and French free of charge by a local group, "Homegrown":

If there's no hope there is no faith
With no faith there is no will
And with no will there'd be no goal
We'd ever hope to fill.

If there's no dream there is no day
With no day there is no night

If there's no wrong then there's no way
There could ever be a right.

If there's no man who'll take a chance
'Cause he's so afraid to fail
There'd be no hope for freedom
There'd be no open trail.

If we had strength and we had love
And courage and desire
We'd have the power within ourselves
To ignite eternal fire.

There came a boy not yet a man
With courage hope and love
And faith and will who had a goal
And was guided from above.

He faced the longest lonely miles
But he never lost his will
And he instilled within our hearts
A love that time can't kill.

He breathed into a countryside
That stretched both far and wide
The hope of God's eternal life
And then one day he died.

A crippled boy with just one leg
And golden curly locks
God only lent us for a while
And then he took home his Terry Fox.

You gave us in your courage
A reason to go on
Though you were here for just a while
You never really will be gone.

For you gave us a chance to know
That we could feel the rain
And Terry I just wish some day
You could pass this way again.

This song's first four stanzas refer generally to the characteristics usually associated with Terry Fox – faith, will, hope, and so on – and to the signifiers of his activities seen in previous poems – dreams, day, night, and fire. It opens with a hierarchical ranking of hope, faith, will, and creation and fulfilment of goals, each one enabling the next in sequence. Hind's express concern is with hope and the Marathon of Hope itself. Though these could be seen narrowly as referring to cancer, she intends a wider significance for Fox in terms of both social values and mythic heroism.

Commentary in the second stanza strongly suggests Shadrock Porter's "Crown Him Hero"; potentially negative aspects of life in Fox's case are enablers of more positive ones – without night, no day; without wrong, no right, and so on. Another echo of Porter is in Fox's symbolic ability to "ignite eternal fire." Others could do the same thing ("If we had strength and we had love" then "We'd have the power"), yet they lack the necessary qualities. A symbolic deficiency in society is filled by an individual embodying those needed attributes. This is in part because Fox is a mythic giant – "He breathed into a countryside."

Unlike Porter, Hind sees Fox as a "boy not yet a man." She intends to show his innocence and thus his appropriateness as a symbolic mythic sacrifice. Fox has an advantage in being "guided from above." To Hind, he is not really one of the community; he was lent, and subsequently taken home, by God. Again we notice a similarity to Christ. Fox is not only an embodiment and example of eternal (Christian) love but also someone who makes such love available to the community. His death is juxtaposed with his bringing hope of eternal life; his resurrection, then, is implied. Fox propagates Christianity and its values.

The penultimate stanza honours Fox's exemplary effects and asserts, like many previous works, that Fox "never really will be gone." This is affirmed when the final two stanzas are addressed to Fox himself in the second person. In the last stanza, unlike other poets, Hind does not show Fox living in community memory. Instead, Christ-like, he exists in the knowledge and lessons that he has imparted. Terry Fox's death, though potentially negative, in fact manifests Christian redemption. Though his effects are on the countryside (stanza seven), they are national in extent, if not nationalistic in results.

Crystal Davies,
"Terry Fox You Never Really Stopped"

Crystal Davies was fifteen when she wrote "Terry Fox You Never Really Stopped." She sent it to the *Toronto Star* and to the *Aurora Banner*, which published it on 23 March 1983:

Terry Fox don't ever stop
You're on the top
You're having fun
We'll help you finish that run.

You died to save
That means you're brave
We're really sad to see you go
But I really hope you know

That you're a part
Of all our hearts
Especially mine
And that's just fine.

Terry Fox don't ever stop
You never really stopped
Run run run.

This work is similar in intention and meaning to Bonnie Hind's. It addresses Fox and asserts both his continuation of the run and the community's participation in it. The first stanza fictively exhorts Fox to run, implying his transcendence over the community ("You're on the top") but also that group's responsibility to Fox ("We'll help you finish that run"). The writer's final comment, "You never really stopped," can be interpreted, as in the Hind song, as pertaining to the man's community and mythical effects. This poem, like others discussed earlier, employs the run as root metaphor, apt because of the annual Marathon of Hope runs and their continuation of Fox's aims and goals. The mythic and social spheres are conflated here; the writer displays Fox's self-sacrifice, implicitly Christ-like, without committing herself to an interpretation.

Laurena Wright, "A Tribute to Terry Fox"

Laurena Wright is a hospital worker in her mid-fifties. She sent her poem, at her childrens' urging, to the *Ottawa Citizen* and to the *Kemptville Weekly Advance*, where it was published:

Through many miles of anguish
Through many miles of pain –
He braved the harshest elements
To help his people gain
The hope of all who suffer

From Cancer, which all do fear –
Remember Terry Fox
A boy we all hold dear.
A boy, who for his country,
Gave his last days of life
In battle with a dread disease
He bravely fought, though long and hard
To help his fellow man;
Canada will ne'er forget
The courageous lad who ran.
He walked so many miles
In sunshine and in rain;
Our Terry kept on trying
E'en though he was in pain.
He never was a quitter
Despite his own heartache
He knew that he was dying
But kept on for our sake.
Though now he's gone forever;
The millions he brought forth –
From across all Canada
Will, well indeed be worth
A great deal to our country
In medicine and research,
To give hope to our people
And that land which gave us birth.

This poem operates in the spheres of national and mythic heroism. References to physical hardships the man faced are expressed as manifesting Fox "helping his people." Explicitly, he is viewed as culture hero; the problems he faces – harsh elements and many miles – are signifiers of Canada. But "his people" include fellow cancer patients as well as fellow Canadians. Like many other poets Wright sees Fox's effect as giving hope, implicitly for a cure.

The poet juxtaposes an exhortation that we remember Fox with a statement of community affection for him. His unifying effects are obvious in that "we *all* hold [him] dear" (my emphasis). His supreme, nationalistic self-sacrifice is that he "gave his last days of life" "for his country." National and community/social spheres are congruent.

Fox's sacrifice is characterized by the battle metaphor, always paired with assertions that "Canada will ne'er forget" and that he "kept on for our sake." To Wright, Fox is a giver more than an exemplar, and what he gives is equally "hope," through cancer research money, and national unity. He is discussed in mythic terms, not only because of his implied Christian self-sacrifice but also for his effect of "bringing forth millions [of dollars]" and for his fight against cancer. Here the mythic aspect is much less prominent than in previous examples; Terry Fox is "gone forever."

Ken Reynolds, "Terry's Marathon of Hope"

In his mid-fifties, Ken Reynolds is a federal public servant in Ottawa. He wrote this poem "following the September ... Terry Fox run" and read it at local "Community Fairs, Country Music Awards night, etc." (Q April 1984). It was also published in a suburban community newspaper, the *Clarion*, on 9 September 1981.

Never before has this country been so united and proud!
We're telling the whole world, yes, shouting out loud –
Terry, we love you, you're the greatest of greats,
You've brought us together and turned off many hates
By showing the courage, unmatching strength and the will
To carry a mighty torch with no concern for your ill.
T'was a cure you strive for cancer that dread of us all
And millions of people have since rallied to your call
Not just coast to coast, but now round the entire globe
Countries, cities, corporations, down to the smallest abode
Have answered his message, an appeal by just one man
This disease must be beaten and there's one way it can
By costly day and night efforts someday this dream will come true
Thanks to a giant lad – Terry, mankind is much indebted to you
Your immeasurable stamina captured our hearts in an indelible way.
Let's all pledge in advance by making the marathon an annual day!
And thank God for TERRY FOX, one man who challenged this test
May his spirit live with us after a hard earned eternal rest.

More mythic than Laurena Wright's, Ken Reynolds's view of Fox is equally nationalistic. His poem works in a number of semantic domains, using the familiar battle ("This disease must be beaten") and dream metaphors but also a more unusual verbal one. Fox calls, appeals, and gives messages. In return, the country shouts, answers, and pledges. Reynolds delineates Fox in enthusiastic, optimistic superlatives; the poem's general mood differs substantially from that of previous examples written after Fox's death. In content, tone, and use of symbolism, this poem resembles Costas Cokkinos's, written at the end of Fox's run.

Reynolds immediately presents Fox as a unique figure: *"Never before has this country been so united and proud"* (my emphasis). Like foreign-born poets Cokkinos and Porter, Reynolds sees the man as the first true Canadian hero. He maintains that in having such a hero, Canada at last can take its place as a mature nation. Like Wright, Reynolds juxtaposes the nationalism and cancer cure aims, extending the latter to "the entire globe."

The superlatives – "greatest of greats," "unmatching strength" – refer to Fox's mythic qualities, as does his carrying "a mighty torch," an image that Cokkinos also uses. Selflessness, used by other poets to refer to the mythic sphere, is also evident here. And as in other works emphasizing the mythic, Fox is presented as a giant. But Reynolds says that Fox's spirit continues in the national sphere as well as getting a "hard earned eternal rest." This poet tends towards the resolution of the memorial poems, where we can approach the everyman Fox's death only with respect to his transcending the human sphere. In most national and mythic poems this was implicit, but Reynolds makes it explicit in his final line.

W.S. Tomlinson, "Terry Fox"

W.S. Tomlinson is a retired construction-company executive. His poem was published in the *Thunder Bay Chronicle Journal* of 20 August 1983 with an article on Terry Fox runs and the dedication of a monument in Thunder Bay to him:

Canada has heroes of yesteryear
But none like Terry Fox
Canada gained fame among its peers
But none like Terry Fox
The human spirit may pass us by
But not "by" Terry Fox.
A giant above the milling crowds
He lives and goads us on
May the lord have mercy on our souls
If we fail to respond.

Tomlinson's view of Fox as a social hero is at variance with that of other poets. Superficially, this poem's symbolic content strongly resembles that of the Grampa G work in the first section. Both poets assert Fox's national uniqueness, and both express it in negative terms – Terry Fox is not like others. Also shared with other poets is

Tomlinson's "giant" analogy. However, his contentious tone, like Zorro's in "Marathon of Hope," is anomalous and generically inappropriate. Likewise, Tomlinson's concept of Fox is truly one of a kind. Here Fox is not an "everyman" hero but "a giant above the milling crowds." In specifying his context of domination, Tomlinson presents Fox's social qualities as autocratic ones. "He lives and goads us on" as a kind of cosmic foreman or overseer. With respect to the community as a whole, Fox is an "other," not a "self," but this view is not unusual. The anomaly is that as an "other," Fox is effective not through inspiration or assistance, as elsewhere in this sample, but coercively, through threat of divine punishment: "May the lord have mercy on our souls / If we fail to respond."

Bob Shrier, "A Tribute to Terry"

Bob Shrier, the local newspaper entrepreneur and editor we met in chapter 2, is in his late forties. He published "A Tribute to Terry" in his own column in *Topic* and in *Focus* on 30 September 1983; he has also read it at meetings of service clubs and other organizations. He sees the message of Terry Fox as one at odds with the "gloom and doom and reverence to him" (T83–52), which he feels the man would not have wanted:

The Fox boy on the run gave us a thought.
One which we heard and simply forgot.
Terry said, "Dreams are made if people only try."
We thought at the time, what a meaningful cry.

It's a lonely process, this hope of tomorrow,
Because everyone else, our mind wants to borrow,
They make their dream ours and we feel alone,
To reach out with purpose, courage must be shown.

He taught us a lesson we soon forgot:
Dreams are for everyone – the have and have not.
If you are satisfied to conform to the tribe,
Be ready always for conformity's bribe.

He knew defeat and to be denied;
That lack of a will was why other dreams died.
That's what the boy on the run gave us for thought,
Something we heard and promptly forgot.

His life was extinguished; for most his idea,
Our hero he was, he raised national hysteria.
Saddened he'd be if he knew that his thought
Was something we listened to and promptly forgot.

Dream a dream that is yours, chase it through pain
Chase it for years; you and others will gain.
When your life is extinguished, maybe you'll leave a thought;
Something someone listened to and never forgot.

If you get a dream like the kid on the run
Go for it! Suffer for it as Ghandi and King and others who won.
When challenged with what can one person do?
Remember the kid and what he said to you.

My God, don't forget that he gave us a thought,
One which we heard and promptly forgot.
Anything can happen if man only knows,
A dream deep inside will beat the mightiest of foes.

We forgot the tremendous odds that he faced,
Just in preparing to run the great race;
Our hurts and our insignificant pain
Are nothing compared to what he did for our gain.

We all feel so comfortable to be part of the pack,
Run alone as he did and never look back,
Terry the boy, Terry the man
Ran because of a cause and a plan.

The hurting will stop for all who desire
To run life's race with their belly on fire,
Impossible you say, what of he with one leg;
He said, chase your dream, he did not say to beg.

If you want to live life in your own special way,
To realize your dream as he did one day,
Don't whine and grovel and look at the dirt,
You must go through the agony the pain and the hurt.

It's lonely out there on your own special run,
But that's part of the price if your dream's to be won;
Believe in miracles, that was his thought,
Something he said, but most people forgot.

Shrier addresses two types of symbolic deficiency. The more obvious is the misunderstanding of Fox's true message, as the poet sees it, and the other is the content of that message, the colloquial "Go for it!" expressed in the poem itself. Shrier argues for a view of Fox in the everyman spheres only; he expressly rejects mythic or nationalistic views. His iconoclasm is evident in his characterization of Terry Fox as "the Fox boy," which possesses neither the personal, friendly tone of "Terry," used by several other poets, nor the more formal, almost iconic "Terry Fox."

As in the Reynolds poem, Fox is metaphorically characterized as a speaker. Shrier quotes Fox's words to show his function as didactic and exemplary. The dream metaphor is appropriate here, associating personal thought with collective inspiration. Yet Shrier's view of Fox's social message – like Tomlinson's – is individualistic, not communal. Fox's "aloneness" is shared with the rest of the community; what sets him apart is not some special essence, but his having followed personal goals. The poet repeats signifiers of Fox's ordinariness: "He knew defeat and to be denied" and "His life was extinguished." Fox's "dream" is a weapon in a root-metaphorical battle: "A dream deep inside will beat the mightiest of foes." It also allows a person to transcend "the agony, the pain and the hurt." Consistent with his anti-mythic view, Shrier sees these negative factors not as enablers but as obstacles to realizing dreams.

In this last group, which covers the widest time-span and has the fewest common meanings, we also find two relatively unusual and individualistic views of Terry Fox, Tomlinson's and Shrier's. Both, by no means coincidentally, are poets who represent a wealthier than usual segment of Ontario society. Not only does this indicate Fox's malleability as a symbolic hero, but it also shows the broad, effective range of his penetration into Ontario culture. These two examples also suggest a psychological dimension to Terry Fox poetry, which I will mention but hesitate to extend to the entire sample. Evidently, both Shrier and Tomlinson identify strongly with Fox, and their poetic exegeses of his character refer to qualities essential to their own self-concepts. As a manager and executive Tomlinson is in a sense also a "giant above the milling crowds," and Shrier, a self-made millionaire, feels that what sets him apart from the rest of the world is his own "go for it" entrepreneurial mentality.

Compare these individualistic views with those of the poets who see the continuation of the Marathon of Hope as Fox's major message: Davies, Wright, and Reynolds especially. To the latter Fox's effects extend beyond individual inspiration, and his implications reach past the community, and sometimes even the nation. However, as we will see next, the archetypification of Fox on the national level is difficult, since the available metaphors and symbols cannot be so specifically applied to it as on the everyman or mythic heroic levels.

This final group of poems, above, returns us to the run as root metaphor. Because of the Marathon of Hope's continuation as a community event, this is clearly appropriate. Though superficially contradictory, the allusions to Fox's stopping his run and to his continuing it are in fact aspects of the same issue: the ongoing marathon. If Fox continues, he does so alongside the rest of the community. If he stops, it is because the community takes his place.

SITUATION CHANGE AND MEANING CHANGE

Conceiving Terry Fox as a hero who overcomes symbolic deficiencies is thoroughly apposite for contemporary Ontario folk poetry. Our discussion of this traditional expressive genre has sought to demonstrate its central preoccupation with cultural rifts, disjunctions, and changes and with their appropriateness and inappropriateness – all of which can be described as being or referring to types of symbolic deficiencies. In so far as a hero is perceived as someone who approaches and/or overcomes such cultural problems, he is appropriate to this type of poetry, and aspects of his character manifesting his relationship to the community are most likely to be expressed in it. The marked exception to this general observation, as we have seen, is Helen Parkin's untitled second poem, a memorial referring to another kind of disjunction, experienced as a result of death in a family, rather than to Terry Fox himself as a heroic figure. If the numerous poems sent to the Fox family on Terry's death had been available for study, I would surely have found more of this type of memorial verse. The sources that were available produced poems and songs directed primarily towards local communities and only secondarily and, in a few cases, privately to the family as well.

A striking feature of these poems is their sociocultural reflection of the province. The sample is to a great extent microcosmic for Ontario and for the province's folk poets. Seven poets are foreign born, four from Britain and three from elsewhere. The occupational and social cross-section is likewise broad, from the "sweaty maintenance man" Grampa G to the self-made millionaire Bob Shrier. There are works by professional or semi-professional writers (Kennedy, Porter, and St. Denis); by known community poets like Bonnie Hind; by one-timers like Bob Shrier; and by topical poets like Anne Boyes.

The sheer number of works in this sample and their collective

extension over more than three years confirms the poetic archetypification of Terry Fox. What these poems mainly share is the view of
Terry Fox as an inspiration to the community. We may regard this
as inherently conservative; the social mores that Fox indexes are
associated with the traditional community. The values themselves
(except for those advocated by Tomlinson and Shrier) are emphatically
those of co-operation, collective effort, and work for community benefit.
Whereas Shrier and Tomlinson see Terry Fox as an icon of individ-
ualism, other poets view him as one of communal effort. In a world
where traditional values are constantly being eroded, the archetypification of Terry Fox shows an intention both to glorify someone who
indexes such values and to reinforce them in the media and in the
nation. Like other Ontario folk poetry – despite its "oil on troubled
waters" ethos – the Fox poems actively contest the transformation of
the Ontario community and its forced incorporation into a crasser,
self-regarding world.

Fox's efforts are presented as anti-materialistic. For instance, Grampa
G maintains "No man is a mountain ... No matter how rich," and
Grant Filson affirms "Fortune and fame were not your aim." Even
Fox's fund-raising is rarely characterized simply in terms of "money"
but often as "gold," "funds," and "donations." This is not irresponsible
individual wealth but largesse intended for use towards the common
good. Such money seems to possess an almost organic life and is
"raised" like a crop, as in St. Denis's "To raise the gold that Terry
always wanted" and also perhaps Parkin's "The fund is swelling by
the hour." Another poet alludes to the same metaphor in her "Donations against cancer started coming in / First by the bag and then
by the bin." This is hardly Marxian commodity fetishism, since it is
collectively directed money. In addition, the metaphors concentrate
not on the money itself as a quasi-organic substance but on Terry
Fox as its cultivator, as suggested in Wright's "the millions he brought
forth."

Money is also described, metaphorically and even less fetishistically
– concentrating on its effects, not on the object itself – as life-giving
water, as in one poet's "Donations started pouring in," Herridge's
"The dollars came reluctantly at first / Then they began to pour,"
or Boyes's "And from every corner of the land / The money began
to pour." Funds raised will enable research to continue and will, it
is hoped, ultimately produce a cure for cancer. Money is a means in
a system of exchange rather than an end in itself.

Further evidence that this poetry is particularly representative of
Ontario community and folk-poetic values lies in how Fox is represented as a hero. Some symbols and tropes are integrally associated

with certain heroic perspectives, while others are more loosely clustered, adhering to the edges of one conceptualization and spilling over into others. The metaphors of the run, the battle, and the dream, for example, are malleable enough (as is Fox himself as an archetype) for use in more than one type of argument or commentary. The notion of Fox as torch-bearer (Cokkinos and Reynolds), however, is tied into his mythic aspect, as are the giant and the mountain.

One crucial heroic sphere that poets find difficult to denote is the national one. Canada is often characterized as lacking a distinctive identity, and this is reflected in the poems' absence of distinct metaphors and symbols to indicate Fox's nationalistic importance. Perhaps Canada's only national metaphor is the railway, built as a symbolic and actual connection between the east and west of the country. It was viewed and constructed as such, and a popular work on the subject calls the railway "The National Dream" (Berton 1970). It is not coincidental that Terry Fox is also seen as a "dreamer."

An analogy between Fox and the national railway, though never explicitly stated, can be drawn from the poems. Most poets who attend to Fox as a national hero refer somewhere to his cross-Canada run – the "east to west," "St John's to BC" aspect – and many also allude to history as the locus of Fox's activities. Analogically, the railway is generally perceived as a symbol more appropriate to the past than to the present, and the physical span of Fox's run, and its understood slow but steady progress, may suggest a similarity to the railway's lengthy construction period. The latter, more than the railway's completion or use, symbolizes the elusive Canadian unity.

Otherwise, distinctive poetic signifiers of nationalism are non-existent. For example, Costas Cokkinos's nationalistic view draws upon his own Greek culture heroes: Prometheus, the Colossus of Rhodes, and the soldier who ran from Marathon to Athens carrying the news of the Persians' defeat by Pericles. There are no Canadian culture heroes to whom Fox can be compared. When Tomlinson says, "Canada has heroes of yesteryear," a Canadian is hard pressed to identify one.[10] In this light Terry Fox's archetypification in folk poetry may prove to be the creation of a prototype; his heroic traits may be incorporated into a figure with which subsequent Canadian heroes can be identified and compared. The archetypified Terry Fox has the potential to be a summarizing symbol for Canadian nationalism.

Perhaps the most telling indicator of Fox's – and Ontario folk poetry's – meaning is the change that occurs in the use of common metaphors and symbols, not their employment by individual poets. The two songs written during the original Marathon of Hope centre on Terry Fox as an individual and as an everyman hero in the human spheres, both spiritual and physical. Fox's social effects receive only minimal attention. The poets assume their audience's knowledge of certain facts – in Ross Knechtel's "Running Man," even the identity of the "runner" is inchoate – and fix their metaphorical and symbolic attention on exhortations and encouragement to Fox. The run is the major organizing symbol for these writers, and the run to which they refer is the actual ongoing marathon. It is less a symbolic run than it is an actual event.

Neither work mentions cancer or the Marathon of Hope. It seems, as suggested above, that the archetype of Terry Fox at this point centres on his physical and spiritual determination. Fox himself is perceived in terms of pride, faith, and courage. His run is seen as an individual effort; the admiring crowds and local support, which are constituent elements of the everyman hero in his community context, are absent or downplayed. The other human presences are people explicitly unlike Fox: Knechtel's scoffers and doubters, and Kennedy's admiring community.

With the return of the cancer and the cessation of Fox's marathon, Ontario poets deploy new symbolic material. They consider more extensively the adversity that the everyman hero faced: environmental and community as well as human spiritual and physical adversity, the latter now extending textually to include cancer and amputation. This poetry begins to involve others besides the runner; the community at large is encouraged to donate, to pray, and to identify. Fox himself is exhorted to continue his "hope" – a newly introduced characterization – for cure and recovery, and a resumption of the run. Even at this early stage the first indications of Fox's nationalistic and mythic meanings enter the poetic repertoire, though as suggested above, the national meaning's expression is blocked by a lack of signifiers.

At Terry Fox's death, root metaphors of the battle and the dream are added to that of the run, which itself becomes more a metaphorical and symbolic concept than a physical event. As a symbol, the run – a continuous, long-term, ongoing activity – cannot sustain the weight of the real life situation. The central adversity and problem of the everyman-human aspect of Fox becomes cancer, and this joins with the "cause," his own aim of fund-raising for cancer research. The battle metaphor allows the possibility of a temporary setback – Fox's own death – without the admission of total defeat, while to stop in the middle of a run is to fail.

Not surprisingly, with this event comes an increasing concentration on others – the community – as well as on Fox himself. He may be portrayed as a lone runner, a teacher, or a dreamer, but his inspiration affects spheres beyond that of the individual. The first-person plural voice increasingly appears, a shift demonstrating a rising common perspective that dominates, even transcends personal views. This also begins the final stage of archetypification, which we can see even more clearly in the final group of poems, where the prevailing tendency – even if the poet wishes to countervail it – is to see Fox as figure, representation, and symbol, not as human, personal, and individual, and where the run returns as a central root metaphor.

Further, the need for a resolution is clear in this material. The undeserved death of an innocent and admirable individual is, of course, a central problem in Christianity, and many writers find and project a resolution in a comparison between Terry Fox's self-sacrifice and Christ's. They oppose Fox's lack of success in his proximate goal (the incomplete run and his death) to his achievement of the penultimate goal, raising money for cancer research. (The ultimate end, to find a cancer cure, was never in Fox's own hands.) This is incorporated in the battle metaphor; though Fox's personal battle ends, the wider battle against cancer continues. The battle and dream metaphors, as suggested above, provide an intersection of his personal goals with wider community, national, and more general human (mythic) values.

Throughout the process of Fox's archetypification, the central metaphors for his activities, the view of Fox himself, the methods for considering both activity and man, and the representation and expression of the archetype in poetry all change. Most of these transformations occur as part of a retroactive evaluation of the abundant material on Fox and his run that was available through the mass media. But poets as representatives of their community's culture choose certain aspects of that culture for emphasis, and this is all the more evident in this case because of the differences in perspective that correspond to changes in the actual situation.

Another question remains. What is the view of the community inherent in this poetry? I have earlier suggested that Terry Fox's special interest for the community was that, although he was an outsider, he very unusually epitomized the values and morality of the traditional community: the importance of physical effort, spiritual determination, love of family and place, and work for communal rather than individual benefit.

To many urban Canadians Terry Fox was nothing more than an object of media hype, a token nationalistic issue, an individual canonized by newspapers, radio, and television, and something of an embarrassment. Fox seemed to this constituency to epitomize rural "hick"-ness, if only because of the widespread emotional adulation he generated. Critic Susan Sontag has suggested that "Cancer is a rare and still scandalous subject for poetry; and it seems unimaginable to aestheticize the disease" (1977, 20), and in this light, making Terry Fox a hero was a step in such a direction. Yet all the evidence shows that this young man was something special to Ontario communities and an object of genuine grassroots concern.

Fox also came to be perceived as a locus for the conflict between traditional popular community values and urban academic sophisticated perspectives. For example, after I gave a talk on Fox as a national hero in a Royal Ontario Museum (Toronto) senior citizens' program, one man warmly shook my hand and commented that he was pleased to see a representative of the academic point of view praising and appreciating Terry Fox. He told me that in the issue in which Terry Fox's obituary was printed, *Maclean's* magazine had also printed a letter from a University of Toronto history professor maintaining that Fox was neither a "historical figure" nor a "great man." My search through back issues of *Maclean's* turned up neither a formal obituary nor any such letter. It is very possible that the articles in question were printed elsewhere or that two separate incidents have been conflated; however, a certain poetic truth (in the vernacular sense) – in the conviction that "Canada's National Magazine" could have contained these items – cannot be denied. To Ontario's traditional communities, *Maclean's* could represent the urban academic sophisticate's perception of society, opposing their values of co-operation over competition.

We should remember that Fox first came to community attention in the national media, where he received considerable publicity. To Ontarians reading about him in the *Toronto Star*, for instance, he must have seemed odd, a national newsmaker who characterized not the usual "bad news" but stood for values the community wanted to see upheld. For them he was an ideal heroic figure: in spirit and by his acts one of the community, yet actually an outsider. Perhaps he manifests the ideal of what an outsider should be but usually is not: one who understands and profoundly respects local values and morality. This is the crux of Terry Fox's importance and meaning in Ontario.

Yet a dialogue between the reality of Terry Fox and his presentation in the media did exist. The media emphasized some of Fox's words and deeds while downplaying others. But Ontario poets, representing their communities, were equally selective with the information they received. A profound change in how the media represented Fox, showing whatever negative qualities he might have possessed, would have made his archetypification more difficult, if not impossible. But the wide popular support – even adulation – for Fox clearly fed the media's interest in him and influenced the positive content of broadcast and newspaper reports. Fox's archetypification by Ontario poets and their communities, as their verse shows, is a negotiated creation. Poets present and represent their community's ideas, or argue with them. There was a real person, of whom we know various facts, who began but could not finish a marathon across Canada to support cancer research. But Terry Fox as a Canadian hero, whether everyman, mythic, or national, is the creation of those who so view him. And this is where we can return to idea of appropriation in its active sense:

The word in language is half someone else's. It becomes "one's own" only when the speaker populates it with his own intention, his own accent, when he appropriates the word, adapting it to his own semantic and expressive intention. Prior to this moment of appropriation, the word does not exist in a neutral and impersonal language ... , but rather it exists in other people's mouths, in other people's contexts, serving other people's intentions ... Language is not a neutral medium that passes freely and easily into the private property of the speaker's intentions; it is populated – overpopulated – with the intentions of others. Expropriating it, forcing it to submit to one's own intentions and accents, is a difficult and complicated process. (Bakhtin 1981, 293–4)

What Bakhtin says about the appropriation of words applies equally to the appropriation in words of Terry Fox as a hero. That is, Fox the person and Fox the national hero are essentially different things. His significance is created by poets and by those who ran for him, donated to his cause, volunteered for the Canadian Cancer Society, and so on; in Bahktin's words, they "populate" him with meaning. Terry Fox as a word, as an idea, and as a symbol is no more neutral than language itself. He is not a hero until he is so described; he exists as a hero in the context of Ontario communities' understanding of him as such. That there is so much similarity among the poets' conceptions of Fox as a hero shows their success and his appositeness in the task, as well as some very profound underlying cultural similarities among Ontario communities and among their poets.

CHAPTER SIX

Folk Poetry and Opposition

Appropriateness, appropriation, and community have been linking concepts for *True Poetry*. I have tried to show how the three interrelate, while at the same time indicating how traditional and popular verse is central to their connection. In this final chapter I would like to comment on some broader issues that pertain to folklore as artistic communication, while suggesting in a general way how all the abundant creativity evident in folk poetry serves the needs of its creators, presenters, and audience.

I have frequently heard the comment that folk artists do their creative "thing," whatever it might be, as a not-so-subtle bid for attention. And in fact it is pretty obvious that some of these peoples' creations are startlingly different and demand not only an audience but a response as well. But it is patently false then to conclude – as some of my interlocutors do – that these artworks are nothing more than a psychological outlet for the lonely. No one who has spent time in a community like those I have described here, or actually talked to yard artists, folk poets, storytellers, or other such creative individuals, would be able to conclude that they are a pathetic lot, using blatantly unconventional methods to gain a measure of regard from others; that without the folk artistic outlet for their strangeness these people would be social outcasts, ignored by their own group or community.

I often feel insulted on behalf of the people with whom I have worked, and on behalf of folk artists in general, that critics might draw such conclusions and separate but one component of creativity – its value as an attention-getter – from all its other meanings and uses. The folk artists I know are as respected and admired as their neighbours who express their creativity in different ways, and any theory that suggests otherwise misconceives its subjects.

In the communities I know, whether they are rural or urban, it is infinitely more difficult to get privacy than it is to get vigilance from others. But even if solitude were rampant, there are any number of other ways – and some much better ways – to gain recognition. Instead of creating wild, colourful whirligigs, a man could gain a reputation for fixing broken machinery. Rather than directing her narrative talents to story-telling, a woman could run for public office. As an alternative to writing folk poetry a versemaker could take interest courses in literature at a local school. All these are creative outlets that gain for those who engage in them a higher profile in their group or community. I am not saying that these expressive activities demand the same talents and abilities or that they would receive the same kind of response as folk artistry does; it is fundamental to my understanding of the significance of such expression that there exists no substitute for it. I am simply claiming that other activities could likewise have the function of attracting some regard from the community.

In fact, one could perversely analyse almost any social activity as a way of drawing attention. That leads the issue back upon itself. If other methods of attention-getting are available, why do folk artists choose the one they do? I hope that my discussion of folk poetry has begun to answer that question. Folk poets appropriate traditional and popular verse because it is the most appropriate expression, not only for them but also for their audiences.

To reiterate, folk poetry as a genre is known and understood within Ontario communities as a way of expressing particular kinds of opinions – especially those that could be interpreted as critical – without risking damage to the community itself as a collective social creation. This verse has serious subjects, but its tone and deployment are playful. It is particularly suited to the sociocultural dynamics of Ontario communities, with their evident rifts between groups and individuals perceived as insiders and outsiders. The contexts in which folk poetry is presented, from the Women's Institute meeting to the community shower to the local newspaper, are themselves loci for working out personal and collective conflicts, and folk verse assists in resolving the problems that inevitably arise. This is especially evident when one compares folk verse with other verbal genres, or examines a situation in which poems, or poets, are opposed one to another.

The verse itself draws extensively upon known prototypes, which are often examples of traditional wisdom, yet the simple reproduction of the prototype is much less common than its re-creation or refiguring. This means that at the same time a poet or presenter takes personal accountability for a statement in verse, he or she may may temper its individuality because it is also something that has been around for a while, whose validity is commonly understood. In effect, the poet or presenter recommends a poem to the community not only on his or her own part but also because it represents an already recognized truth, from tradition and from other poets. Such a comment is worthwhile partly because the poet or presenter feels it is, but this is confirmed by the fact that that the verse – its wording, its structure, and its genre – ultimately originates in the sociocultural milieu that is recognized, and for the most part accepted, by its local audience. This is quite obvious in the Terry Fox verse: similar concepts, words, images, and metaphors are used to describe him and evaluate his significance. Yet the poets themselves represent a broad cross-section of Ontario's population. A common milieu and shared sources have lead to common, shared expressions.

Clearly, practising some traditional or popular art is not considered a weird or socially unacceptable thing to do as long as the individual who does it is not weird or socially unacceptable for some other reason. Remember that folk poets' identities are based on their relationships to their communities through family, school, homestead, and so on, and not primarily on what they do. The folk arts are not particularly unusual or uncommon. Urban dwellers may be unaware of them, but this is because they fail to identify, or simply ignore, the creative expressions they encounter in their own milieux. Such expressions range from the pointed use of a photocopied cartoon to the artful retelling of a personal experience, and beyond. Traditional and popular verse in the province of Ontario is not only locally recognized as a standard communicative form; it is quite common in a number of different contexts.

Another misconception I often encounter is that folk artists are engrossed in worlds of their own making and that their "primitive" or "naïve" creations ignore what's going on in the community or beyond. *True Poetry* has shown traditional and popular verse engaging in an important dialogue about Ontario's political economy and participating in shaping the province's sociocultural configuration. The creators and presenters of this verse, like other folk artists, are offering perceptions and analyses that are anything but primitive or naïve. Their form of expression may superficially appear unsophisticated, but it is in fact as symbolically complex as any other form of verbal art. Cultural and artistic awareness mingle in this work.

The majority of Ontario folk poets whose works and commentary I have quoted see the Ontario community as a dying entity and traditional culture as equally moribund. If they did not see their way of life as being in jeopardy, they would not have to create and present, through traditional and popular verse, another vision of society. They are genuinely and reasonably concerned about the quality of the future, and so they continue to express and communicate the alternatives and thus to participate in creating their own culture. A shared quality of folk arts – and this certainly applies to folk poetry in Ontario – is that they are alternative and oppositional, or, differently put, they are "contestative" (Lombardi-Satriani 1974). They present – and usually actively advocate – alternatives to the status quo, to mainstream culture, to "progress," or even to change. A recent characterization of folklore catalogues these qualities, or "orientations," in the subject: "the *communal* (a group or collective), the *common* (the everyday rather than the extraordinary), the *informal* (in relation to the formal and institutional), the *marginal* (in relation to the centers of power and privilege), the *personal* (communication face-to-face), the *traditional* (stable over time), the *aesthetic* (artistic expressions), and the *ideological* (expressions of belief and systems of knowledge)" (Oring 1986, 17–18).

Seeing folklore as informal, marginal, common, and ideological certainly confirms its oppositional, alternative stance. But the communal, personal, traditional, and aesthetic can also present cultural alternatives: to the individualistic, the impersonal, the new-fangled, and the anaesthetic. This can be reactionary; in Ontario communities it may appear to be so because the advancers of traditional and popular culture want to preserve an ideal they themselves associate with the past. Yet most of the advocates of these values want to preserve the best of modernity without losing what is worthwhile from former times. So traditional and popular culture can also be revolutionary, in the sense that the solutions presented and the ideas created are built as much of present circumstances as they are of yesterday, and because the past is reconstituted, as it is in the appropriation of folk poetry, in order that history might become an essential, conscious element in the creation of the future.

Notes

1 In Ontario, the charivari (often called "shivaree") usually follows a wedding, and involves surprises and tricks directed at the newly-weds (see Greenhill forthcoming).

1 Semiotics is the study of signs and symbols, and how they are used.
2 I collected the following version of "Barbara Allen" from Edward Miller of Haliburton:

'Twas in the merry month of May
When flowers were a-blooming,
Sweet Willie on his deathbed lay
For the love of Barbara Allen.

He sent his servant to the house
The house that she did dwell in,
Saying "Master dear has sent me here
If your name be Barbara Allen."

Slowly, slowly she got up
And slowly she went to him
And all she said when she got there
Was "Young man, I'm feared you're dying.

"Do you remember the other day
When we were in the tavern

You drank a health to the ladies there
And slighted Barbara Allen."

"Yes I remember the other day
When we were in the tavern
I drank a health to the ladies there
But gave my heart to Barbara Allen."

As she went on through the town
She heard his death bells ringing
And every stroke it seemed to say
"Oh cruel Barbara Allen."

"Oh Mother dear go make my bed
Make it long and narrow
Sweet Willie died for me today
And I die for him tomorrow."

They buried Willie in the old churchyard
And Barbara in the new one
From Willie's grave there grew a rose
From Barbara's a sweet briar.

They grew and grew to the old church top
Where they could not grow any higher
And there they tied in a true love knot
The rose bush and the briar. (Edward Miller, T84–26)

3 See Luigi Lombardi-Satriani's "Folklore as Culture of Contestation" (1974).
4 Worldview refers to the sum of ideas, beliefs, and attitudes that individuals or groups hold vis-à-vis the world around them. Ethos refers to value systems; "the essential meaning of ethos lies in norm, in the conceptions people have as to the good" (Redfield 1960, 80).
5 See Bronson (1959, 2:131) for this version of "Barbara Allen."
6 Dalhart and Carter were country and western recording stars of the 1920s to 1940s.
7 Modern folklorists recognizing the dialectical quality of folklore include Barbara Kirshenblatt-Gimblett (1975) and Regna Darnell (1975).
8 Liminality refers to periods of transition (see Van Gennep 1960).
9 The "green side" and "dry side" refer to aspects of the production

of planks in logging mills and the consequent separation of the mill into a "green" side, which deals with raw logs, removing bark and preparing them for the "dry" side, in which the logs are sawed into planks.

CHAPTER TWO

1 Prior to its entry into Canadian confederation in 1867, Ontario was called Upper Canada. "Upper Canadian" is now a pejorative term for Anglo Ontarians among other Canadians.
2 Both traditional and revival quilting continue to be popular in the province.
3 William Davis, recent head of the provincial government.
4 John Szwed describes Newfoundland songmaker Paul E. Hall as a marginal individual who uses his songs to negotiate a viable position within his community (Szwed 1970).
5 John Slykhuis kindly loaned me his file of unpublished poetry submitted to *Topic*.
6 See Burke (1969, 70–1) for further discussion of these kinds of rhetoric.

CHAPTER THREE

1 In spring 1984 Metroland published newspapers in Acton, Aurora, Ajax-Pickering, Bolton, Brampton, Etobicoke, Georgetown, Markham, Milton, Mississauga, Newmarket, North York, Oakville, Oshawa, Richmond Hill, Thornhill, Scarborough, Stouffville, and Woodbridge.
2 In memoriams are selections of verse, usually four or eight lines long, published on the anniversary of an individual's death.
3 The portions of this transcript (T84–43) that are conventional poetry are so transcribed. In Mrs G.H.'s story, spoken in ethnopoetic lines (see Tedlock 1972), ends of lines indicate speech pauses. Read prose is presented in standard form.
4 A presentation is a gift, sometimes money, from the community collectively.
5 Although the rest of the transcription comes from my tape 84–48, I have presented Eagan's poem as it is given in his written version.
6 In northern England "the most common setting in the newspaper for a local poem was in the letters-to-the-editor section" (Renwick, N 14 Oct. 83).
7 The verse is probably from the *Bolton Enterprise*. I am uncertain

because my copies come from Raymes's own undocumented collection of his work.

8 Structural anthropologist Claude Lévi-Strauss (1969) suggests that most simple societies evaluate nature as threatening and culture as benign, the very opposite of what is seen in many aspects of Ontario culture. For further discussion of this point, see Greenhill (1985, 230–83).

9 Brown and Levinson (1978) discuss politeness mechanisms in terms of the preservation of personal face. They suggest that special language is used to mitigate the force of orders, suggestions, and so on. This clearly applies to Ontario folk poetry's function. See also Bauman (1983) for an application of Brown and Levinson's concepts to a social interactional study of folkloric materials, the speech of seventeenth-century Quakers.

10 Brown and Levinson (1978).

CHAPTER FOUR

1 Anthropologist Michael Taussig explains the distinction between use value and exchange-value as follows:

As a commodity the shoe has properties that are in addition to its use-value of providing comfort, ease of walking, pleasure to the eye, or whatever. As a commodity the shoe has the exchange-value function: it can generate profit for its owner and seller over and above the use-value that it holds for the person who eventually buys and wears it. In its exchange-value the shoe is qualitatively identical with any other commodity, no matter how much they may differ in terms of their use-value properties ... By virtue of this abstraction, which is based on market exchange and the universal equivalence of money, a palace is equal to a certain number of shoes, just as a pair of shoes is equal to a certain fraction of an animal's hide. (1980, 25–6)

2 I thank John Slykhuis, editor of the newspaper, for making this material available to me.

3 For example, Pocius (1976) discusses how the role of singer is passed on through families in one Newfoundland community.

4 See Renwick's supplement to Coffin's work for an outline of recent scholarship on the subject.

5 See Radcliffe Brown (1965) on teasing relationships. Joking takes place on the subject of the most problematic relationships in the social structure – those between sons- and mothers-in-law.

6 Kenneth S. Goldstein defines the recitation as "a solo spoken

performance of any passage, or selected piece, of prose or poetry" (1976, 8).

7 The *Family Herald* was a national weekly paper published in Montreal. It was very popular in Ontario until its demise in the 1960s. The "Old Favorites" column published requested and submitted versions of songs and poetry. "Somebody's Mother" was published in the column on 1 Apr. 1903, 15 Aug. 1906, 28 Mar. 1923, and 27 Sept. 1939. This information was provided from her files by Edith Fowke.

8 Jeanne Greenhill recalls that "Somebody's Mother" was one of her recitations at a public school concert in Highland Grove.

9 The *Oxford English Dictionary*, for example, defines parody as "a composition in prose or verse in which the characteristic turns of thought or phrase in an author or class of authors are imitated in such a way as to make them appear ridiculous, especially by applying them to ludicrously inappropriate subjects; an imitation of a work more or less closely modelled on the original, but so turned as to produce a ridiculous effect."

10 Though I know of one variant, possibly a parody, modelled on "In Flanders Fields" (Davis 1978, 138), its serious tone makes it an unlikely prototype except in very limited circumstances.

CHAPTER FIVE

1 The friendly co-operation of the staffs at Toronto area Canadian Cancer Society units, including Agincourt, Bramalea, Mississauga South, Scarborough, and York, and from the Ontario division, especially Coreen Villemere and the Nepean unit in Ottawa, made the location of many poems and songs possible. I am also indebted to Leslie Scrivener for making her files available to me.

2 I employ the apparently non-inclusive term "everyman" because I was unable to come up with a reasonable alternative.

3 Legend usually refers to narratives involving a cultural truth, even if its historical facts are distorted.

4 The following information is from a "Terry Fox Fact Sheet" supplied by the Ontario division of the Canadian Cancer Society. For more information on the runner's life, see Scrivener (1981).

5 A similar effect has been noted in native American balladry. In her study of the murdered girl stereotype in the ballad and newspaper, Anne Cohen notes that aspects of the events that do not fit the pattern – the second murderer, for instance – are ignored or dropped (1973).

6 The ages given in this chapter refer to the time of writing, 1985.

7 This line refers to Dick Traum, the amputee who inspired Fox's run by completing the New York City marathon.

8 One of the workers there kindly photocopied it for me.

9 These are organized and promoted by a private organization supported but not directly administered by the Canadian Cancer Society. The money raised goes directly to another independent organization, the National Cancer Research Institute of Canada, which is funded primarily by the Cancer Society. The latter supports patient care and education in addition to research.

10 A very informal survey on the question "Name a Canadian hero" failed to bring any immediate response. On considerable reflection, several individuals suggested Billy Bishop, a First World War flying ace. No one mentioned Sir John A. Macdonald, Canada's first prime minister, or even current hockey great Wayne Gretzky.

Bibliography

Atwood, Margaret. *Survival: A Thematic Guide to Canadian Literature.*
Toronto: Anansi 1972.

Bakhtin, M.M. *The Dialogic Imagination.* Trans. Michael Holquist and
Caryl Emerson. Austin: University of Texas Press 1981.

Bauman, Richard. *Verbal Art as Performance.* Rowley, Mass.: Newbury
House 1977.

– *Let Your Words Be Few: Symbolism of Speaking and Silence among Seventeenth-Century Quakers.* Cambridge: Cambridge University Press 1983.

Ben-Amos, Dan. "Toward a Definition of Folklore in Context." *Journal of
American Folklore* 84 (1971): 3–15.

Berton, Pierre. *The National Dream: The Great Railway 1871–1888.*
Toronto: McClelland and Stewart 1970.

– *Canadians as Winners.* St John's, Nfld: Memorial University of
Newfoundland Faculty of Engineering and Applied Science 1975.

Bronson, Bertrand H. *The Traditional Tunes of the Child Ballads.* Princeton:
Princeton University Press 1959.

Brown, E.K. *On Canadian Poetry.* Toronto: Ryerson Press 1943.

Brown, Penelope, and Stephen Levinson. "Universals in Language
Usage: Politeness Phenomena." In *Questions and Politeness,* ed. Esther
N. Goody. London: Cambridge University Press 1978.

Burke, Kenneth. *The Philosophy of Literary Form: Studies in Symbolic
Action.* Baton Rouge: Louisiana State University Press 1967.

– *A Rhetoric of Motives.* Berkeley: University of California Press 1969.

Burke, W.J., and Will D. Howe. *American Authors and Books.* New York:
Crown Publishers 1972.

Campbell, Helen Richards. *From Chalk Dust to Hayseed.* Belleville, Ont.:
Mika Publishing 1975.

Campbell, Joseph. *The Hero with A Thousand Faces.* Princeton: Princeton
University Press 1968.

Canadian Catholic Readers. *Second Book*. Toronto: Copp Clark 1899.

Caraveli Chaves, Anna. "Bridge between Two Worlds: The Greek Woman's Lament as Communicative Event." *Journal of American Folklore* 93 (1980): 129–57.

Child, Francis James. *The English and Scottish Popular Ballads*. Vol. 2. Boston: Houghton, Mifflin, and Company 1885.

Coffin, Tristram Potter. *The British Traditional Ballad in North America*. Rev. ed., supp. by Roger deV. Renwick. Austin: University of Texas Press 1977.

Cohen, Anne B. *Poor Pearl, Poor Girl! The Murdered-Girl Stereotype in Ballad and Newspaper*. Austin: University of Texas Press 1973.

Creighton, Helen. *Songs and Ballads from Nova Scotia*. Toronto: J.M. Dent 1932.

Darnell, Regna. "Correlates of Cree Narrative Performance." In *Explorations in the Ethnography of Speaking*, ed. Richard Bauman and Joel Sherzer. New York: Cambridge University Press 1974.

Davis, N. Brian. *The Poetry of the Canadian People, 1900–1950*. Toronto: NC Press 1978.

Deacon, William Arthur. *The Four Jameses*. Toronto: Macmillan 1927.

Dorson, Richard M. "A Theory for American Folklore." *Journal of American Folklore* 72 (1959): 197–215.

Ellis, Bill. "'The Blind Girl' and the Rhetoric of Sentimental Heroism." *Journal of American Folklore* 91 (1978): 657–74.

Ernest, Edward P. *The Family Album of Favorite Poems*. New York: Grosset and Dunlap 1959.

Farber, Carole. "High, Healthy, and Happy: Ontario Mythology on Parade." In *The Celebration of Society: Perspectives on Contemporary Cultural Performance*, ed. Frank E. Manning. London, Ont.: Congress of Social and Humanistic Studies 1983.

Foucault, Michel. "What Is An Author?" *Partisan Review* 43 (1975): 603–14.

Fowke, Edith. "British Ballads in Ontario." *Midwest Folklore* 13 (1963): 133–62.

– and Norman Cazden. *Lumbering Songs from the Northern Woods*. Austin: University of Texas Press 1970.

– and Alan Mills. *Canada's Story in Song*. Toronto: Gage 1960.

Geertz, Clifford. *The Interpretation of Cultures*. New York: Basic Books 1973.

Gibbon, John Murray. *New World Ballads*. Toronto: Ryerson Press 1939.

Giuliano, Bruce. *Sacro O Profano? A Consideration of Four Italian-Canadian Religious Festivals*. Ottawa: Canadian Centre for Folk Culture Studies Mercury Series, no. 17, 1976.

Goldstein, Kenneth S. "On the Application of the Concepts of Active and Inactive Traditions to the Study of Repertory." *Journal of American Folklore* 84 (1971): 62–7.

– "Monologue Performance in Great Britain." *Southern Folklore Quarterly* 40 (1976): 7–30.

Greenhill, Pauline. *So We Can Remember: Showing Family Photographs.* Ottawa: Canadian Centre for Folk Culture Studies Mercury Series, no. 36, 1981.

– "Portuguese Outdoor Household Shrines." Paper presented at the Folklore Studies Association of Canada meetings 1982.

– "Lawrence McGuire: Voice From a Community." *Rotunda* 18, no. 1 (1985a): 24–9.

– "Contemporary Folk Poetry in Southern Ontario." PhD diss., University of Texas at Austin 1985b.

– "Welcome and Unwelcome Visitors: Shivarees and the Political Economy of Rural-Urban Interactions in Southern Ontario." *Journal of Ritual Studies* forthcoming.

Halpert, Herbert. "Vitality of Tradition and Local Songs." *Journal of the International Folk Music Council* 3 (1951): 35–40.

Harrison, Dick. "Popular Fiction of the Canadian Prairies: Autopsy on a Small Corpus." *Journal of Popular Culture* 13 (1980): 326–32.

Hiebert, Paul. *Sarah Binks.* Toronto: McClelland and Stewart 1964.

Hind, Bonnie. *Poems by Bonnie Hind.* Wardsville, Ont., 1981.

Hirsch, Edward. "A Structural Analysis of Robert Service's Yukon Ballads." *Southern Folklore Quarterly* 40 (1976): 125–40.

Inglis, Stephen. *Something out of Nothing: The Work of George Cockayne.* Ottawa: Canadian Centre for Folk Culture Studies Mercury Series, no. 46, 1983.

Ives, Edward D. *Lawrence Doyle, The Farmer-Poet of P.E.I.: A Study in Local Songmaking.* Orono: University of Maine Studies 1971.

Jakobson, Roman. "Concluding Statement: Linguistics and Poetics." In *Style in Language,* ed. Thomas A. Sebeok. Cambridge: MIT Press 1960.

Johnston, William Victor. *Before the Age of Miracles: Memories of a Country Doctor.* Toronto: Fitzhenry and Whiteside 1972.

Jorgensen, Marilyn. "Anti School Parodies as Speech Play and Social Protest." In *The World of Play: Proceedings of the Annual Meeting of The Association for the Anthropological Study of Play,* ed. Frank E. Manning. West Point, NY: Leisure Press 1983.

Kirshenblatt-Gimblett, Barbara. "A Parable in Context." In *Folklore: Performance and Communication,* ed. Dan Ben-Amos and Kenneth S. Goldstein. The Hague: Mouton 1975.

Lévi-Strauss, Claude. *The Raw and the Cooked: Introduction to a Science of Mythology.* New York: Harper and Row 1967.

Lombardi-Satriani, Luigi. "Folklore as Culture of Contestation." *Journal of the Folklore Institute* 11 (1974): 99–121.

Long, Eleanor. "Ballad Singers, Ballad Makers, and Ballad Etiology." *Western Folklore* 32 (1973): 225–36.

McIntyre, James. *Oh! Queen of Cheese*. Intro. by Roy Abrahamson. Toronto: Cherry Tree Press 1979.

McKeon, Richard. *Introduction to Aristotle*. New York: Modern Library 1947.

Macmillan, Ernest. *A Canadian Song Book*. Toronto: Dent 1929.

Mark, Vera. "Ways of Telling: Social Dimensions of Written Gascon in Lectoure, France." PhD diss., University of Texas at Austin 1984.

Matthews, John Pengwerne. *Tradition in Exile: A Comparative Study of Social Influences on the Development of Australian and Canadian Poetry in the Nineteenth Century*. Toronto: University of Toronto Press 1962.

Miner, Jack. *Wild Goose Jack*. Markham, Ont.: PaperJacks 1969.

Moir, John S. *Rhymes of Rebellion*. Toronto: Ryerson Press 1965.

Moss, John. *Bellrock*. Toronto: NC Press 1983.

Narvaez, Peter. "The Folk Parodist." *Canadian Folk Music Journal* 5 (1977): 32–7.

Ontario Readers. *Second Reader*. Toronto: Canada Publishing Company 1884, 1909, 1923.

Opie, Iona and Peter Opie. *The Oxford Dictionary of Nursery Rhymes*. Oxford: Clarendon 1951.

Oring, Elliot. *Folk Groups and Folklore Genres: An Introduction*. Logan: Utah State University Press 1986.

Ortner, Sherry. "On Key Symbols." *American Anthropologist* 75 (1973): 1338–46.

Pocius, Gerald. "'The First Day That I Thought of It since I Got Wed': Role Expectation and Singer Status in a Newfoundland Outport." *Western Folklore* 35 (1976): 109–22.

Radcliffe-Brown, A.R. *Structure and Function in Primitive Society*. New York: Free Press 1965.

Reader, H.J. *Newfoundland Wit, Humor and Folklore*. Ottawa 1958.

Redfield, Robert. *The Little Community and Peasant Society and Culture*. Chicago: University of Chicago Press 1960.

Renwick, Roger deV. "Two Yorkshire Poets: A Comparative Study." *Southern Folklore Quarterly* 40 (1976): 239–82.

– *English Folk Poetry: Structure and Meaning*. Philadelphia: University of Pennsylvania 1980.

Rollin, Roger. "The Lone Ranger and Lenny Skutnik: The Hero as Popular Culture." In *The Hero in Transition*, ed. Ray B. Browne and Marshall Fishwick. Bowling Green, Ohio: Bowling Green University Popular Press 1983.

Rosaldo, Michelle Z. *Knowledge and Passion: Ilongot Notions of Self and Social Control*. Cambridge: Cambridge University Press 1980.

Royal Canadian Series. *Second Reading Book*. Toronto: Canada Publishing 1883.

Sahlins, Marshall. *Culture and Practical Reason*. Chicago: University of Chicago Press 1976.

Scrivener, Leslie. *Terry Fox: His Story*. Toronto: McClelland and Stewart 1981.

Service, Robert. *Collected Poems of Robert Service*. New York: Dodd, Mead and Company 1940.

Sharp, Cecil. *English Folk Song: Some Conclusions*. London: Novello 1907.

Sontag, Susan. *Illness as Metaphor*. New York: Farrar, Straus and Giroux 1977.

Spaeth, Sigmund. *Read 'Em and Weep: The Songs You Forgot to Remember*. Garden City: Doubleday Page and Company 1926.

– *Weep Some More My Lady*. Garden City: Doubleday 1927.

Steckmesser, Kent Lad. *The Western Hero in History and Legend*. Norman: University of Oklahoma Press 1965.

Szwed, John F. "Paul E. Hall: A Newfoundland Song-Maker and His Community of Song." In *Folksongs and Their Makers*, ed. Henry Glassie, Edward D. Ives, and John F. Szwed. Bowling Green, Ohio: Bowling Green University Popular Press 1970.

Taussig, Michael. *The Devil and Commodity Fetishism in South America*. Chapel Hill: University of North Carolina Press 1980.

Tedlock, Dennis. *Finding the Center: Narrative Poetry of the Zuni Indians*. New York: Dial Press 1972.

Turner, Victor. *The Ritual Process*. Ithaca: Cornell University Press 1969.

Van Gennep, Arnold. *The Rites of Passage*. Trans. Monika B. Vizedom and Gabrielle L. Caffee. Chicago: University of Chicago Press 1960.

Williams, Raymond. *The Country and the City*. London: Chatto and Windus 1973.

Woods, Randy. *The Better Poems of Peter Paul Van Camp*. [Winnipeg] 1978.

Index